45-

To Father Jim:
　　Without your help pg 162 would not have been possible, and I consider it (along with pg 139) as one of the prize photos.
　　　　　Gratefully
　　　　　John T. Dwyer

CONDEMNED TO THE MINES

CONDEMNED TO THE MINES

THE LIFE OF EUGENE O'CONNELL
1815–1891
Pioneer Bishop of
Northern California and Nevada

by
JOHN T. DWYER

priest of the
Archdiocese of San Francisco

VANTAGE PRESS
New York   Washington   Atlanta   Hollywood

FIRST EDITION

All rights reserved, including the right of reproduction in whole or in part in any form.

Copyright © 1976 by John T. Dwyer

Published by Vantage Press, Inc.
516 West 34th St., New York, New York 10001

Manufactured in the United States of America

Standard Book Number 533-02130-8

"DAMNATUS SUM AD METALLA"

These were the words, taken from the Roman Martyrology, spoken by Father Eugene O'Connell in November, 1860, to Pope Pius IX when the Holy Father declined to release him from his appointment as the new vicar apostolic of northern California and Nevada. Condemnation to the metal mines was a form of punishment inflicted by the emperor Diocletian on the early Christians.

DEDICATION

On August 20, 1938, the Sisters of Mercy at Mt. St. Mary's, Grass Valley, California, celebrated the Diamond Jubilee of the arrival of the first Sisters on August 20, 1863. Present for the occasion as presiding Prelate was the most Rev. Thomas K. Gorman, then Bishop of Reno. Present also was the author, who was then a seminarian, a graduate of Mt. St. Mary's School, and a resident of Grass Valley in the last half of the 1920's. Among his friends who had entertained him by the hour with tales of the past were such pioneers as Sister Agnes Ryan, who had entered the Grass Valley Mercy Convent in 1876; Sally Carson Hare, who had graduated from the school in 1876, both friends of Bishop Eugene O'Connell. In the course of the day's conversation, Bishop Gorman, finding out the background of the seminarian, urged him to research and write the history of the church in the old Grass Valley Diocese. This seed, sown on that day in 1938, has finally come into bloom. Because of his inspiration, this book is dedicated to

THE MOST REV. THOMAS K. GORMAN, D.D.

former Bishop of Reno
retired Bishop of Dallas-Fort Worth

ACKNOWLEDGMENTS

The author wishes to express his deepest gratitude to many people who contributed substantially to make this biography a reality:

To the Rev. John B. McGloin, S.J., of the University of San Francisco, for his most gracious cooperation in making available the materials in his outstanding collection of western Catholic Americana, and his help and encouragement in correcting the text.

Likewise, to the foremost authority of Catholic Americana in the southern part of the state, the Rev. Francis Weber, archivist of the Archdiocese of Los Angeles, for making available the materials found in the Los Angeles archives and for his constructive and helpful suggestions.

To Sister Sara Ann Rude of the Religious of the Sacred Heart, for the hours spent in correcting the English and improving the style.

To Betty Gardiner for the countless hours spent in editing and preparing the final manuscript for the publisher.

To the Most Rev. Alden J. Bell, bishop of Sacramento, sixth successor of Bishop O'Connell, for his assistance in financing the publication of this book.

To the Rev. Michael Walsh of All Hallows College, Dublin, Ireland, for his patient research of the records of the College and his prompt response to many questions.

To the Rev. Larry Lorenzoni of the Salesian Fathers, who translated the documents which were in Italian, and to Mark LeBeau of Ontario, Canada, who translated the French documents.

To Sister Montserrat Santos, O.P., and to Carmel Lynch,

who gave many hours of their time to typing the original manuscript with its corrections and additions.

To the Sisters of Mercy of Grass Valley, for the use of their valuable photograph collection.

To Mr. Gerard Sherry of *The* (San Francisco) *Monitor* for outstanding cooperation and help in the use of *The Monitor* files.

To Miss Kelp of the Mullen Library, Catholic University of America, in Washington, D.C., for her graciousness and cooperation in making available the *National Catholic Directories*.

To Mr. Ivan K. Edelman of the Marysville-Yuba County Library, for several courtesies and photos.

To Mr. Eugene Tyler of Gilroy, California, whose outstanding photographic skill provided many of the photos which were reproduced from very old pictures.

To Miss Dorothy Bear of the Mendocino Historical Research, for many photos and courtesies during the period of research.

To everyone who assisted in even the smallest way and made it a joy to bring to the light of day the hidden works and accomplishments of this pioneer bishop of northern California and Nevada.

THE RT. REV. EUGENE O'CONNELL, 1815–1891
Titular Bishop of Flaviopolis
Vicar Apostolic of Marysville, 1861–1868
First Bishop of Grass Valley, 1868–1884
Titular Bishop of Joppa, 1884–1891
(Photo, courtesy of Society of California Pioneers, San Francisco)

CONTENTS

	Essay on Sources	xv
I.	Major Events in Irish History, 1845–1850	1
II.	Events in Far-off California, 1840–1850	15
III.	Volunteer Missionary, 1851–1854	26
IV.	Seminary Professor to Vicar Apostolic, 1854–1861	38
V.	Pastoral Journeys, 1861–1884	50
VI.	Supplier of Priests, 1861–1864	64
VII.	The Years as Vicar Apostolic, 1861–1868	80
VIII.	Extraordinary Concerns	103
IX.	Years of Major Decisions, 1868–1871	123
X.	The Care of the Indians	144
XI.	The Busy Years, 1871–1876	156
XII.	Administrator of Affairs	181
XIII.	The Difficult Years, 1874–1881	194
XIV.	The Quest for a Coadjutor, 1874–1881	215
XV.	The Unsettled Years, 1881–1886	231
XVI.	The "Los Angeles Years," 1886–1891	257
XVII.	Holiness of Life	265

APPENDIXES

A.	Poetical Tribute of the Rev. Joseph Phelan to the Memory of Bishop O'Connell	276
B.	Succession of Pastors of the Parishes in the Grass Valley Diocese, from Their Start Up to 1900	279
C.	Biographic Sketches of Priests for Whom There Are No Photographs	291
	Index	297
	Index of Photographs	301

ESSAY ON SOURCES

When the writer undertook to do the life of this pioneer bishop, his first disheartening discovery was that there were no archives. Nothing was preserved covering the years of the vicariate of Marysville (1861–1868) or the Diocese of Grass Valley (1868–1886) or even the early years of the Diocese of Sacramento (1886–1900). No letters of appointment, no records, no diaries, no biographical sketches of the priests—nothing was preserved either in Marysville or Sacramento for the historian. This situation is not unusual. Rare was the pioneer among priests or bishops who for a moment thought that what he was doing might someday be important. Bishops even had to enforce the keeping of the necessary parochial records, the baptismal and marriage books. Whether Bishop Eugene O'Connell, first bishop of northern California and Nevada, kept any records we will never know, for if he did they were lost or destroyed as being worthless. Evidence seems to indicate that he most probably did not.

His Letters

However, Bishop O'Connell was a prolific letter writer. In his twenty-six years in California he sent back to his alma mater, All Hallows College in Dublin, one hundred six letters in which he revealed the status of his vast diocese, his problems, his concerns, his scholarship, his wit, his personal holiness. These letters were all handwritten in English. Luckily, the seminary authorities considered them worth preserving.

His ultimate superior, the one to whom he was responsible,

was the Cardinal Prefect of the Sacred Roman Congregation known as Propaganda Fidei, the arm of the church which rules all mission lands (and this was mission territory all during Bishop O'Connell's days). To the various cardinals who ruled that Congregation, he wrote fifty-five letters revealing his needs and concerns. These letters were all handwritten in Latin. They were preserved in the Propaganda archives and were translated by the author.

Finally, the "Oeuvre pour la Propagation de la Foi," based in Paris and Lyons, was the arm of the church which doled out the "Mission Funds" collected from all over the world for the support of the missions. In order to obtain the much-needed funds, Bishop O'Connell had to keep the president of the Society informed of the needs of the diocese and pleading letters were addressed for this purpose. These letters and reports were all handwritten in French. They, too, were preserved by the Society, and were translated with the help of Mark LeBeau of Ontario, Canada.

It was not necessary, however, for the writer to make a trip to Dublin to consult the All Hallows archives. Nor was it required that a trip be made to Rome and the necessary permissions be sought to consult the Propaganda archives. Nor was a trip necessary to Paris to the archives of the Society for the Propagation of the Faith. All that was needed was a series of visits to the University of San Francisco where photostats and photographs of all these materials have been amassed. In 1957 and again in 1963, the University and the Society of Jesus granted a sabbatical leave to the Rev. John B. McGloin, S.J., professor of History at the University of San Francisco, to research the foundation and development of the Catholic church in western America. He spent many months in Europe going to all places, religious communities, and institutions that had anything to do with his research. At that time, all these materials and much more besides were photographed, photostated, or microfilmed for the University's Department of History and made available for the use of the historian.

Archives of the Archdiocese of San Francisco

Archbishop Joseph Alemany, first archbishop of San Francisco, was the exception to the rule regarding record-keeping and preservation of early church history. His well-kept books of records, letters, and documents often reveal important aspects of Bishop O'Connell's life, for the two men were very close friends. Archbishop Alemany was responsible for his being in California, and Bishop O'Connell was dependent on the Archbishop, both as his metropolitan and as his friend.

The principal records in this collection are:

The "Libro Borrador," the last fourteen pages of which cover 1850–1882 and contain references to Bishop O'Connell.

The "Liber Gubernii Sedis St. Francisci" contains the records of such events as ordinations, consecrations, erections of dioceses, and other important events.

There are several volumes of Roman documents, some of which pertain to Bishop O'Connell and problems he was faced with in his diocese.

Archives of the Archdiocese of Los Angeles

Another outstanding source of material can be found in the archives of the Archdiocese of Los Angeles, where the archivist, the Rev. Francis J. Weber, has amassed many documents pertaining to the history of the church in California. All the materials, for example, on the Osuna case were found in these archives, together with many other important documents.

Archives of the Congregation of the Passion

The Roman archives concerning the foundation of the Passionist Order in North America, 1853–1895, provided more letters by Bishop O'Connell and the events pertaining to the foundation in Nevada.

Archives of the University of Notre Dame

This collection contains twenty-nine letters from Bishop O'Connell found among the papers of James Edwards, James McMaster (Editor of *Ave Maria Magazine*), the Rev. Daniel Hudson, C.S.C., and Orestes Brownson, and eleven letters by others to these same people in which the bishop is mentioned.

Newspapers

Principal source among newspapers was *The Monitor*, the Catholic paper of the Archdiocese of San Francisco, which, although it does not have all issues prior to the 1906 fire, has a rather complete file, some in bound volumes, some on microfilm. Since *The Monitor* had correspondents spotted throughout California and Nevada, the activities of Bishop O'Connell were fairly well recorded, reported, and published.

Likewise, the local daily paper, the *Marysville Appeal Democrat*, kept an eye on one of its most prominent citizens and reported on him in some detail.

United States Documents in the Propaganda Fide Archives

A Calendar in five volumes, edited by Finbar Kenneally, O.F.M., published by the Academy of American Franciscan History, Washington, D.C. This admirable compilation complemented the letters of Bishop O'Connell to Propaganda Fide because they indicate the responses made by Rome to his many questions. The volumes contain summaries of the letters received and the answers given.

The National Catholic Directory

Since the very early days of the organized church in the United States, the bishops of the nation have published annually (except the Civil War years 1862–1863) a *National Catholic Directory*. This detailed listing of each diocese and of the U.S. clergy depended, of course, for its accurateness on an annual report by the bishops to its headquarters in New York. Again, the human element of considering the report unimportant sometimes produced no report or partial reports. Bishop O'Connell was no exception. This source is not totally reliable for this reason. Likewise, in each case the statistics given and the location of clergy were all as of the previous year since it took months to gather, compile, and publish this national directory.

Henry Walsh, S.J.

A most important, prime printed source was the outstanding work *Hallowed Were the Gold Dust Trails*. This remarkable compendium, published in 1946, was commissioned by Bishop Robert Armstrong of the Diocese of Sacramento, the first of the California bishops to recognize that there was another "Gold Mine" as yet undiscovered and unrecorded, and which would soon be lost unless the records and recollection of the pioneer priests, sisters, and lay people were captured and preserved. For two or three years, Father Henry Walsh of the University of Santa Clara traversed parish after parish the length of northern California and Nevada, county by county, from Tuolumne County to the Oregon border, talking with pioneers, recording late at night their observations and stories, poring over baptismal registers to find the succession of pastors, assistant pastors, and famous names of pioneers. All this was recorded in his significant book which this present study of Bishop O'Connell has proven to be remarkably accurate. Sometimes the book has been criticized for having "romanticized" various persons. But that does not detract from its remarkable accuracy, especially considering its scope in time and area.   *"Savages"*

Bishop Thomas K. Gorman

One final original printed source is the 1935 publication *Seventy-Five Years of Catholic Life in Nevada*, written by the first of the western bishops to recognize the need to preserve the early history, Bishop Thomas K. Gorman, first bishop of the Diocese of Reno. This very accurate account of the church in the state of Nevada was also compiled from original sources. Father Henry Walsh relied on it for his chapter on Nevada State.

James P. Gaffey, Citizen of No Mean City

The Life of Patrick W. Riordan, Archbishop of San Francisco (Washington, D.C., Catholic University Press, 1975), is the recently published life of San Francisco's second archbishop, 1884–1914.

Cecil Woodham-Smith, The Great Hunger

This outstanding work on the Potato Famine in Ireland provided most of the background material for the first chapter, since Eugene O'Connell experienced the great famine and was eventually caught up in the resulting emigration from Ireland.

Andrew F. Rolle, California, a History

This excellent work by the professor of History at Occidental College provided much of the background for the development of California in the days of the Gold Rush and the resulting emigration to California which was to affect so dramatically the life of Eugene O'Connell.

Unpublished Manuscripts

Hanagan, Sister Barbara, S.N.D. "The Sisters of Notre Dame in Marysville, California, 1856–1972." University of San Francisco, 1973.

Hehr, Sister Fredrick Ann, O.P. "History of the Catholic Church in Virginia City, Nevada." University of San Francisco, 1969.

La Voy, Sister M. Gerald, O.P. "The Foundation and Early Growth of St. Mary's Hospital, Reno, Nevada." Catholic University, Washington, D.C., 1960.

Ley, Harry P. "Eugene O'Connell, Pioneer Bishop of Northern California." Master's thesis, University of San Francisco, 1968.

Renner, Pamela. "History of Catholic Activity in Rohnerville." Dissertation for Senior History Seminar, Humboldt State University, Arcata, California, December, 1967.

Sanguinetti, Sister M. Rose, O.P. "A Survey of Education in Virginia City, Nevada, 1859–1897." Dominican College, San Rafael, 1965.

For someone who consciously left no archives, Bishop O'Connell, through his letter writing, his marginal notes in parish records, and his dynamic appeal to *The Monitor* correspondents, left a trail behind him that made the reconstruction of his life, the nature of his personality, and the heroic sacrifice of himself easy to discover and a pleasure to record.

Abbreviations for Principal Sources

AAHC	Archives of All Hallows College, Dublin, Ireland
AALA	Archives of the Archdiocese of Los Angeles, Los Angeles, California
AASF	Archives of the Archdiocese of San Francisco, San Francisco, California
ASPF	Archives of the Société pour la Propagation de la Foi, Paris, France
ASRC	Archives of the Sacred Roman Congregation of Propaganda Fidei, Rome

AUND   Archives of the University of Notre Dame, Notre Dame, Indiana

Gorman, *Seventy-Five Years.* Gorman, Thomas K., *Seventy-Five Years of Catholic Life in Nevada.* Reno, Nevada: Journal Press, 1936.

Kenneally, *U.S. Documents.* Kenneally, Finbar, O.F.M. *United States Documents in the Propaganda Fide Archives, a Calendar.* Washington, D.C.: Academy of American Franciscan History, 1974.

Walsh, *Hallowed Were.* Walsh, Henry L., S. J. *Hallowed Were the Gold Dust Trails.* Santa Clara, California: University of Santa Clara Press, 1946.

Photography

The amassing of the photographs which accompany this historical presentation was even more illusive and more challenging. The ferreting out of pictures which date back almost a hundred years proved difficult and often frustrating. The greatest single source for these photos was provided by the author himself who, over a period of forty years, had photographed the buildings which constituted the Catholic church in the Grass Valley area, most of which no longer exist. These photographs were donated in 1972 to the Historic Preservation Committee whose task it is to preserve the remaining buildings.

The second greatest source, owned by the Sisters of Mercy, Grass Valley, was a beautifully bound, century-old album containing twenty-six photos of the priests of the old Grass Valley Diocese, none of them with a name attached. Identification was made of fourteen. All efforts to identify the remaining twelve were fruitless.

The largest single source of photos outside of these two private collections was that of the Nevada Historical Society, which possesses an admirable collection of old Nevada photos and from whom pictures of most of the churches in the Nevada State portion of the diocese were obtained.

Some excellent pictures were found in the files of St. Mary's in the Mountains, in Virginia City. All efforts to locate a photo of the old Virginia City orphanage failed.

The Mendocino Historical Research also shared some valuable photos which they possess.

These photos were gathered in order to enhance the story and demonstrate the hardships and sacrifices endured by the priests and people who pioneered the American Catholic church in the West, especially in the old Grass Valley Diocese.

CONDEMNED TO THE MINES

Chapter I

MAJOR EVENTS IN IRISH HISTORY, 1845–1850

The Ireland into which James and Judith O'Connell were about to bring their firstborn child was a far cry from the pastoral scene the visitor finds today. The last quarter of the twentieth century is as different from the first quarter of the nineteenth as human imagination can envision.

For one thing, Ireland was a land of almost nine million people in 1815. An official census taken in 1841 placed the population at 8,175,124 but readily admits that due to the impossibility of getting an accurate count the true population may have exceeded that figure even by twenty percent.[1] The population in the mid-twentieth century barely exceeds four million.

It should be easy to understand, therefore, that every square mile of Ireland was densely populated. Since the country was almost totally agricultural, Disraeli stated that on arable land the population of Ireland was denser than that of China.[2] Land was the most cherished possession, because land meant food. Unless an Irishman could get hold of land on which to grow his crops, he had no means of sustenance. The consequence was that land was divided and subdivided, split into the smallest fragments, even into acre and half-acre holdings.

Farms had already been divided by landlords and middlemen, but in the era in which the O'Connells began to raise their family, further subdivision was made by the families themselves. Parents allowed their children to occupy a portion of their own holdings because the alternative was to turn them out to starve. The same census of 1841 showed that forty-five percent of the holdings were of fewer than five acres.[3]

But matters were even worse. Almost all held land as tenants. Tenants could be quickly turned off the land should circumstances go against them and they be unable to pay the rent. Therefore, the average Irish tenant farmer held his land with no security and with starvation as the only alternative should he lose that land.

Of course, things were worse in the west of Ireland than in the Province of Leinster. The northeast corner of Ireland, clustered around the city of Dublin, fared much better than the Province of Connaught with its rocky land, its plunging cliffs and the wild Atlantic Ocean. The O'Connell plot of land was in Leinster but near the Ulster border, actually outside the village of Rolagh in County Meath, but the responsibility of the parish of Kingscourt which is in County Cavan.[4]

Conditions in any locality depended on the landlord, the owner of vast acreage whose lands were let and sublet either by the landlord himself, or, if he were an absentee, by his agent. Unfortunately, the vast majority of Irish landlords were absentees, some of them beholding the source of their income but once or twice in a lifetime. The chance that James O'Connell of the parish of Kingscourt was anything more than a tenant farmer is very remote indeed.

Nor were the houses in which these tenant farmers lived the cute little white Irish cottages often seen by the tourist in the twentieth century, nestled against a green hill, the smoke pouring from its chimney against the Irish sky. The Irish tenant farmer had no money with which to build himself a decent house. He used the rocks, the mud and straw, the thatch for his roof, and thus he kept his family secure against the elements and warm against the cold. Since his rent was determined partly by the size of his plot of land and partly by the size of his house, he kept it small. And later, when the taxes on Irish landlords were raised, the size of the windows was even considered in fixing such rates. The average Irish dwelling then was little better than a mere shelter. It had no conveniences, no sanitary facilities, little more than was needed for bare subsistence.

Into such a household James and Judith O'Connell welcomed their firstborn child, a boy, on June 15, 1815. The following day, as was the custom, they took him to St. Mary's Church at Kingscourt and the name they gave him was Eugene.[5]

Other children followed. Next was Mary, then another boy, and probably some who did not survive the rigors of those days, until finally in 1832 their last son was born, to whom they gave the name of Patrick. The four children went to the local school, and among the brightest was Eugene.

Considering the hardships of the times, it is difficult to know how James O'Connell could afford to send his oldest son off to school in the nearby city of Navan. Yet, around 1833, when young Eugene expressed a desire to become a priest, the family managed somehow to make a further sacrifice. The fall term found Eugene O'Connell enrolled among the students at the diocesan seminary in Navan, only nineteen miles from home. When he finished his course in 1837, he made a move farther away from home to the major seminary at Maynooth, twenty miles west of Dublin on the Dublin-Galway Road.

Eugene O'Connell was an excellent student and became well versed in the classical training of the times. He seems to have had no great trials on the road to the priesthood and on June 3, 1841, the order of subdeaconate was conferred on him. One year later, on May 20, 1842, he was ordained a deacon and on the following day, in the chapel at Maynooth, Archbishop Daniel Murray of Dublin ordained Eugene O'Connell a priest of God in the service of his home Diocese of Meath.[6]

His talents were quickly recognized and he was invited one year later to return to his diocesan seminary at Navan as a professor. He was in his second year of teaching at Navan Seminary when disaster hit Ireland in 1845.

Events both in Ireland and in the western part of the United States which took place in the five-year span between 1845 and 1850 were to have a profound effect on the life of this young seminary professor. He, in turn, was to exercise a profound influence on the events which followed those of 1845 to 1850.

The whole structure of Ireland in 1845—the division of land into tiny acreage, the frantic competition for land—all this was produced by the potato. The conditions of life in Ireland and the existence of the Irish people depended on the potato entirely and exclusively.

The potato, provided it did not fail, enabled great quantities of food to be produced at a trifling cost from a small plot of ground. Sub-division could never have taken place without the potato: an acre and a half would provide a family of five or six with food for twelve months, while to grow the equivalent grain required an acreage four to six times as large and some knowledge of tillage as well. Only a spade was needed for the primitive method of potato culture usually practised in Ireland. Trenches were dug and beds—called "lazy beds"—made; the potato sets were laid on the ground and earthed up from the trenches; when the shoots appeared, they were earthed up again. This method, regarded by the English with contempt, was in fact admirably suited to the moist soil of Ireland. The trenches provided drainage, and crops could be grown in wet ground, while cultivation by the spade enabled potatoes to be grown on mountain sides, where no plough could be used. As the population expanded, potatoes in lazy beds were pushed out into the bog and up the mountain, where no other cultivation would have been possible.

The potato was, moreover, the most universally useful of foods. Pigs, cattle and fowls could be reared on it, using the tubers which were too small for everyday use; it was simple to cook; it produced fine children; as a diet it did not pall.[7]

Meanwhile, a report had come across the seas that some kind of blight had hit the potato crop in North America in 1844.

At the beginning of July, 1845, the potato crop in Ireland promised remarkably well; the weather was dry and hot. Then followed three weeks of continued gloom, with low temperatures, chilling rains, and fog. Nevertheless, at the end of July the crop was exceptionally heavy and on July 23, 1845, *Freemans Journal* reported that the "poor man's property, the potato crop, was never before so large and at the same time so abundant."[8] By the end of September, when the crop was due for harvest, some blight had appeared in various places throughout Ireland, but not enough for any general alarm; yet, as the harvesting continued the alarm grew. Crops that were dug up turned in a couple of days into stinking masses of corruption. Whole fields turned black overnight.

The consequence of this potato failure was not felt at first. Plenty, not scarcity, was the first result as every farmer tried to unload his crop before the blight attacked it. It was not until five or six months later when every available scrap of food, even partially diseased potatoes, had been eaten that actual famine would hit the land. Thus various schemes could be prepared, to be ready in April and May of 1846.

The reaction of the English government to the crisis in Ireland was one which readily demonstrates why there has never been any love on the part of the Irish for England. The government policy was that the property of Ireland was to pay for the poverty of Ireland. Any money raised for relief was to come from the landlords. Nothing was to be done which would interfere with or compete with private enterprise. Public works were instituted, but they were to be paid for out of the "rates" imposed on the landowners. The landlords reacted by immediately eliminating from their lands all those who could not pay their rents. This began a long history of evictions which were to add to the distress of the people; not only were they hungry, but many were due also to become homeless.

Between the public works and the Indian cornmeal which the English government obtained from America, Ireland managed to survive the loss of the potato crop of 1845.

One of the anomalies of the time was the amount of food exported for sale out of Ireland at the very time that the people were on the verge of starvation. John Mitchel, the Irish revolutionary, wrote: "During all the famine years, Ireland was actually producing food, wool and flax to feed and clothe not nine but eighteen millions of people."[9] Yet no Irishman would dare touch these products of the soil. They were his rent money, and the payment of the rents rated higher than filling his stomach with food. It must also be kept in mind that in many parts of Ireland, especially the west, the art of cooking had been lost. Father Mathew, the great temperance leader of his time, once wrote: "The potato deluge has swept away all other food from our cottagers and sunk into oblivion their knowledge of cookery."[10] In other words, the bulk of the population at that time would not have known what to do with the wheat, the barley, or the oatmeal, just as they had to be given instructions on how to prepare the Indian cornmeal shipped over from America.

In the year 1846, the people looked forward to a bumper crop of potatoes, although the acreage planted was about one-third less than in 1845. But Irish optimism assured one and all that it couldn't happen again, yet happen again it did! Even while the blight was reappearing all over Ireland, the English government prepared to wind up its public works schemes and close down its Indian corn relief stations that resulted from the failure of 1845. The summer of 1846 brought nothing but misery. The harvest in general was poor, the blight more universal, the people already weakened and despairing, the weather extraordinarily bad, and even the country around Dublin was flooded. Death from starvation was not only a possibility, it was now a probability.

Naturally, the seminaries of Ireland were affected by the conditions of the country. The problems of the procurators in trying to obtain food for their large households must have been challenging. The young Father Eugene O'Connell was only one of many who had to go hungry when food became scarce.

However, in the midst of all this turmoil and travail the seminary authorities of the missionary College of All Hallows in the Drumcondra district of Dublin had heard of the ability of the professor at Navan and issued him an invitation to join the All Hallows faculty for the fall term.[11] Thus, right at the time when the famine would see its worst, Father O'Connell, now age 31, moved from Navan to All Hallows College in Dublin and began his duties there in the fall as professor.

Autumn was now passing into winter. The nettles and blackberries, the edible roots and cabbage leaves on which most of the people had been eking out an existence began to disappear. Children began to die first; then nature took over to add to the troubles of Ireland.[12]

The winter of 1846 was the most severe in memory, and the longest. The normal Irish winds are from the Atlantic, but this winter they came from the northeast and brought with them biting cold. By the middle of December, the Thames in London was a mass of floating ice. Normally, the Irish were well protected from the cold. Their turf fires kept their cabins warm. But in 1846 the Irish peasant was forced to go out in bad weather to his work in the public works in order to make a few pennies to survive. In the spring, which continued cold and wet, scarcely anyone worked in the farms; hardly any crops were planted. This was not only because he had to work on the public works to make a few cents, but also because he had nothing with which to buy the seed to sow the next year's crop. Reports came in that some farmers were actually so hungry that they ate the very seeds they had received for planting. But there was a hidden reason why the tenant farmer was reluctant to plant; he was convinced that if he did, the landlord would seize the crop to pay the rents. So why plant?

The relief for the starving victims took a different form in the spring of 1846. First of all, when the word of the second disaster reached countries outside of Ireland, many private relief committees sprang up. Help came from Calcutta, India; from London; and from the United States.[13] The Society of Friends, the Quakers, were the most active and the best organized; with them originated the idea of "soup kitchens." The British Association, established in London, alone raised £70,000; on their subscription list can be found the name of Queen Victoria and a gift of £2000.

As soon as the soup kitchens were established, the public works were supposed to close down. These schemes were costing the British government £40,000 per day and were availing very little real good. However, the number of starving peoples exceeded the ability of the soup kitchens to reach them. It became impossible to close down the public works projects.

As if Ireland had not enough troubles, yet another disaster lay in wait for the Irish people. Typhus fever or some other pestilence usually followed periods of crop failure and famine. By the fall of 1846, the fever had broken out all over Ireland. The abnormal severity of the weather had drawn people even closer together. The number of dispossessed and wandering beggars had increased, and Irish hospitality provided a welcome to all who were down and out. These very conditions provided perfect breeding grounds for the spread of disease. Once infection had been brought into a district, it spread with lightning rapidity among the crowds in the soup lines and in the public works projects where men worked so closely together.[14] To meet this epidemic, nothing was prepared. The fever was raging for three months before the government acknowledged its existence and passed laws for the relief of the fever victims. By September, 1847, the epidemic began to subside. The total of those who died during the fever epidemic will never be known, but probably ten times more people died from disease than from starvation.

Desperation was at such a high pitch, the Irish now began to think in terms which heretofore had not been considered, namely the idea of fleeing from Ireland. Until the time of the famine, emigration from Ireland was almost unthinkable. For years there had been an annual temporary migration to England for the harvesting of the crops, affecting perhaps 60,000 people. Likewise, certain numbers of able-bodied Irishmen, but never more than 5,000 in any year, had been attracted to America for employment in construction work. It was these Irish gangs who had built the canals of the eastern states, but the idea of leaving Ireland on a large scale had been unthinkable. However, desperation drives people to strange solutions.

There was to be one other major difference in this emigration of 1847. Those who had emigrated had always been the strong, the able-bodied, the ambitious. But the thousands who left Ireland for England and America in the summer of 1847 were to consist of the sick, the starving, the destitute, the unskilled, the dispossessed—who had no skills, no strength, and no ambition except to get away from hopelessness. Two things were in their favor. The lumber ships which brought building materials from the Canadian forests were glad to have ballast for the return trip to America, and the fares were extremely low, within the grasp of almost everyone. Although there had been some emigration in 1846, more than usual, it was only a trickle compared to the flood which began in the spring of 1847. Most went to Liverpool and there caught passage to America. However, more than 85,000 sailed from Irish ports alone in 1847.[15] Accommodations on these ships were abominable even at their best; a wooden berth between the decks; cooking facilities in a grill on the deck; an issue of water daily; no sanitary facilities of any kind; and each passenger brought his own food. So great was the demand for passage that every craft, seaworthy or not, was commandeered for passage. Often there was not enough water on board or it became unfit for human use, and, of course, the starving emigrants of 1847 had no food to bring along.

It is important to point out that while it was the ambition of the vast majority of these emigrants to go to the United States, yet that was not their immediate destination, as the ports of the United States were not available to these refugees from starvation and disease. The United States had strict laws governing ships which brought passengers to its shores, and since the cost of providing somewhat decent conditions increased the fare, the vast majority of the emigrants of 1847 could not afford passage to the States. The destination of most of the ships was Quebec. The Canadian government had a quarantine station at Grosse Island. This was the actual destination of the passenger-carrying vessels.

The opening of the St. Lawrence River was late in 1847. Ice was thick until the middle of May when the first ship was able to discharge its passengers. Out of a list of 241 passengers, 9 had died at sea and 84 had the fever. Four days later, eight ships arrived. These had 430 fever cases. Three days later, seventeen more ships were anchored offshore and all had fever cases. On May 26, thirty vessels with 10,000 emigrants on board were waiting at Grosse Island. By May 31, forty ships, extending in a line two miles down the river, were lying at anchor. The little hospital at Grosse Island had 1,100 cases of fever, and more lying on pallets in sheds and tents and in the little church. In 1847, it is estimated that 109,000 people left Ireland for British North America.

The conditions on the fever-laden ships when they arrived beggar description. The conditions on Grosse Island, despite the heroic efforts of those willing and able to nurse the sick, were unforgettable. Eventually, the landing emigrants who were not sick were allowed to proceed to Montreal, but since they were on the crowded steamer for two days, many had come down with fever by the time they reached Montreal. Fever sheds had to be erected there also.

When ice closed the St. Lawrence River for the winter season, and the emigration ended, thousands rested in graves along Canada's shores. In Montreal where the fever sheds once stood, there stands a large memorial stone in reverent memory of "6,000 immigrants who died from ship fever, A.D. 1847–48." At Grosse Island, a monument carries an inscription which reads: "In this secluded spot lie the mortal remains of 5,294 persons who flying from pestilence and famine in Ireland in the year 1847 found in America but a grave."[16]

It is estimated that about 20,000 died in Canada that year, and almost an equal number lie in watery graves stretching from Liverpool to Quebec across the sea.

One consequence of this emigration was felt in the United

States. Though comparatively fewer emigrants landed in the United States, most of those who survived slipped across the border and headed for the cities of the United States, especially Boston. By a curious piece of reasoning, the Irish starving in Ireland were regarded as unfortunate victims and Americans had opened their hearts and purses to assist them; but when these same Irish crossed the sea and landed in the cities of America, they were looked upon as the scourings of Europe and an intolerable burden on the taxpayer. Because these starving emigrants had no skills and little strength, they drifted into unskilled, irregular, badly paid work, such as cleaning yards and stables, unloading ships, pushing carts—forming a mass of underpaid, casual labor, living in the slums. Coming from wretched housing in the farms of Ireland, they flocked to any place that provided shelter—lofts, basements, sheds, and cellars.[17]

It must not be thought that no emigration came to the United States. In the seven months of the 1847 emigration, 52,946 Irish emigrants landed in New York alone.[18] There is a prevalent idea that an emigrant necessarily possessed some of the qualities of a pioneer, but the famine emigrants were the reverse of pioneers. They had not set out to find wider horizons but had fled from hunger and pestilence. They were miserably poor and stayed where they landed. Furthermore, although they were agricultural people, very few took up farming of any kind. They rooted themselves in the cities and there they multiplied faster than the death rate of childbirth in city slums. They soon created a world of their own in New York, in Boston, and in Philadelphia.

Back in Ireland, as the summer of 1847 progressed with excellent weather, the crops were described as magnificent, although only one-fifth of the normal acreage of potatoes had been planted, completely insufficient to feed the hungry masses. As usual, the small farmer dared not eat these grain crops. Those were destined to pay the rents. The public works projects had all been closed down in August. In spite of the emigration and the deaths, there were still thousands of destitute people wandering the countryside, begging in the alleys and lanes of the cities. These had no money with which to buy available food such as Indian corn. The soup kitchen operation was destined to close down by October 1, 1847. Meanwhile, the British government had determined to spend no more public funds on Ireland. Whatever had to be done had to come from the property owners. There began a relentless severity in the collection of rates, and since landlords were responsible for holdings valued at £4 and under, an equally relentless series of evictions began.[19] Landlords were determined to clear their estates of all small holdings for two reasons. First, they could not pay the rates on the smaller holdings and, secondly, they needed larger acreage to plant crops which were not subject to the blight and for which there was a market.

Once again the weather conspired against the poor Irish people. The spring of 1848 was cold in Ireland; the people sacrificed everything they had to obtain seed and plant potatoes. More than twice the acreage of 1847 was planted. Landlords looked forward to the rents being paid, the people toward enough to eat. In May and early June the weather was excellent. Hopes were high; a feeling of relief was everywhere. But in the middle of June the weather changed and became continuously wet. By mid-July, the terrible story of 1846 was repeated blow by blow. Blight was everywhere. Through August, rain fell in torrents, day and night. Everything was ruined, not only the potatoes by the blight, but the wheat and grain crops as well. Landlords lost as well as tenants. The state of Ireland was as bad as in 1846.[20]

The Marquess of Sligo, one of the best of the landlords, was in receipt of £7,200 annually from his estate at Westport, County Mayo. His costs ran £6,000. He had been active in relief work, had twice supported the insolvent Westport workhouse at his own expense and, since the famine, had kept "no establishment," not even a carriage. Even this good man was left with little choice now except to evict. He had received no rents for three years and had borrowed £1,500 to pay the rates levied on him.[21] Indebted landlords could not even sell their estates. The law stated that a debt was on the entire property, not any parcel of it, and such property could not be transferred to a new owner until all debts and encumbrances had been satisfied. Evictions at this time were wholesale, there being more than 1,000 cabins pulled down in County Clare alone in the spring of 1848.

With the start of travel across the Atlantic, there began another wave of emigration, but this time one which was to do the most harm to Ireland itself. Changes had taken place across the Atlantic; Canada was not about to allow a repeat of the tragedy of 1847. New laws governed ships that landed, requiring more expensive and better-provided-for transportation. All these things meant that the impoverished, the beggars, the homeless could not flee Ireland as in 1847. This time the emigrant group was a better class of farmers, whom Ireland could ill afford to spare. However, the English government looked upon it as a blessing. If small farmers left, then landlords would be induced to sell portions of their estates to persons who might have some capital to invest. Small holdings would be reduced.[22]

The devastation of parts of the country was not likely to induce investing. In some counties, especially in the west, whole townslands were uninhabited, the former tenants having died, emigrated, or been evicted. Landlords, who often owned thousands of such derelict acres, were shut up in their huge houses, with no income, no crops, no one to work them even if they had been planted, and existing on rabbits that ran across their abandoned and overgrown estates.

Once again, as if there were a curse on the land, the famine was not enough. To it was added an epidemic of Asiatic cholera which raged from January to June of 1849. There are indications that James O'Connell died around this time, perhaps a victim of the cholera. We know that Father O'Connell's mother was referred to in 1850 as his widowed mother. The cholera epidemic claimed many victims in the Meath and Cavan area.

The total population of Ireland dropped about two and a half million people in the ten years between the census of 1841 and 1851.[23] Because of deaths and emigration, Ireland had seen an almost one-third reduction in population, a reduction which was to continue. Once the tide of emigration began to flow, it continued for nearly one hundred years. It had been estimated that between 1848 and 1864, thirteen million pounds were sent home from America to bring relatives out to America. Because the British government took no steps to restructure the distribution or ownership of land, because no efforts were made to reduce the dependency of the Irish people on the potato, the land lost its best and most enterprising citizens to enrich other countries, especially the United States of America. As someone put it so well, Ireland's greatest single export for a century was its people, a people who were to enrich the country of their adoption.

Meanwhile, Father Eugene O'Connell continued his round of orderly duties as professor at All Hallows College in Dublin. As he read about and often watched people preparing to emigrate to the shores of North America, one wonders if he ever envisioned himself as a potential emigrant. Yet this very migration from Ireland was to be the cause of a great change in the life of this young priest. He, too, was destined for the shores of North America in the very near future.

Sources for Chapter I

1. Cecil Woodham-Smith, *The Great Hunger* (New York: Harper & Row, 1962), p. 31.

2. Ibid.

3. Ibid., p. 324.

4. Harry P. Ley, "Eugene O'Connell, Pioneer Bishop of Northern California," Master's thesis, University of San Francisco, 1968.

5. Ibid., p. 2.

6. Ibid., p. 5.

7. Woodham-Smith, op. cit., p. 35.

8. Ibid., p. 38.

9. Ibid., p. 75.

10. Ibid., p. 76.

11. Ley, op. cit., p. 6.

12. Woodham-Smith, op. cit., p. 141.

13. Ibid., p. 157.

14. Ibid., p. 191.

15. Ibid., p. 216.

16. Ibid., pp. 236–237.

17. Ibid., p. 248.
18. Ibid., p. 253.
19. Ibid., p. 319.
20. Ibid., p. 362.
21. Ibid., p. 364.
22. Ibid., p. 371.
23. Ibid., p. 411.

Chapter II

EVENTS IN FAR-OFF CALIFORNIA, 1840–1850

While the tragic circumstances in Ireland were causing a great migration of the Irish people across the Atlantic to the eastern shores of America, events were taking place three thousand miles to the west which would eventually draw many of these emigrants to the shores of the Pacific.

California came under three different civil jurisdictions in the course of the nineteenth century. It had been a possession of Spain since its discovery in 1542. Over the two centuries it was occasionally explored and visited from Mexico by ship and by land expeditions, but it was inhabited only by the native Indians up and down its almost one-thousand-mile shoreline from Oregon to Mexico. Actual attempts to colonize and to civilize the Indians of Alta California were not begun until 1769 when Spain introduced what was to become the famous "Mission system" for the conversion and civilization of the Indians and the protection of colonists at the same time. The establishment of the twenty-one Mission settlements took fifty-four years, from the founding of the southernmost Mission at San Diego in 1769 to the establishment of the northernmost of Sonoma in 1823. These Missions eventually were only a day's journey apart, a day's journey on horseback, thirty miles more or less, so that it became possible by 1804 to travel from San Diego to San Francisco and sleep each night under the protection of and with the warm hospitality of the Franciscan Friars during the 400-mile journey. These Missions, when they were fully developed, were not only centers of religion, including a church and rooms for religious instruction, but also they included quarters for the priests and Indians who lived and worked at the Mission, industrial schools for weavers, carpenters, masons, agricultural skills, furniture making, blacksmithing and every other skill needed for the building, maintenance, and support of the Mission and its large holdings. These often included groves of lemons, figs, and olives, and fields of corn, grain, and other crops needed for the support of the Indian residents; huge ranges of cattle, and all the auxiliary enterprises such as tanning of hides, making of tallow, manufacture of sandals, etc. They eventually were completely self-sustaining, supporting, training, and civilizing hundreds of formerly nomad savages. Often the Missions included in their reports hundreds of horses and thousands of head of cattle, making them actually very rich holdings. The design of the Missions with their thick adobe brick walls, the tile roofs, and wide colonnades connecting the buildings which housed the church, the residence, the workshops, and storerooms all built around a large central quadrangle, became a unique style of architecture now known as California Mission style. By the time the founder, Father Junípero Serra, died in 1784, nine Missions had been founded; by the time his successor, Father Fermín Lasuén, died in 1802, nine more had been established. The remaining three were established in the nineteenth century, that of Santa Inez in 1804, San Rafael in 1817, and the last, San Francisco Solano, at Sonoma in 1823.[24]

It is interesting to note that these twenty-one centers of civilization, culture, and Christianity extended along the coast from San Diego to Sonoma, north of San Francisco. Because of the secularization process in the 1830s, there were to be no Missions or efforts to colonize north from the San Francisco Bay area to the Oregon border, another four hundred miles; nor were there any establishments in the huge central valleys of the Sacramento and the San Joaquin rivers, much less along the foothills of the Sierra Nevada mountain range, which runs like a spine along the eastern California border separating it from Nevada.

The second change of jurisdiction took place in 1821. Just as suddenly as California had become "New Spain" in 1542 by the planting of a flag and the claiming of the lands for the king of

Spain, so just as quietly California passed out of the jurisdiction of Spain when Mexico declared its independence from Spain in 1821.[25] Unfortunately, far-off California was ruled better from Spain than it was from nearby Mexico. Within ten years would come an edict known as the decree of secularization which would spell the death knell of the Mission system. Ideally, the plan was not bad: the Missions were to become pueblos or towns; each Indian family was to receive an allotment of land and livestock, a plan which in modern society would certainly be approved as a step in the right direction from the paternal system of the Missions to a self-sustaining system which included ownership of land and independence. Unfortunately, the Indians were not yet ready for this step. A further decree of 1833 completely removed the missionaries from control. [26] The Missions became parochial churches, with the clergy acting only as parish priests. All the holdings of the Missions, their cattle, their fields, orchards, vineyards, became available for private ownership. Mission administrators were appointed, most of whom had little or no concern for the Indians. They enriched themselves, took little care of the Mission properties, failed to cultivate the land, and exposed the Indians to all kinds of corruption. Thus, within a few short years the whole Mission system collapsed. The missionaries were helpless except to stand by and watch years of hard labor vanish before their eyes. Most of them were old, worn out by years of difficult work and devotion, too old to resist or even protest.

There was a further development which took place while California was under Mexican rule. Anxious to have the vast country settled with colonists, Mexico encouraged a system of "land grants" by which any Mexican of good character, or any foreigner willing to become naturalized and to accept the Catholic faith, might petition for as much as eleven square leagues of land.

In contrast with the division and subdivision of acreage in Ireland was this distribution of vast holdings of land. A square league was 4,438 acres. Thus eleven square leagues amounted to close to fifty thousand acres. Although this "land grant" system had started with Spain, there were only nineteen such private "ranchos" in 1790. But by 1830 there were some fifty of them. Among them were such ranchos as that of Francisco Pacheco, totaling 125,740 acres, 14,000 head of cattle, 500 horses, and 15,000 sheep.[27] One of the ranchos which was to play an important part in later California history was that owned by the Swiss captain John Sutter, located on the site of the present city of Sacramento, eleven leagues extending some sixty miles in length. The rancho of Don Luis Peralta, called the Rancho San Antonio, included what is now the cities of Oakland, Alameda, and Berkeley. By 1840 these ranchos, extending up the Sacramento valley and down the San Joaquin valley, numbered over one thousand, of all various sizes, with about 800 of them stocked with cattle, each rancho averaging 1,500 head.

This period in California history has been greatly romanticized. There was a style of living, a great degree of hospitality, and a definite Spanish culture of a California brand, all of which was about to come into a clash with the "Americanos."

Two events occurred in 1848 which were to change all this and bring about a wholly new "culture," if it may be called that. First of all, Mexico had been at war with the United States since 1846. Although it was no great war and the skirmishes were few and relatively unimportant, the net result was the transfer of California, when the Treaty of Guadalupe Hidalgo was signed on February 2, 1848. By the terms of this treaty, California, as well as New Mexico and Texas, passed from Mexican to American jurisdiction. Residents had the option of becoming American citizens or of leaving former Mexican territory. The United States paid Mexico $15,000,000 for the land. Thus California was now American territory.[28]

It is doubtful whether this simple transaction on the part of two governmental agencies would have made much of an impact on California had it not been for an event which occurred at the same time some miles from Captain John Sutter's rancho. The Swiss captain found it necessary to invest in a lumber mill in order to supply lumber to the immigrants who were gradually increasing. He sent one of his employees, James W. Marshall, to locate, set up, and operate this sawmill. Marshall chose a little valley which the local Indians called Cullomah. It was about forty-five miles northeast of Sutter's Fort on the south fork of the American River at about fifteen hundred feet in elevation. Here Marshall built the lumber mill. To operate the huge saw, water was diverted into what was called a tailrace, an artificial flume which brought water rushing to the wheel which operated the saw. On January 24, 1848, Marshall was inspecting this tailrace when he spotted some shining flakes in the sand and gravel in the tailrace. It was gold. Soon John Sutter found his employees walking off their jobs and heading for the streams to search for gold.[29] The actual publicity that was to touch off the famous Gold Rush began about two months later when a Mormon named Sam Brannan walked down the streets of the pueblo of San Francisco waving a bottle of gold dust and shouting, "Gold, gold, gold from the American River."[30]

This simple event touched off one of the greatest migrations which the United States has ever seen. The word that gold had been discovered in California reached not only the east coast but even Europe. Needless to say, rumor exaggerated actuality; an ounce of gold became a pound nugget. By June, 1848, two thousand men were digging for gold and by July the number had doubled. Every able-bodied man, be he sailor on a ship that docked in San Francisco, worker on a rancho, or merchant in Monterey or San Francisco, abandoned his trade and headed for the hills.[31] Of course, by November, 1848, all these original gold seekers had to face the reality of leaving the mountains, as the winter in the California foothills would not tolerate the kind of camp living that these original gold seekers pursued.

The year 1849 has gone down in history as the year of the Gold Rush. At the start of the year, there were about 26,000 persons in California, not counting the Indians. As soon as travel became available, men from every part of the country headed for California. Those in the East either took ship for California, some going all the way around Cape Horn, a trip of six months minimum; others stopping at Panama or Nicaragua and crossing the Isthmus, a trip of 6,000 miles; or they ventured across the plains in covered wagons. By summertime in 1849, there were 50,000 men seeking gold in the streams and the rivers of California. By the end of the year it has been estimated that there were 115,000, four-fifths Americans. The scene at the end of 1849 was almost unbelievable. Forced to leave the mines, certainly by November when the rains came, the miners flocked to the port towns. San Francisco literally exploded in size. Sacramento suddenly came into existence. So did Marysville, at the junction of the Feather and the American rivers. In March, 1848, there had been only 812 residents in San Francisco. By 1850 it was a boom town of 25,000. A photo of San Francisco in 1851 shows the waterfront with its hundreds of masts in the background, all ships abandoned by passengers and sailors alike as soon as they arrived. Records show that between April 12, 1849, and December 31, 1850, eight hundred five vessels docked in San Francisco and discharged 62,000 passengers on its shore.

Needless to say, this initial wave of gold seekers was almost exclusively male. Very few women came in the first two years, and often those who did were seeking gold in an indirect manner. It took time for a family man to obtain the money, the equipment and the companions needed to make a safe trip across the plains with his family. For instance, in Nevada County, a census in 1852 showed 12,448 white males in the entire county but only 920 females together with 721 foreign males and 61 foreign females. Chinese and Indians were counted separately, each with over 3,000 individuals. So there were less than 1,000 women in a population of over 20,000.[32]

With the arrival of the immigrants of 1851, 1852, etc., the picture slowly changed. With the coming of families, a more settled form of life began to appear and schools for the children became a necessity, as well as other amenities of settled American life such as churches, theaters, etc.

It might be well to get some idea of the spread of the Gold Rush to explain roughly the geography of northern California. The Sierra Nevada Mountains, many of whose peaks reach over 9,000 feet elevation and whose passes are all in excess of 6,000 feet, stretch like a giant spine or backbone down the eastern boundary of California, separating it from the state of Nevada. Although the Nevada plain remains about 4,000 feet in elevation, the California side gradually slopes to sea level. Someone has said that the California side resembles a giant comb pressed by the Creator into the land so as to form dozens of rivers flowing west from the spine of the comb, the Sierra Nevada. Rivers with such names as Feather, Yuba, American, Bear, and Consumnes formed the norther mines, with headquarters in Sacramento. The southern mines were located along the rivers named Mokelumne, Calaveras, Tuolumne, and Merced, with headquarters in Stockton. The original form of mining, the kind pursued by these early gold seekers, is known as placer mining. It was not so simple to do. The sifting of sand and gravel from river and creek beds, both those flowing with water and those which were dry most of the year, through screens to trap the loose gold which lay along these streams in abundance—this was backbreaking work. Many camps or towns sprang up, some along the river beds, others along the ridges of hills which separated the many tributaries of these rivers and their branches. Colorful names were given most of them. Some simply described the place from which the early settlers came: Iowa Hill, Michigan Bluff, Oregon Gulch, French Corral, Dutch Flat; others were named for individuals with "-ville" (French word for city) attached, such as Downieville, Marysville, Weaverville, Smartsville, or Birchville. Still others ended up with such names as Rough and Ready, Red Dog, You Bet, Poker Flat, Whiskey Diggings, Port Wine, Hangtown, and many others.

By 1854, the "easy pickings" of placer mining had practically disappeared. Meanwhile, there had come into existence a more permanent form of mining known as quartz mining by which gold was extracted from veins contained in rock buried deep in the earth. This form of mining required machinery, capital, and perseverance, as well as good luck. It was to become the stabilized form of mining for many years. However, the boom of the Gold Rush was over in a few years and life became more settled and diversified.

On September 9, 1850, California became the 31st state in the American Union. There was no doubt now that it was American. Since most of the area south of San Francisco was unaffected by the Gold Rush, it remained for the most part Mexican in culture, customs, and often in language. But north and east of San Francisco was totally American, with its own culture, customs, and needs.

All of this was to have a profound effect on the Catholic church, and was to produce needs that required special solutions. California had been separated from Mexico City into a separate diocese in 1840 with Fray Francisco Garcia Diego as the first bishop. However, when he died in 1846, no one was appointed in his place. Therefore, when California passed into American ownership, the bishopric was vacant. Likewise, the condition of the church in the old Missions was sad indeed.

One of the first attempts by the American hierarchy to assess the needs of the California church was made by Bishop John Hughes of New York who, in December, 1848, had written to an outstanding Spanish Catholic layman in Santa Barbara, Don Jose de la Guerra, asking him for a report on the conditions of the church in California. The letter took four months to reach Santa Barbara.

"El Gran Capitan," as he was known in California and Mexico, replied that the clergy consisted of four secular priests, one of whom was so sick as to be often unable to celebrate Mass, one Dominican who belonged to Baja California, two missionaries from the Sandwich Islands, one priest sent by the archbishop of Oregon, and seven Franciscans, two at Santa Barbara and the other five scattered among the old Missions, three of them being too old and too infirm to be of much service. Don Jose wrote his report at the start of the Gold Rush, which was over three hundred miles to the north of Santa Barbara.[33] Therefore he knew nothing of the needs of the Americanos nor of the presence of any priests.

The American hierarchy responded to the report by petitioning Rome to appoint a bishop for California, and preferably one who could deal with the bilingual and bicultural situation which existed in the different halves of the state. Accordingly, on November 20, 1849, Rome appointed as bishop of Monterey (the capital of the new state at that time) a Dominican Father, Charles Montgomery, a native of Kentucky. But California was not yet to get a bishop. Father Montgomery declined the honor. Rome had to look elsewhere.

Meanwhile, one month later, the provincial of the Dominicans in the United States, Father Joseph Sadoc Alemany, a native of Spain, set out for Rome from his headquarters in Somerset, Ohio, to attend a General Chapter of the Order which was scheduled for May in Naples. When he arrived in Paris, he learned that Pope Pius IX had canceled the chapter. Father Alemany then traveled to his hometown, Vich, to visit his mother, then proceeded to Barcelona, Marseilles, and Genoa, and arrived in Rome on June 8, 1850. Meanwhile, disturbed at the refusal of their first choice for Monterey, the American bishops again sent recommendations to Rome. It was on May 31, 1850, that the official appointment was made of the Dominican provincial, Joseph Sadoc Alemany, as bishop of Monterey. He had been in Rome only five days when he was told this news. The dismayed friar consulted his confessor, then the Vicar Gen-

ARCHBISHOP JOSEPH SADOC ALEMANY, O.P., 1814–1888
Dominican Missionary in Ohio, Tennessee, and Kentucky, 1840–1848
Provincial of American Province, 1848–1850
Bishop of Monterey in Upper California, 1850–1853
Archbishop of San Francisco, 1853–1884
Titular Archbishop of Pelusium, 1884–1888
(Photo, Courtesy of Sisters of Mercy, Grass Valley)

eral of the Order. Finally, on June 16, 1850, he proclaimed his unworthiness to Pius IX himself.

"You must go to California; there is no alternative; where others are drawn by gold, you must go to carry the cross. God will assist you," was the reply of the Holy Father.[34]

The bishop-elect made an eight-day retreat at the ancient Dominican Convent of Santa Sabina in Rome, offered Mass at the tomb of St. Peter on June 29, 1850, and was consecrated a bishop by Giacomo Cardinal Granzoni, Prefect of Propaganda Fidei, on June 30, 1850.

It was to be five months before the new bishop would set foot in California. He had another audience with the Pope on July 6, spent seven days in bed with a fever, offered his first Pontifical Mass on July 28, and left Rome on July 30, 1850. He headed for France, calling at the Lyons and then at the Paris headquarters of the Society for the Propagation of the Faith, the source of funding for the missions. By August 30, the new bishop was ready to leave Paris for London, where he contacted Fathers Faber and John Henry Newman regarding the possibility of getting oratorians for the California mission. From London, Bishop Alemany proceeded to Ireland where he visited and pleaded for California at the seminaries of All Hallows near Dublin, St. Patrick's in Maynooth, and St. Patrick's in Carlow.[35] After these visits, he returned to England and headed for Liverpool, the point of embarkation for America.

On September 11, 1850, Alemany and his companions sailed for New York, and on October 12, 1850, landed there after a comparatively uneventful voyage. The voyage to the Isthmus began on October 27, and Chagres was reached on November 6. For three days, the party endured the hardships of crossing the Isthmus of Panama and arrived in Panama City on November 12th. They sailed from there on November 16, and into San Francisco Bay on December 6, 1850. The next day, the new bishop of California set foot for the first time on the soil of San Francisco. The following day, Sunday, December 8, 1850, he offered Mass in San Francisco's only church, that of St. Francis. The next day the pastor, Father Anthony Langlois, returned to San Francisco and was presented with the necessary documents proving that Alemany was really the long-awaited bishop of California.[36]

Sources for Chapter II

24. Andrew F. Rolle, *California, A History* (New York: Crowell Co., 1969), p. 73.
25. Ibid., p. 131.
26. Ibid., p. 155.
27. Ibid., p. 114.
28. Ibid., p. 208.
29. Ibid., p. 213.
30. Ibid., p. 215.
31. Ibid., p. 217.
32. Thompson & West, *History of Nevada County* (Oakland, 1880), p. 55.
33. Francis J. Weber, *Documents of California Catholic History* (Los Angeles: Dawson's Book Shop, 1965), p. 57.
34. John B. McGloin, *California's First Archbishop* (New York: Herder & Herder, 1964), p. 93.
35. Ibid., p. 100.
36. Ibid., p. 108.

Chapter III

VOLUNTEER MISSIONARY, 1851–1854

The call of California's Bishop Joseph Alemany in Ireland at the two seminaries of All Hallows in Dublin and St. Patrick's in Carlow was to be one of the most productive visits he would ever make. His appeal to the students fell on willing ears and by 1854 he was able to report that he had fourteen students in the seminaries of Carlow, All Hallows, and the Propaganda in Rome. But the crowning achievement was that he did not have to wait for two or three years for the first one to come from All Hallows. He wrote in his diary on September 5, 1850: "Received Father O'Connell, a very good priest, who wants to come to California if his College of All Hallows allows it. The President, Father David Moriarty, agrees if an annual sum of £5 can be set aside to provide for his elderly mother."37

What motivated Eugene O'Connell to accept this challenge set before the faculty and students by the visiting Spanish Dominican bishop of Monterey, California? Perhaps the appeal for priests so urgently needed presented a challenge which was made all the more clear by the abundance of priests in Ireland. Perhaps he felt that he would be a better trainer of future priests for the missions if he himself had experience in the missions. Whether these were his primary reasons he did not reveal. But a secondary reason is revealed in his future writings; namely, that the gold fields could be a source of help for the much-impoverished All Hallows. Father O'Connell had previously gone on begging expeditions to Liverpool with Father Bennett seeking funds for the struggling seminary.[38] California might be a good place to find substantial amounts to send back to relieve the poverty of the seminary, so poor that Father O'Connell had been working all these years without salary.[39]

On November 21, 1852, he wrote suggesting that "the All Hallows authorities ask Bishop Alemany to allow me to collect for All Hallows for two or three months from Sacramento to Los Angeles, otherwise my service is of no use to All Hallows."[40] Previously he had written that such a collection was underway in Santa Barbara. So, quite evidently, this motive was at least a secondary one prompting the young professor to volunteer his services.

Bishop Alemany wrote on September 7, 1850, that the news from All Hallows concerning Father O'Connell was favorable. One of the last things the bishop did before leaving Ireland on September 11, 1850, was to write an encouraging letter to his future missionary.[41]

Arrangements were completed by early April, 1851, and Father O'Connell bade farewell to his friends and family and set out for Cork City and the ship that was to bring him to New York. (The Atlantic voyage in that era took fourteen days.) He arrived in New York on Wednesday, April 23, 1851, and was met by a classmate, Father McCarron of St. Joseph's Church, where he received the customary Irish hospitality for three weeks during which he rested from the voyage and renewed his strength for the rigorous trip ahead.[42]

He was asked to escort several nuns to California. Two Dominican sisters from Ohio were going to Monterey and four Notre Dame sisters were destined for San Jose. The steamer to the Isthmus of Nicaragua, a route made famous by the Argonauts of the early fifties, sailed on May 13, 1851. For the next six weeks it was constant travel.

To give some ideas of the trials that awaited the six nuns and Father O'Connell, we have recourse to a description of this trip across the Isthmus recorded two years later when undertaken by Father Hugh Gallagher and the pioneer group of Mercy nuns.

On reaching San Juan del Norte, Nicaragua, all passengers

and luggage had to be transferred to grossly overcrowded river boats which took hours of tortuous navigation (and several dead stops in the shallows) to get as far as the Castilian Rapids. Here another laborious transfer to a lake steamer was necessary; the trip across Lake Nicaragua in the moonlight was the only pleasant episode in the major business of crossing the Isthmus. Then a fourth transfer of passengers and baggage was in order for the twelve mile trip through steep mountains to the Pacific. This last stage, until 1853, was taken on mules.

San Juan del Sur was the port of embarkation for the Pacific portion; however, the description continues:

As there were no wharves provided, the final flourish of the crossing was for the passengers enroute for the North to be picked up bodily by natives unencumbered with much clothing and thus be carried about fifty yards out to a waiting skiff.

It then took another two weeks for the ship, loaded for the most part with a motley crowd of gold seekers, to wend its way up the coast to San Francisco.[43] At last, on July 1, 1851, the weary travelers reached their destination and presented themselves to the clergy at St. Francis. Whether the bishop met them in San Francisco or at his see city, Monterey, is not known.

Little time was lost in giving Father O'Connell an assignment. To his great surprise he was not sent north to the mines but instead south to the old Mission at Santa Inez to take care of the parish and the tiny seminary which the Diocese of Monterey struggled to maintain there. We know he was in Santa Barbara on July 11, 1851. On that date he wrote back to All Hallows to state that there had been no priest in Santa Inez since June and that the only one who spoke English there was the steward of the Mission.[44] His letters during 1852 speak of the loneliness and the solitude. What a contrast from the community life of All Hallows where companionship was so available and where conversation among learned men was so easily found. In a letter of November 21, 1852, he writes that he looks on his sojourn at the lonely Mission of Santa Inez as just punishment for his past sins and negligences, and prays that he will be able to bear it with perfect resignation and accept it as such. He dreams of Ireland, he writes, and "longs for an associate from our Alma Mater to cheer and help me in the discharge of my duties."[45]

During 1852, one letter written in February and another in March describe his Mission and his occupation as pastor of the parish. He wrote:

> The Mission of Santa Inez extends along the Pacific some sixty miles and is bounded on the east by the Sierra Nevada, an immense mountain chain, which runs almost parallel to the Pacific, throughout the continent of America. Santa Inez Mission is about thirty-six miles north of Santa Barbara, which is a seaport, and twenty-one miles south of La Purisima Concepcion. Both these Missions, once so flourishing, were formerly attended by the zealous Franciscan Fathers till the spoilers came and deprived them of the temporalities.
>
> Though this country is almost one continued series of undulating hills and steep sierras which render the passage from one Mission to another exceedingly difficult and dangerous, yet the Indians are not deterred by distance or danger on Sundays and Festivals of our Lady. They set out on horseback or afoot at an early hour in order to assist at High Mass and sermon, and long for the following Sunday to give vent to their piety in hymns and canticles.
>
> If my flock are few they are far between. From Santa Inez, with its hundred Indians clustered, to La Purisima, it is at least twenty-one miles over an unusually level plain, stretching along between undulating hills on either side. Only then imagine to yourself a solitary missioner suddenly summoned after Mass on New Year's Day to attend a sick call at such a distance. Of course, the Mission is provided with a horse, equipped in California style with wooden stirrups, and armed, if he wish, with a lasso coiled around the pommel of the saddle, for the purpose of ensnaring bears which he is liable to meet after dusk. Yet it is not so much the distance, or the grizzly bears, or the rattlesnakes that may appall the missionary as he wends his way through the mountain passes and along the hillsides of Alta California,

because he believes in his heart that "ex his omnibus liberabit eum Dominus;" and in gratitude to God I must confess that He preserved me from more than one rattlesnake; but I repeat it, it is not so much the fear of wild beasts as the fact of not finding the sick person alive, that weighs heavily on the heart of the missionary; and so it happened on the occasion just alluded to. I afterwards ascertained that at the very moment I got the first notice of the sickness of Dona Catalina Carillo of La Purisima, her lifeless remains were being carried to the grave, at the distance of twenty-one miles.

From my residence at Santa Inez, my faithful Indian guide accompanied me back and forth, and whenever he spied a bear in the distance, he used to tell me to stop till he had scared away our grizzly friend with the help of his pack of dogs.

Thus did poor Dona Carillo pass to her account without the rites of our holy religion, while your citizens in their agonies have the happiness of being fortified with the last sacraments. Surely the ways of God are wonderful; sometimes it was my lot to be called to the sickbed of the dying, whom I found in full possession of all their faculties. After administering the last rites, they expired. At other times, no matter what haste I made, it was all in vain; I found the sick person a lifeless corpse.[46]

Father O'Connell managed to keep busy over and above the sick calls he alludes to and the Sunday Masses. Bishop Alemany came for a visit on August 22, 1851, and confirmed eleven persons. Between his arrival in July, 1851, and the end of the following year, Father O'Connell performed thirteen baptisms. On September 24, 1851, he had his first marriage. By July 18, 1852, just one year after his arrival, he could state that he had learned enough Spanish to converse and read and that he now had four seminarians, all sons of American or Irish fathers.[47]

On January 21, 1852, a summons was issued by Bishop Alemany to the forty priests scattered from San Diego to Sacramento to come together at St. Francis in San Francisco on March 10, 1852, for a retreat and to attend the first Diocesan Synod from March 19 to March 23, 1852.[48] Although there is no evidence whether Father O'Connell attended these two events or not, the presumption is that he did. To Father O'Connell, loyalty and obedience to his bishop were second nature; that he would not have attended is most unlikely, but he makes no mention of it in any letter that has been preserved.

The only other recorded instance that Father O'Connell attended any function in San Francisco was for the laying of the cornerstone for the new cathedral (present Old St. Mary's), which event took place on July 17, 1853, and at which "Father O'Connell, Superior of the Seminary," was listed as present.

His letters during this year, 1852, reflect two positive matters: his own very good health since his arrival and the magnificence of the California climate. In a postscript he writes:

> In point of climate, upper California is not inferior to any other country on the face of the globe; nay more, it is superior to many, not even Italy or the south of France excepted; it abounds not only in the necessaries, but even the luxuries of life. The vine and olive flourish; immensely large watermelons and pineapples, lemons and oranges are all the production of California.[49]

He even succeeded during 1852 in getting some money collected for All Hallows. On September 8, 1852, he forwards £250, asking that £10 be given to his brother Patrick. At the same time he speaks of his present situation as an "unprofitable Mission."[50]

Meanwhile, the bishop was occupied with two matters which would affect the life of Father Eugene O'Connell. For one, the First Plenary Council of Baltimore had been held at Baltimore in May by the American bishops at which California's bishop presented a convincing case for dividing the enormous Diocese of Monterey which extended from the Mexican border below San Diego all the way to the Oregon border, approximately one thousand miles. When he returned to Monterey, Bishop Alemany knew the division would take place and that he was destined to go to San Francisco as archbishop. It was time, therefore, to prepare to transfer the "paltry Seminary" to the new see city. However, an emergency had arisen in San Francisco. A great scandal had occurred in San Francisco's Church of St. Francis. At that time there were only two priests there, the pastor Anthony

Langlois, a French Canadian, and a young Irish priest, John Scanlan, who was considered the priest for the "English speaking people." Although no details have been preserved, this young priest allegedly absconded with a very large sum of money, thus creating quite a scandal.[51] The bishop was determined to undo the scandal by sending an exemplary priest in the place of the former one. He chose Father Eugene O'Connell and in a letter to Dr. Moriarty, the president of All Hallows in 1854, the Archbishop states why: "He affects more good in one year than others might in a longer time."[52]

Therefore, sometime shortly after November 21, 1852, Father O'Connell bade goodbye to his little flock and set out for San Francisco and the tiny Church of St. Francis.

By February 3, 1853, Father O'Connell was able to send another donation to All Hallows, this time $200, and he asks that whatever his brother Patrick might need of this be given him to pay his expenses to the United States, "as he wants to try his fortune in California."[53]

The same letter also contains the comment: "You are certainly doing a great work of charity in allowing me to help poor Dr. Alemany because he is yet so badly off for priests." However, this zeal was tempered by a great loneliness for All Hallows and for the life to which he was so inclined. This great yearning prompted him to write on May 23, 1853:

> Now to come to myself, Dr. Moriarty, how long do you intend my sojourning here to be; if you think that the interests of All Hallows would be promoted so much by me remaining here as by my return say: "Stay," but if not, say: "Come," and I will come, yet I am sure Dr. Alemany would not let me go until he sees some representatives worthy of All Hallows.[54]

In the meanwhile, three things were taking place which would determine the date of the return of Father O'Connell to Ireland.

In the first place, the division of California had been approved in Rome and the Archdiocese of San Francisco was separated from the Diocese of Monterey on July 29, 1853. Archbishop Alemany now transferred his own residence to St. Francis and also transferred the tiny seminary from Santa Inez. Father O'Connell was the logical one to take charge.

His appointment to Mission Dolores is dated September, 1853.[55] This made him the first non-religious pastor of the Old Mission Dolores, and the first pastor under the jurisdiction of the Archdiocese of San Francisco. At the same time, a seminary under the patronage of St. Thomas Aquinas was opened in the old Mission quarters.

Father O'Connell wrote that he had six Spanish seminarians. Two of them were destined to be ordained within one year, both having come from Spain: Juan Comapla and Juan Comellas. But the turnover in the tiny seminary was great. By December 30, 1853, he wrote to say that he now had three Spanish seminarians, one Mexican, two Irish and one French.[56] The Irish seminarians probably included John P. Harrington, who would be ordained from the little seminary in 1855, and the Frenchman was probably Louis Auger (1856). Both of these men were to give yeoman service to the early California church. Both were ordained from St. Thomas Seminary located at Mission Dolores.[57]

Once again, Father O'Connell's appointment had an overtone of compensation for scandal. The famous Father Flavian Fontaine of the Picpus Fathers had been his predecessor at Mission Dolores and had left because of financial concerns. In his letter of September 30, 1853, Father O'Connell told Dr. Moriarty the story of Father Fontaine's attempt to build a college near Mission Dolores without reckoning its cost or where the funds would come from. When he found himself in a serious financial situation, unable to face his creditors, more from shame than any dishonesty, he simply left. He died a few months later in Callao, Peru, en route home to Belgium.[58] Once again, Father Eugene O'Connell was expected by the Archbishop to counteract the resulting scandal by his own personal goodness and example.

The second matter which changed the picture was the beginning of the flow of priests to staff the archdiocese. The first fruits of Bishop Alemany's recruitment at the Irish seminaries began to arrive in early 1853 when Father John Quinn arrived from Carlow.[59]

But one other event was to turn the tide sooner than expected. The dioceses in Oregon had been flourishing long before the California Gold Rush. A continuous flow of priests for this

MISSION DOLORES in 1856
Rev. Eugene O'Connell first diocesan priest,
pastor, and rector of St. Thomas Seminary there, 1853-1854.
(Photo, courtesy of Mission Dolores, San Francisco)

mission had already been coming from the Irish missionary seminaries. Now, all of a sudden, because of the California Gold Rush, Oregon became depopulated. When gold was discovered, the settlers in Oregon were the first to get the word and, being the closest, were the first to get the fever and rush to California to try their luck. Most of the gold seekers of the year 1848 were from Oregon. The result was that the church in Oregon no longer had the need for the priests destined for it. Father O'Connell tells in his letters about the arrival of Father Myles O'Reilly and Father William Kenny. Both were destined for Oregon, but negotiations were underway for the Archbishop to keep them both for San Francisco. Father Dominic Bowles and Father Thomas Dalton were also soon to arrive, both destined for the far north but also to remain in San Francisco.[60]

The long-awaited letter finally arrived which, though written on March 5, 1853, had been sent to Santa Inez and reached Father O'Connell in June. In it was an invitation from Dr. Moriarty to "come home." But the joy of this prospect was tempered by the zeal and loyalty of Father O'Connell who wrote: "I can't leave until some of the All Hallows men arrive. You would really pity the poor Bishop. I trust you will think well of my remaining a few months longer for the reasons given."[61]

The news of the invitation to come home was a great disappointment to the Archbishop, who wrote to Dr. Moriarty: "I did not think you would contemplate to recall Father O'Connell so soon considering the immense distance between Dublin and San Francisco. The least stay should be five years!" He then begged to keep Father O'Connell longer—"or at least find me another one like him."[62]

Matters proceeded rapidly. Father Macken, also destined for the north, had arrived. The Archbishop had been allowed to keep Father Kenny and Father Dalton. Young Richard Carroll from Carlow also arrived. Archbishop Alemany ordained him on December 18, 1853. Although Father Carroll was appointed pastor of Placerville in January, he was recalled on May 16, 1854, to take Father O'Connell's place as rector of the seminary and pastor of Mission Dolores.

Once again, for Father O'Connell, there was the long journey down the coast to the Isthmus, the crossing, the voyage to New York, and then the sailing across the Atlantic; but this time it all seemed so different. Instead of the unknown there was the welcome thought of the companionship of All Hallows, the stimulating conversation of equals, the regular peaceful life of the seminary, and a wealth of experience to make him a better teacher of the future missionaries of California.

Eugene O'Connell's return to All Hallows was an occasion of great joy. When the scholastic year began in 1854, he settled down to the life he was so well suited for, the life he loved so much. His appointment as dean of All Hallows was accepted with equilibrium: to this life Father Eugene O'Connell was temperamentally well suited. California was a memory. His experiences were conversation pieces. His loyalty to "poor Bishop Alemany" was active as the flow of priests to San Francisco continued through the years, encouraged by Father O'Connell. The next six years were to be happy ones for Father O'Connell, filled with memories of far-off California which he never expected to see again.

Sources for Chapter III

37. AASF, "Libro Borrador," H–16, entry of September 5, 1850.

38. AAHC, letter of April 23, 1862.

39. ASPF, letter of November 23, 1860.

40. AAHC, Santa Inez, November 21, 1852.

41. AASF, "Libro Borrador," H–16, entry of September 5, 1850.

42. AAHC, New York, letter of Low Sunday, 1851.

43. Sister Mary Aurelia McArdle, *California's Pioneer Sister of Mercy* (Fresno, California: Academy Library Guild, 1954), p. 29.

44. AAHC, Santa Barbara, letter of July 11, 1851.

45. AAHC, Santa Inez, letter of November 21, 1852.

46. AAHC, Santa Inez, letter to Father Richard O'Brien, February, 1852.

47. AAHC, Santa Inez, letter of July 18, 1852.

48. McGloin, op. cit., pp. 135, 142.

49. AAHC, Santa Inez, letter to Father Richard O'Brien, February, 1852.

50. AAHC, Santa Inez, letter of September 8, 1852.

51. AAHC, San Francisco, letter of April 15, 1853.

52. AAHC, San Francisco, Alemany to Dr. Moriarty, July, 1853.

53. AAHC, San Francisco, letter of February 3, 1853.

54. AAHC, San Francisco, letter of May 23, 1853.

55. AASF, "Libro Borrador," H–17, entry of September, 1853.

56. AAHC, San Francisco, letter of December 30, 1853.

57. *Catholic Directory*, Archdiocese of San Francisco, 1962, p. 332.

58. AAHC, San Francisco, letter of September 30, 1853.

59. AAHC, San Francisco, letter of February 3, 1854.

60. AAHC, San Francisco, letter of January 14, 1854.

61. AAHC, San Francisco, letter of June 15, 1853.

62. AAHC, San Francisco, Alemany to Dr. Moriarty, July, 1853.

Chapter IV

SEMINARY PROFESSOR TO VICAR APOSTOLIC, 1854–1861

To describe the character of Eugene O'Connell as a seminary professor is a difficult task, not because his personality is not clearly manifested, but rather because the conclusion that all seminary professors were of the same kind could easily be drawn. It is true that Eugene O'Connell was a typical example of a certain kind of seminary professor of bygone days. But it would be wrong to conclude that all were the same type.

Seminary professors, whether in Irish or French or American seminaries, were like all other university professors, as different as personalities differed. Yet there was a type, a breed of them, which had much in common, of which Father Eugene O'Connell was a most typical example. For one thing, they were well educated in the classics. They had an excellent foundation in Latin and Greek and in the classics of these languages. The classical allusions, the quotations from Latin and Greek which are to be found in Eugene O'Connell's letters, especially to his fellow professors, give ample evidence that he was an educated and cultured man in these areas. Eugene O'Connell had a talent for languages. He wrote Latin fluently, correctly, and with ease. He was so at home in this area that he was appointed "Writer of Latin Letters" at the II Plenary Council of Baltimore by his fellow bishops in September, 1866.[63] His letters to Rome, all written in Latin, in his own hand have very few errors and a wide vocabulary. We have already seen that he learned Spanish within one year's time to the point where he could read and converse in it readily. For a long time it was thought that he knew French, but he himself confesses that he did not.[64] The conclusion is that others wrote for him the many reports he sent in French to the Propagation of the Faith in Paris. Likewise, he was well versed in the Sacred Scriptures, as references and quotations abound in his letters.

But one of the characteristics of his type of seminary professor was the tendency to be very critical of the students under his care, a characteristic which he never lost or changed, even when dealing with his former students who were adult, ordained, experienced men and who were his fellow laborers. They very much remained "students" and were criticized as students generally are by this kind of professor. Quick to blame for mistakes, slow to praise for doing what was plainly considered to be duty, this was a hallmark of this kind of character. And if praise were due and merited, although given, it was veiled from the student himself. It could be described as a "keep them guessing" attitude. This was the kind of seminary professor that Father Eugene O'Connell appears to have been. As time went on, he settled more and more into this character. He had thirteen years of this kind of life, this kind of attitude, and it left its mark on his character and mental attitude.

While Father O'Connell was pursuing this kind of life which suited him so well temperamentally, matters were progressing in far-off California. As the 1850s approached the 1860s, Archbishop Alemany's chores increased. All Hallows and other seminaries began to send a supply of priests to the far west, and Archbishop Alemany began to make parishes stretching as far north as Yreka and as far east as Carson and Virginia City. As the mines developed, settlements grew up and priests were needed. Marysville, Nevada City, and Downieville became supply centers for the mines. Sacramento became an active and busy port. The thousands of miners and settlers scattered through the foothills needed churches and priests. Once again the size of the territory to be covered was too large and Archbishop Alemany felt that his archdiocese should be divided.

He began a series of consultations. He had made his first proposal for such a division to Rome on March 19, 1858, but either it never reached Rome or was not taken seriously. The next time, Archbishop Alemany was in earnest. On February 8, 1859, he wrote to Archbishop John Purcell of Cincinnati, a leading prelate at the time, asking his advice. In his letter, he told Archbishop Purcell that the Archdiocese of San Francisco had at that time 57 churches and 9 chapels, 60 priests and about 100,000 Catholics. The territory was too large and required him to be absent from San Francisco for long stretches of time, thus forcing him to leave important business at home unattended. Archbishop Purcell and others he consulted all encouraged him to apply for a division.⁶⁵

On May 20, 1859, the Archbishop wrote the proposal to Alessandro Cardinal Barnabo, prefect of the Sacred Roman Congregation of Propaganda Fidei. In it he proposed boundaries and candidates for the office of bishop.

His first alternative was that the new diocese should stretch from the 39th to the 42nd parallel and from the Pacific Ocean to the Colorado River. The Archbishop pointed out that this territory had 60,000 inhabitants, about one-third of whom were Catholic, and that it had 17 churches and 10 priests. He proposed that the see city be Marysville, one of the larger cities in this territory, a city of seven or eight thousand people, about one-fourth of whom were Catholic. Marysville also had a beautiful church, and a convent of sisters with a school for the education of girls.

The alternative boundary line proposed by the Archbishop was parallel 38⅓ from the Colorado River to Sacramento River, then north to its intersection with the 40th, and then a straight line to the 42nd, with Sacramento as the see city. In favor of Sacramento as the see city, the archbishop pointed out that it was the seat of the California State government. It had a population of 16,000, one-fourth of whom were Catholic, and also had a beautiful church and a convent of sisters for the education of girls.⁶⁶

In the presentation were included observations of Bishop Thaddeus Amat, Alemany's successor in the see of Monterey. He had written his opinions to Rome because Archbishop Alemany had asked him to do so. It is a very humble letter, stating that he doesn't know the northern country nor the priests proposed to be made bishop. However, he favored Marysville over Sacramento as the see city because it is farther removed from San Francisco and therefore more important for the inland population, whereas

40

Sacramento is of easy access to San Francisco. Finally, he suggested a vicariate apostolic rather than a diocese, thus giving some freedom of choice later on to the new bishop.[67]

In regard to the candidates for bishop of this new territory, Archbishop Alemany proposed three names. In the first place, as "most worthy," was Father James Croke, at that time Alemany's Vicar General and pastor of (Old) St. Mary's Cathedral. The archbishop then listed the many excellent qualities of mind and soul which would qualify Father Croke for the office of bishop. He next proposed Father Eugene O'Connell, professor of All Hallows, Dublin, as his second choice and as "extremely worthy."

We quote in full the Archbishop's estimate of Father O'Connell:

... the second, Eugene O'Connell is endowed with the same qualities; more or less 40 years of age, he was born in Ireland, and is a man of great prayer, purity of conscience, piety, docility, obedience and humility, great zeal, charity, who by his preaching moves the hearts of the faithful. Besides English, he has knowledge of Spanish and perhaps French. He is a professor at All Hallows, Dublin, Ireland, and enjoys a knowledge especially of Theology, and sufficient skill in business matters. He was proposed to the Holy See as especially worthy for the Diocese of Monterey in the Council of Baltimore in 1852, and although he belongs by right to the College of All Hallows he was for some years my subject in the California Missions in which he labored with great fruit of souls and the love of all, and in which he is willing now to work if he merits to obtain the consent of his Superiors. Furthermore it is important to the Church to have good Shepherds, so that it would be, unless I am mistaken, very useful for the work of Religion if Father O'Connell was deemed worthy to be sent to our California Missions.

In third place, as "worthy," the Archbishop proposed the name of Father Thomas Foley, secretary to the archbishop of Baltimore.[68]

All this had taken place without Father O'Connell's knowledge. Little did he dream while he was in Santa Inez that his name had been proposed as a candidate for bishop when the first division of California was being planned. His name was then in third place because, as it was pointed out, he was quite young, only 37. Now again, unknown to him, it was proposed by Archbishop Alemany that Father O'Connell return to the California mission.

This time the Archbishop's request received prompt attention in Rome. Cardinal Barnabo prepared the document to be set before the members of the Sacred Congregation. It set forth the proposals of the Archbishop with necessary reasons and statistics. All was in readiness for the meeting of the Congregation set for September 18, 1860. Just about the time that Father O'Connell was returning to his classroom at All Hallows, the seven members of the Congregation met at the Vatican and considered carefully the proposal, the alternatives, and the candidates. The results were an affirmative decision regarding the suggestion that the archdiocese be divided and the selection of the first alternative for the boundary lines, with Marysville as the see city. However, following Bishop Amat's advice, it was thought better that the new area not be made a diocese but rather a vicariate apostolic, a division lower in rank and dependent on the mother diocese, a structure which had a missionary status and which could be easily changed or suppressed if it did not work out. The final decision was that Eugene O'Connell was to be the bishop.[69]

The Cardinal Prefect had an audience with the Holy Father, Pius IX, on September 23, 1860, at which the Holy Father approved these decisions. The Cardinal Prefect then set about informing the parties concerned. The letter from Rome to Father O'Connell was written on October 12, 1860. When he received it is not known. His reaction is. It was a completely unexpected shock. The letter informing Archbishop Alemany was written on October 10, 1860. The Archbishop was delighted.[70]

Those days were troublesome ones for the dean of All Hallows. He was torn between his loyalty and obedience to the will of God as expressed in this appointment from the Holy See, and also his pity for "poor Dr. Alemany," whom he realized wanted him and needed him, and his reluctance to return to California and take on the awesome responsibility of shepherd of the flock in northern California and Nevada. He had witnessed some of the difficulties Archbishop Alemany had faced and he felt inadequate in taking on these burdens. These were days of prayer and consultation, days of indecision, of seeking advice. The final decision was that he would go to Rome and ask the Holy Father to change his mind about the appointment. If Pius IX declined, he would accept the responsibility and leave the matter in God's hands.

Early in November, the worried Father Eugene O'Connell left Ireland for Rome. He arrived at the Irish College in Rome on November 9, 1860, where he was to be a guest during his stay. There he wrote letters and arranged for appointments.[71] His audience with Pius IX must have been immediate and, of course, the answer was negative. Eugene O'Connell, missionary, seminary professor, dean of his college, was to become the Titular Bishop of Flaviopolis and Vicar Apostolic of Marysville in far-off California. The die was cast. The bishop-elect, summoning his courage and using his wit and knowledge of the Roman Martyrology, said to Pius IX: "Most Holy Father, I am condemned to the mines [damnatus ad metalla]."

Now that his future was determined, the new bishop-elect set about taking care of urgent matters: such things as money to get to California, personnel to help him, and the obtaining of the necessary jurisdiction (faculties) he would need in the administration of his vicariate. The necessary jurisdiction was to be obtained from Cardinal Barnabo to whom he was to be directly responsible. Whenever Bishop Eugene O'Connell had to "write to Rome," that meant to the Cardinal Prefect of Propaganda Fidei, the arm of the church which has jurisdiction over all the mission lands. Eugene O'Connell put in writing to Cardinal Barnabo on November 15, 1860, his initial concerns: "Please let me know how I am to go to the Vicariate assigned me and whence I am to obtain the funds since I don't have the necessary money to undertake such a journey." He then requested the necessary faculties and asked a question about the application of a certain law on marriage in California.[72] Cardinal Barnabo replied the very next day by granting him the necessary faculties in person and informing the bishop-elect that the Society for the Propagation of the Faith in Paris would supply the funds.

On December 21, 1860, the bishop-elect wrote that he planned to return to Ireland after Christmas and that he was seeking another audience with the Holy Father. He would return to Ireland via Paris so that he could visit the headquarters of the Society for the Propagation of the Faith.[73] He was in Paris at the Irish College on January 12, 1861. On that date he wrote to Monsieur Certes, the lay administrator of the Society. He told him that he now had only five priests in his vicariate. Father Daniel Slattery, pastor of Marysville, had died in October; two or three had preferred to remain attached to San Francisco and left their posts. So all he had now was five. This information had been sent to him via All Hallows which had received a letter from Father James Largan of Placerville in California. Bishop-elect O'Connell hoped to recruit helpers, but the fare for each one would be 1,500 francs. Monsieur Certes promised to send him needed funds. The departure date was set for March 1, 1861.[74]

Bishop-elect O'Connell was home in All Hallows by January 24, 1861, as on that date he wrote the first of very many letters to Cardinal Barnabo submitting to him cases for solution and problems to be solved. Eugene O'Connell demonstrated early his unfamiliarity with canon law, especially the laws on marriage, so that he did not feel capable of solving the kind of complicated cases found in America. But there also begins to appear an evidence of indecision, the lack of ability to use general guidelines and resolve his own problems, a certain scrupulosity concerning the observation of the law to the letter and the need to ask permissions before varying from the letter of the law. These showed themselves almost immediately.

There is evidence that after a while Rome began to ignore some of Eugene's requests hoping he would make up his own mind. The first letter to Cardinal Barnabo dated January 24, 1861, asks for four permissions and submits five questions regarding marriage.[75] It is safe to state that hardly ever did a letter go to the Cardinal Prefect from that date on without one or more questions regarding the application of the laws of marriage being included.

His consecration as bishop took place in the chapel of All Hallows on February 3, 1861. The principal consecrator was Archbishop Paul Cullen of Dublin, and the co-consecrators were Bishop Edward Walsh of Ossory and Bishop James Walsh of Kildare. The archbishop of Dublin gave him a mitre as a gift, and he received a pectoral cross from the mother of the Jesuit Father Segrave of the English province. The bishop of Killaloe, Dr. Flannery, was the donor of an episcopal ring.[76] It was a jubilant day for All Hallows, the faculty, and students. Eugene O'Connell was now Bishop O'Connell, Titular Bishop of Flaviopolis and vicar apostolic of Marysville in California.[77]

The next month was a busy one. He succeeded in getting one recruit, Father Francis Joseph Blake, former rector of the minor seminary of Newry and at that time assistant pastor of the Dublin parish of St. Michael and St. Joseph.[78]

Evidently he also brought along a young man named Bernard Fitzpatrick and there are also hints that a sexton or custodian was included in the group, although this last cannot be stated with accuracy.[79]

The first pecuniary draft arrived from Paris at the end of January, practically on the eve of his consecration. It contained the news that a total of 15,000 francs had been allocated to the new vicariate. Four-fifths of the total, 12,000 francs, accompanied the letter. The balance of 3,000 francs was to be sent in care of the president of All Hallows for forwarding to Bishop O'Connell.[80] In sending his letter of appreciation to the Society for the Propagation of the Faith two days after his consecration, the bishop stated:

> Your alms, because they spring from charity and are watered by prayer, have relieved that voluntary poverty which I had here embraced by devoting my services such as they were, for so many years to serve the missions gratuitously in this institution. I intend to sail from Cork on March 7, 1861 with the Missioners whom I have already obtained.[81]

Most of the faculty bade Bishop O'Connell farewell at Dublin's Kingsbridge Railway Terminal. The college president, Father Bartholomew Woodlock, and Father Conroy saw him off at Queenstown when he boarded the ship for New York. The voyage was a rough one, taking fourteen days. A storm struck when they were close to New York, during which one passenger committed suicide by throwing himself overboard. They arrived safely on Holy Thursday, March 28, 1861. They stayed in New York for the Holy Week and Easter services, then sailed for California on the Monday after Easter, April 1, 1861.[82]

At this time, the travelers from east to west were using the Isthmus of Panama rather than the Nicaraguan route that Eugene

O'Connell had used on his first voyage ten years previously. The steamer *Champion* took them from New York to Aspinwell in Panama. They boarded the steamer *Golden Age* on the Pacific side and sailed for San Francisco. Thirty-eight days after leaving Cork, the party arrived in San Francisco, on April 24, 1861. They were met by Archbishop Alemany and Father James Cotter of St. Mary's Cathedral. Bishop O'Connell wanted to proceed at once to Marysville but, prudently, Archbishop Alemany advised delaying the installation in order to have Bishop O'Connell rest.[83]

One of the highlights of the week in San Francisco was Eugene O'Connell's return to Mission Dolores, where he had been pastor and rector, and now returned as bishop. Father John Prendergast, an All Hallows alumnus in 1859, was then the new rector of the seminary, having succeeded Father Carroll who had died the previous month. Father Prendergast gathered as many of the All Hallows alumni as could be assembled and their former professor, now bishop, received a grand welcome and, to top it off, a purse in the amount of $1,000. Eugene O'Connell was overwhelmed by this display of affection and sacrifice. He was urged to keep the money, since the church in Marysville was not in good condition and he would have to build a new rectory.[84]

On May 2, 1861, the two bishops boarded a steamer bound for Sacramento, and on the next day changed there to one bound for Marysville. Bishop Eugene O'Connell set foot in Marysville for the first time on Saturday, May 4, 1861. His installation, on the following day, was described by the local daily paper in the following words:

> Rt. Rev. Bishop O'Connell was presented to his Congregation at the Roman Catholic Church in this City last Sunday by Most Rev. Archbishop Alemany, who preached an able and eloquent sermon in the morning. The attendance was large and the exercise interesting and imposing. In the evening the new Bishop preached to a large congregation.[85]

Present at the event were the current pastor of St. Joseph's in Marysville, the Rev. Robert A. Maurice; the assistant pastor, the Rev. Bernard Morris, an All Hallows Alumnus ordained in 1858, and the Rev. Francis Blake.

When Archbishop Alemany took the "down" steamer a

couple of days later, Bishop O'Connell was alone with his new responsibility. The conversations of the past few days did not exactly encourage him, for he had discovered that his see was in debt from the beginning. The Archbishop had revealed that there was still an outstanding debt on St. Joseph's in Marysville, and there was a debt on a non-existent church in Shasta which had to be paid off. In both cases, the discouragement came from the fact that the construction was not complete. There were only the foundations of a church in Shasta, and the Marysville church was incomplete and already needed a new roof.[86]

The rectory was even more discouraging. It is best to let Bishop O'Connell describe it.

A comfortable house is absolutely necessary for a missionary priest or bishop. Such a house we have not as yet, but what they call a wooden shanty—the debris of the first Catholic Church in Marysville, infested by flies, mosquitoes and rats, so that really it is more tolerable to live out of it than inside its wooden walls.[87]

The Bishop is here talking about a wooden building 32' x 48' which Father Peter Magagnotto, the first resident pastor, had built in 1852 to serve as a temporary church until St. Joseph's was finished in 1855.[88] The interior had then been carved up into rooms and had served as a rectory since that time. Bishop O'Connell felt that the first order of business was the building of a new residence. He kept his confreres at All Hallows appraised of the proceedings. On July 16, 1861, he wrote, "Father Morris is engaged at present, as I have been myself, collecting funds to build a habitable house which we need so badly."[89] The new house was completed, and the Bishop, Father Morris, and the newly arrived Father Griffin moved into it on St. Patrick's Day, March 17, 1862.[90] But there was to be no rest. Immediately, Father Morris began a second collection, this time to repair and enlarge St. Joseph's Church, "which I assure you is sadly in need of it," wrote the Bishop. On September 26, 1862, he wrote to All Hallows,

I assure you, in this golden country, money doesn't flow

into me. I was obliged to collect in person for the repairs of our church in Marysville, and during my month's trip in the mountains, I did not make as much as I used to on the Meath circuit [reference to when he collected for All Hallows in County Meath, Ireland]. I could only put a tin roof on the Church.[91]

He related that after his own and Father Morris's expenses, and after paying £6 per month to the housekeeper and £5 to James, "once of All Hallows," out of stipends and Sunday collections, there was nothing left.[92]

Bishop O'Connell now had a respectable house in which to live and entertain visiting priests, and he had a more than respectable cathedral for the times. We can now begin to consider his chief labors for the good of the souls committed to his care.

Sources for Chapter IV

63. Peter Guilday, *History of the Councils of Baltimore* (New York: The Macmillan Co., 1932), p. 214.

64. ASPF, letter of December 28, 1869.

65. McGloin, op. cit., p. 174.

66. ASRC, Vol. 386, F682, letter of J. S. Alemany, May 20, 1859.

67. AALA, Amat to Barnabo, July 9, 1860.

68. ASRC, Vol. 386, F679, document prepared by Cardinal Barnabo for Propaganda meeting.

69. McGloin, op. cit., p. 175.

70. ASRC, Vol. 18, F1237, letter of November 15, 1860.

71. Kenneally, *U.S. Documents*, Vol. V, #351, F679.

72. ASRC, Vol. 18, F1237, letter to Cardinal Barnabo.

73. AAHC, letter of December 21, 1860.

74. ASPF, letter from Irish College, Paris, January 12, 1861.

75. ASRC, Vol. 19, F74, letter of January 24, 1861.
76. AUND, James F. Edwards Papers, letter of January 27, 1887.
77. Joseph B. Code, *Dictionary of the American Hierarchy* (New York: Jos. Wagner), p. 221.
78. *Marysville Daily Appeal*, April 30, 1861.
79. AAHC, letter of April 30, 1861.
80. AALA, letter of February 5, 1861.
81. ASPF, letter of February 16, 1861.
82. AAHC, letter of April 30, 1861.
83. Ibid.
84. Ibid.
85. *Marysville Daily Appeal*, May 7, 1861.
86. AAHC, letter of April 30, 1861.
87. AAHC, letter of July 16, 1861.
88. Thompson & West, *History of Yuba County* (Oakland, 1879), p. 54.
89. AAHC, letter of July 16, 1861.
90. AAHC, letter of March 28, 1862.
91. AAHC, letter of September 26, 1862.
92. AAHC, letter of August 12, 1861.

Chapter V

PASTORAL JOURNEYS, 1861-1884

One of the most appealing characteristics of the late Pope John XXIII, the one which most attracted people to him, was his great pastoral approach. Since his time, bishops have found that more and more emphasis is placed on their being "shepherds of the flock" than on their being "administrators of dioceses." The vicar apostolic of Marysville would very much have pleased Pope John XXIII. This is somewhat surprising since he was primarily a seminary professor by inclination and experience; yet his three years as pastor of the Missions of California at Santa Inez and Dolores had made a great impact on him. A personal inclination to be a pastorally oriented priest also contributed to this outstanding characteristic of his twenty-three years as bishop of the flock.

No sooner was he somewhat settled in Marysville than Bishop O'Connell felt it was his prime duty to visit the parishes of his vicariate. But for him a visitation was no short stay. He did not come to be entertained; he came to work and work he did. We are fortunate that several glimpses into the nature of these pastoral visits have been preserved.

But first there was the very difficult task of reaching the place of the visitation. At the time he undertook his first visitation, he had only six parishes. There was Marysville. Then the nearest neighbor was Grass Valley about thirty-five miles away and Downieville another fifty miles beyond. The other three priests and their flocks were far to the north on the way to the Oregon border. This was the first area Bishop O'Connell decided

ST. PATRICK'S CHURCH, Weaverville, California
Built by the Rev. Patrick O'Reilly in
1860 after fire destroyed
Most Holy Trinity Church. Served as
parish church until fire of 1897.
(Photo, taken in 1887, courtesty of Trinity County Historical Society)

to visit. He tells the story himself in a letter to All Hallows just two months after his arrival.

> I set out from Marysville, my residence, en route to Weaverville; the first place I reached (through clouds of dust) over a rugged road in a four wheeled vehicle called a stagecoach here (or a day coach in Ireland) was Oroville, twenty eight miles distant; a considerable town without any priest. Thence we hurried under a burning sun (early August) and thru volumes of dust by stage to Red Bluff (tota nocte itinerantes—travelling the whole night) sixty three miles from Oroville—no resident priest. Thence we hurried to Shasta, forty miles more; and if I proceed to Yreka, I shall have a hundred more miles to travel, not to speak of climbing a huge mountain called the Backbone of the Salmon River.[93]

He wrote the letter on the fifth day of his visit in Weaverville with Father Patrick O'Reilly. He later wrote again and described the journey from Weaverville to Yreka.

> The Salmon Mountain (which is now called Scott Mountain) is so high that it takes nearly a whole day to cross it on mule back; the ascent is by means of a zigzag or worm trail (as Americans would call it). Just wide enough for a single man or mule along the hillside, in some places sandy, in other rugged and rocky. The distance from the base to the top of this almost perpendicular mountain is almost eight miles, the descent on the northern side is reckoned to be four miles, and the yawning chasm beneath is deep enough to engulf a regiment.[94]

This then brought the Bishop to Yreka and to Father Thomas Crinion. Whether he was able to see Father Florian Schwenninger, the Benedictine priest who cared for the mines along the Salmon River at Sawyers Bar, is unknown, but probably he did. On his return from this arduous venture the Bishop stayed briefly in Marysville and then set off again, this time for Downieville and a visit with Father Cornelius Delahunty.[95] He had two choices as to routes to Downieville. He could go the longer way—to Grass Valley and Nevada (City) and up over the ridge and down the

IMMACULATE CONCEPTION CHURCH, Downieville, California
There is some evidence that the first church in Downieville was a simple structure erected by Father John Shanahan in 1853. However, early in 1856 Father Dalton purchased a former Baptist Church for $2,300 and on June 22, 1856, Archbishop Alemany came from San Francisco and dedicated it under the title of "The Assumption." When this church burned on January 1, 1858, Father Dalton built the present church about 150 yards north of the former site and dedicated it under the title of "The Immaculate Conception." It still serves as the parish church.
(Photo, courtesy of Historic Preservation Committee)

other side to the forks of the Yuba River, up the next ridge and down again, and once again up and down over a tortuous road to Downieville; or he could take one of the advertised stage routes direct from Marysville to Downieville. We will let the advertisement in the September 11, 1862, issue of the *Marysville Appeal* tell the story.

> U S Mail Line for Downieville. Leaves Marysville every morning at 4 o'clock for Goodyears Bar, Brandy City, Eureka, Monte Cristo and Downieville. Passengers booking their names will be called for in any part of the City. Office corner of D and 3rd Sts. St. Nicholas Hotel, Marysville.[96]

We can easily imagine the stagecoach pulling up in front of the flimsy rectory at 7th and C at the end of September to pick up its episcopal passenger and then dashing off in a whirl of dust for the long trip to Downieville. Bishop O'Connell was in the little rectory of Downieville with Father Delahunty on October 1, 1861, for he performed a baptism on that date.[97] There is an indication that his return was via the other route. He confirmed three boys and two girls in Moores Flat on Sunday, November 10, 1861.[98] Thus he would have returned via Grass Valley, completing his visitation for the year 1861.

Each time he received more priests and was able to establish more parishes, the visitations became longer and more distant. The first parish the Bishop created was St. Joseph's in Forest Hill, twenty-two miles from the present city of Auburn. On July 14, 1861, Father Francis J. Blake, the priest he had brought with him from Ireland, took up his residence in Forest Hill.[99] This became an important parish over the years. In 1867, the Pastor was Father James J. Callan. In his extensive pastoral visit of that year, Forest Hill was on the itinerary. Luckily an eyewitness correspondent tells us of that visitation in June, 1867.

> Rt. Rev. Eugene O'Connell, Vicar Apostolic of Marysville visited us for the first time in two years, and during the eight days of his visit, he was from early morn until late at night unceasingly in the confessional, where many a weary soul found rest.
>
> After the Sunday Mass by Father Callan an able and instructive sermon was delivered by his Lordship.

On Monday the Church burial grounds were solemnly consecrated and on Thursday 30 persons received Confirmation. In the evening the children (82 pupils) of St. Joseph's School entertained him from 7:30 until 10:30. Over 400 persons were present for this occasion. On Friday evening the Bishop was taken by surprise as members of the Society of the Sacred Heart formed a semi-circle in front of Father Callan's house accompanied by the Forest Hill Brass Band. At the end the Bishop was given a purse of $200.00. The latter he absolutely refused to accept only on condition that they would permit him to send every dollar of it to All Hallows College for the education of young Missionary priests for the Vicariate. The donors, altho they intended it for his own use, acceded to his proposition.[100]

This pattern of work in each place he visited did not change with the years. As late as 1883, when he was now an old man by the standard of the times, we read this account of his visit to Eureka, California, in August, 1883:

Bishop O'Connell is making his visitation in Humbolt County. He spent many days in Eureka with Father Sheridan in instructing the children for Confirmation which he administered on Sunday August 19, 1883 to forty persons. A few days later he was in Arcata, twelve miles north of Eureka. Now he is in Ferndale with Father Kennedy.

The zeal of Bishop O'Connell knows no rest. When the voice of duty calls, and though feeble in health and in the autumn of life, he is strong to obey. During the week he will administer Confirmation in Table Bluff.[101]

Besides the hardships of travel, there was the expense involved which taxed not only the physical strength of the bishop but also his meager pocketbook.

An article in *The Monitor* of November 14, 1868, describes a trip via stagecoach to eastern Nevada, where Bishop O'Connell would go in the 1870s after he founded a parish at Hamilton in the White Pine District:

It now costs hard upon $100.00 to make the journey from San Francisco to White Pine, Nevada, the time consumed

ST. PATRICK'S CHURCH, Grass Valley.
Built by the Rev. Thomas J. Dalton, 1858
(Photo, courtesy of Historic Preservation Committee, Grass Valley)

being nearly a week. The route and cost of travel are as follows.
 To Sacramento by steamer (120 miles) one night and fare including stateroom and supper: $7.00
 To Wadsworth (188 miles)—one day: fare with meals $17.00
 To Austin by stage (160 miles) one day and two nights: fare with meals $32.00
 To White Pine (120 miles east of Austin)—one day and night: fare with meals including lying over one night at Austin $26.00 with the certainty of having to pay at present from $10.00 to $20.00 in addition, thru delay either at Wadsworth or Austin, sometimes at both places. [102]

Someone remarked it was no wonder the Bishop spent a week or more in these places. It took days to recover from such a trip. Yet this round of visitations went on every year.

When visiting places close to Marysville, the Bishop did not travel by stagecoach. In Father Dalton's account book, preserved in Grass Valley, we get a glimpse of the Bishop's mode of conveyance and its cost while on a visit to Grass Valley to lay the cornerstone of the new orphanage under construction:

April 29, 1865 to Fr Griffin for buggy and other expenses from Marysville to Smartsville	$19.00
Horses and buggy from there to Grass Valley	8.00
May 4, 1865 Team and buggy with Dr. O'Connell to Marysville	20.00

The cornerstone laying was on May 2nd; two days later the bishop was ready to return to Marysville. Evidently the "other expenses" included Father Griffin's fare on the stagecoach to get to Marysville to begin the complicated process of bringing and returning the Bishop who had no mode of conveyance of his own.

A typical circuit of his visitations can be seen for 1867. While the visit in Forest Hill occurred in June, 1867, the following month found him in Eureka, California, a journey which required transportation by water.[103] First, Bishop O'Connell boarded a steamer in Marysville which took seven hours to reach Sacramento; then he boarded another which took overnight to reach San

Francisco. Then he caught an ocean vessel sailing for Eureka, not always a pleasant voyage either. A *Monitor* article on October 11, 1882, stated: "Rt. Rev. E. O'Connell returned on Sunday last from an Episcopal visit to Crescent City where he arrived after a rough voyage during which he suffered much from sea sickness."[104] Scarcely rested up from his journey to Eureka, the Bishop now headed east to the far-flung Nevada portion of his diocese. At the end of August, he was in Virginia City where again he administered confirmation. Highlights of this trip were the dedications of two new churches: the second St. Patrick's in Gold Hill, a prosperous mining town just east of Virginia City on September 1, 1867, and then one week later on September 8th, the beautiful new St. Augustine's Church in Austin, Nevada, said to have cost $50,000.[105] Bishop O'Connell was still in Austin on October 1, 1867. On that date he was presented with a purse which again he refused unless he could send it to All Hallows.[106] But the Bishop's rounds were not completed until November when we find him in Nevada (City), four miles from Grass Valley, giving confirmation to eleven boys and eleven girls.

The year 1871, the year following his return from Rome and attendance at Vatican Council I, had a typically rigorous schedule, considering the difficulties of travel and the distances involved. The first recorded confirmation for that year was in Cherokee in Nevada County on April 23, 1871.[107] On May 23, he was in Nevada (City) for the same purpose, and on the following day in Grass Valley.[108] Forest Hill was included in this visitation, but the date in May was not recorded.[109] The Bishop was at home by the 28th. On that date he confirmed the class of 1870 who waited an extra year since their bishop was absent in Rome.[110] In June, Bishop O'Connell went to Weaverville as he had ten years previously. There on June 22 he administered confirmation.[111] By July 17 he was in Gold Hill, Nevada, for confirmation, and in Virginia City on July 21.[112] He was home in Marysville for the confirmation of the 1871 class on August 16th.[113] Early in October he set out for Downieville where he confirmed on October 2 and in Howland Flat on October 8.[114]

Another itinerary confirms the rigorous pace that had become habitual for him. The year 1873, for example, found him in Carson City, Nevada, on June 30,[115] in Virginia City on July 2, in Gold Hill on July 4,[116] and in Austin a few days later. By July 15, he was confirming in Weaverville.[117] On August 3, he was in Los Angeles as co-consecrator of the new coadjutor bishop, Francis Mora, of the Monterey diocese,[118] and on September 26 he gave confirmation in Camptonville,[119] on the 28th in Downieville, and on September 30 in Howland Flat. On October 1, he was in Port Wine, and October 2 at La Porte, in each place conferring the sacrament of confirmation. On the way home, he confirmed in Nevada (City) on October 8, 1873.[120] This kind of schedule continues on through 1876 at a breathtaking pace. When we consider how pastorally involved he was in each of these places, hearing confessions, baptizing, marrying, helping prepare the children for confirmation, one wonders at the stamina of Eugene O'Connell.

Evidently, in his early days he had excellent health. The only reference that can be found to any kind of poor health is an interesting entry in *The Monitor* on February 22, 1868. The letter published is actually an advertisement for a patent medicine to the merits of which Bishop O'Connell gave his testimony, stating that he received immediate relief for his neuralgia when he used "Bladwins Neuralgia Liniment." His words were: "I have suffered severely from inveterate neuralgia."[121] Considering the hundreds of miles he traveled each year in stagecoaches, it is understandable that he might have neuralgia. That the Bishop was indeed laid low by this neuralgia is confirmed in a letter of Father Manogue to Paris written on February 12, 1868. "His Lordship, the Bishop of Marysville, being indisposed, requested me to write this communication."[122] There were indications of poor health on the part of the Bishop in his later years. A serious illness occurred in April, 1883, when he was sixty-eight years old. A *Monitor* notice on May 2, 1883, stated:

> We regret to learn that our esteemed friend, Bishop O'Connell of Marysville, has been seriously indisposed during the past week, and we ask the prayers of our readers that his life may be spared, as the loss of a Prelate, possessing such wisdom, prudence and charity, would be a serious calamity to the catholic community in general.[123]

The enormous expanse of his vicariate was difficult to explain to either his friends at All Hallows or to the Propagation of the Faith in Paris. These seemed never to get the concept of the vastness of the territory contained within the vicariate of Marysville. It is interesting to read the various efforts to convey this idea to his readers. To say that the vicariate extended from the 39th to the 42nd degree of latitude and from the Pacific Ocean to the Utah border does not make much of an impression on the average reader, especially those who live in Europe. The best description of the vastness of the territory for which Bishop O'Connell was responsible and over which he exercised such pastoral solicitude is to be found in a report written by Father Manogue of Virginia City at the Bishop's request during his illness in 1868. Father Manogue wrote:

> To give an idea of the extent of this laborious Mission, it will suffice to say that it contains about 197,000 square miles—England, Ireland, Scotland, and Wales united contain but 119,600, the Diocese of Marysville exceeding Great Britain and Ireland by 77,400 square miles. From this calculation you are enabled to infer that our Vicariate is almost equal in extent to the Empire of France the latter exceeding it by only 7,800 square miles.[124]

This explains such outbursts as the following in the letters Bishop O'Connell sent back to All Hallows:

> How soon, my dear Father, will you be able to send me one or two more priests? Oh, would you, as soon as possible? Consider Nevada Territory, or Washoe, with its ten counties without a single resident priest; again Humbolt County, stretching along the Pacific, and Del Norte, both without priests. How many children and adults seek bread and there is no one to break it for them.[125]

> Imagine a country as large as Ireland depending on six priests; if there be not an extreme necessity, I leave you to judge. I wrote from Yreka in Siskiyou County to the Pastor of the adjoining parish on Friday and my letter reached him on the following Friday, so difficult is the communication between some places. I must leave a great portion of the north, the whole of Sierra County, without a priest besides the whole western district of the Vicariate is in the same condition.

I haven't yet visited Mormondom or Utah territory, but the Catholics in that quarter are so destitute that they don't see a priest except once a quarter. I can only send them the loan of a priest, who must return to his flock after a month's stay. In the same territory there are three important places viz Carson City, Virginia City and Genoa, without a resident priest, where they report that the Catholics are dying without the Sacraments.

Another great obstacle to priests and people in this Country are the mountain ranges, which in some instances quite surround a district and hardly allow an entrance or exit for several months in the year, owing partly to the immense heights of the ridges, which besides are covered with snow during winter and spring.[126]

It should be very obvious from the above that one of the first concerns of Bishop O'Connell was to obtain a supply of priests for his enormous territory. Who was in a better position to obtain them from All Hallows than this man whose heart and soul was devoted to this beloved institution? Who could work on the sympathies of his Irish readers better than this professor become missionary bishop?

Sources for Chapter V

93. AAHC, letter of August 12, 1861.

94. AAHC, letter of September 16, 1861.

95. Baptismal Register, Marysville, September 13, 1861.

96. *Marysville Appeal*, September 11, 1862.

97. Baptismal Register, Downieville.

98. Baptismal Register, Vol. I, Grass Valley.

99. Baptismal Register, Forest Hill, "Veni ad Forest Hill July 14, 1861."

100. *The Monitor*, June 22, 1867.

101. Ibid., September 5, 1883.

102. Ibid., November 14, 1868.

103. Walsh, *Hallowed Were,* p. 293.

104. *The Monitor,* October 11, 1882.

105. Gorman, *Seventy-Five Years,* p. 90.

106. *The Monitor,* October 19, 1867.

107. Confirmation Register, Marysville, April 23, 1871.

108. Baptismal Register, Nevada City, May 23, 1871.

109. Baptismal Register, Forest Hill, May, 1871.

110. Confirmation Register, Marysville, May 28, 1871.

111. Baptismal Register, Weaverville, June 22, 1871.

112. Baptismal Register, Gold Hill, Nevada, July 17, 1871.

113. Confirmation Register, Marysville, August 16, 1871.

114. Baptismal Register, Downieville, October 2 and October 8, 1871.

115. Baptismal Register, Carson City, Nevada, June 30, 1873.

116. Baptismal Register, Virginia City, July 2, 1873.

117. Baptismal Register, Weaverville, July 15, 1873.

118. Code, op. cit., p. 207.

119. Baptismal Register, Downieville, September 26, 1873.

120. Baptismal Register, Nevada City, October 8, 1873.

121. *The Monitor,* February 22, 1868.

122. AALA, Manogue to Propagation of the Faith, February 12, 1868.

123. *The Monitor,* May 2, 1883.

124. AALA, Manogue to Propagation of the Faith, February 12, 1868.

125. AAHC, letter of January 28, 1862.

126. AAHC, letter of September 16, 1861.

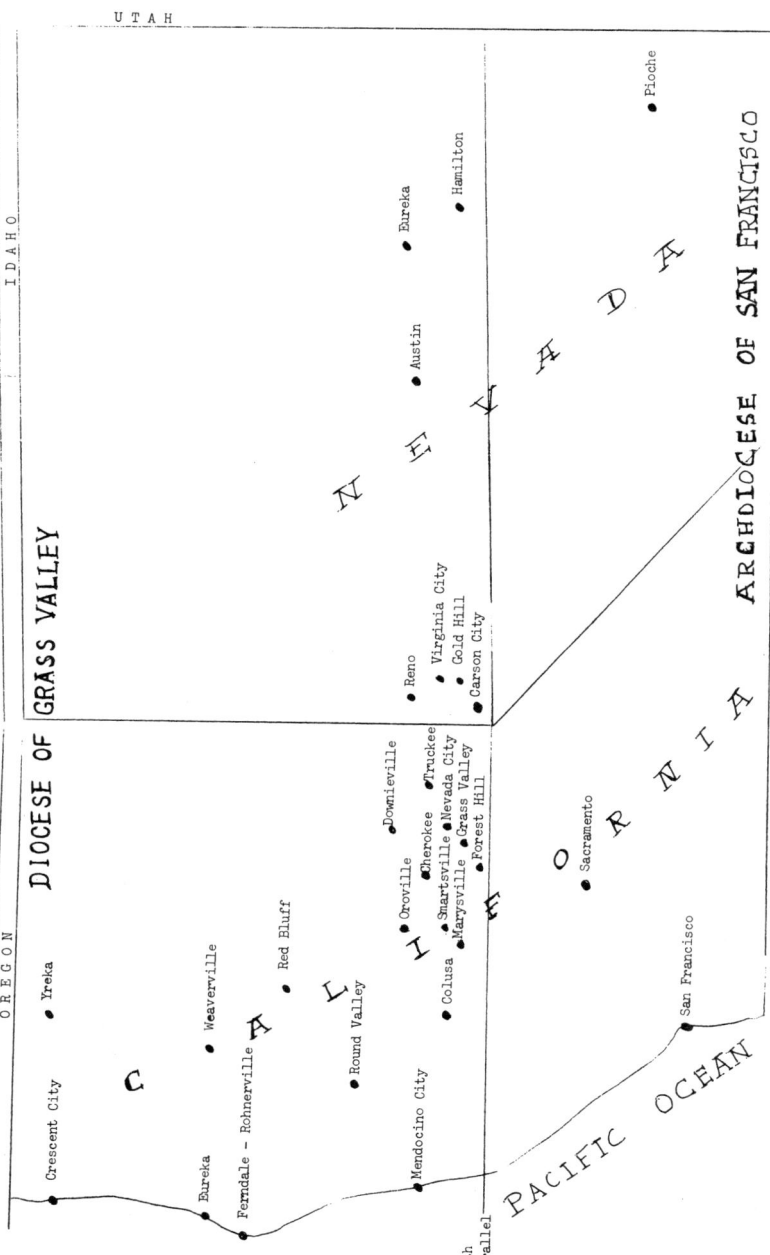

Chapter VI

SUPPLIER OF PRIESTS, 1861–1864

Bishop O'Connell's all-absorbing preoccupation was to obtain priests to serve the people of his far-flung vicariate. We have already seen his concern that there were no priests in Nevada, nor on the Pacific Coast, nor in some of the major towns in the upper Sacramento Valley. The first fruits of his efforts were obtained in 1862. The first to come was Father John Griffin. A native of Kilmacow, County Kilkenny, Ireland, John Griffin was ordained a priest in Dublin for the Diocese of Boston on August 11, 1861. Because Father Griffin was not too robust in health, arrangements were made between Bishop O'Connell and Bishop Fitzpatrick of Boston so that the newly ordained priest was released for service in the Marysville vicariate. He left Ireland in November, 1861, and arrived in San Francisco on December 26, 1861. Bishop O'Connell was impatient for his arrival. "What can I do until the arrival of Father Griffin, whom I look on as a godsend?"[127] He tells about his arrival in a letter he wrote on January 28, 1862:

> Father Griffin arrived in San Francisco on St. Stephen's Day and came by slow marches to Marysville about a fortnight [two weeks] after. He was the delight of the Marysvillians by reason of his sermons and personal appearance, as long as I could keep him. But, alas, Father Dalton's brother George, having killed his adversary in an affray, I

was obliged to send Father Griffin to Grass Valley, some thirty miles distant, in order to come to poor Father Dalton's rescue. The latter couldn't face the people in consequence of his brother's doings.[128]

This arrangement was temporary, just for the months of February and part of March, for by March 20, 1862, Father Griffin was a regular assistant at Marysville.[129]

The Bishop now had two assistants in Marysville, Father Bernard Morris and Father John Griffin. The former pastor, Father Robert A. Maurice, had terminated his service in the vicariate at Bishop O'Connell's request at the end of April, 1861.[130] It seems the Bishop was not satisfied with Father Maurice's handling of finances, and having suffered through two scandals involving mismanagement of funds when he was a missionary in the early '50s, the Bishop was reluctant to chance another. Father Maurice was an Englishman, a convert to Catholicism, evidently ordained for Glasgow, Scotland, who had given outstanding service to the Archdiocese of San Francisco as founding priest of the Boys' Home, St. Vincent's in San Rafael, California, in 1855, as pastor of St. Mary's in Stockton from 1856–60, and then as successor in Marysville to Father Daniel Slattery.[131] Father Maurice evidently returned to Great Britain. Actually, with the arrival of Father Griffin and the departure of Father Maurice, Bishop O'Connell had only a change of personnel, not the increase for which he had pleaded.

The Bishop was very pleased with his two assistants as he wrote back to All Hallows on March 28, 1862:

> When will you send me another missioner like Father Griffin who is giving great satisfaction as a preacher? Father Morris is called a bully preacher. Nothing without preaching satisfies the audiences in this country, and really they deserve it for many reasons, no matter how long he may hold forth. Let my subjects in All Hallows prepare all the sermons they can, otherwise they can produce little or no fruit in this country.[132]

The next young priest to arrive was to prove to be one of his best: six-foot-three Patrick Manogue, a former miner in Moore's

THE REV. PATRICK MANOGUE
Founding Pastor of Virginia City, Nevada 1862–1881
Coadjutor Bishop of Grass Valley, 1881–1884
Second Bishop of Grass Valley, 1884–1886
First Bishop of Sacramento, 1886–1895
(Photo, courtesy of St. Mary's in the Mountains, Virginia City)

Flat who had saved his money, gone to college in Chicago, and to the seminary of St. Sulpice in Paris. Father Manogue had been ordained in Paris on December 21, 1861, and presented himself to Bishop O'Connell on Ascension Day in May, 1862.[133] The Bishop had the answer to his prayers for Nevada. He assigned Father Manogue to the priestless area of Virginia, Carson, and Genoa. Father Manogue went to visit his friend Father Dalton in Grass Valley and assisted him on June 21 and 22.[134] He then left for Nevada and began a missionary career there of twenty-two years.

The next one in All Hallows destined for the vicariate was James Callan. On April 23, 1862, the Bishop wrote as follows:

> I request of you, dear Fr Bennett, to provide Faculties from the Apostolic Delegate for Mr. Callan [the terms Mr. and Father were often interchangeable in those days] the most ample that his Grace can confer—between the College and San Francisco, in a straight line, for I wish Mr Callan to come quamprimum [at once] and this does not mean three months. For mercy sake, hasten his departure from the Ireland of Saints and tell him of his responsibility for the souls of the Mary's-villians. Give him the price of a suit of clothes along with whatever else he may require and I will repay as soon as possible.[135]

On August 20, 1862, came the glad tidings. The Bishop wrote five days later:

> From my heart I thank you for your welcome letter which gladdened me with the good tidings of Fr. Callan's departure from Ireland, although he hasn't come to hand as yet. May God bless you for hastening the arrival of these young men at their destination in order to help their tottering Bishop, who has to bear the heat and weight of the day not infrequently alone.[136]

Father James Callan arrived in Marysville together with Father George Rigby in September, 1862. Father Rigby was a priest of the New York diocese who was loaned to Bishop O'Connell. When Father Callan arrived in New York, the two came to-

THE REV. JAMES J. CALLAN 1836–1887
Assistant at Marysville, 1862–1864
Pastor of Forest Hill, 1864–1868
Pastor of Marysville, 1869–1871
Pastor of Mendocino City, 1871–1873
Pastor of Yreka, 1873–1878
Pastor of Reno, Nevada, 1879–1880
Pastor of Weaverville, 1880–1881
Pastor of Marysville, 1881–1887
(Photo, courtesy of Sisters of Mercy, Grass Valley)

gether to Marysville, but the great joy of the Bishop at the arrival of these young men was to be short-lived. About the same time a letter came from the archbishop of Dublin summoning Father Blake back to Dublin.[137] The Bishop then had no choice but to replace the departing Father Blake with one of the new arrivals. He chose to send Father Rigby as the replacement in Forest Hill.

Father Blake had done good work in Forest Hill in the fifteen months he had been there. The church which he inherited on his arrival, located at Forest Shade, had been built by Father Dalton of Grass Valley. Father Blake had twenty-four new pews made by a carpenter at a cost of $294 in May, 1862. He established a flourishing school, called St. Joseph's, in the parish with a Miss O'Connor as teacher, whose salary for the year was $586. But since the total income from the school for the year was only $168.75, two anonymous donors from Forest Shade made up the deficit between July, 1861, and June 6, 1862.[138] But now in November, 1862, Father Blake had to terminate his work there and return to Ireland. The two priests exchanged places in mid-November, 1862.

One other problem had to be faced by the Bishop: a problem which bothered him seriously over the years and about which he expressed himself quite openly and frankly. Father Delahunty had been alone too long in Downieville and there was a drinking problem. He had been alone in that remote place taking care of Sierra and Plumas counties since 1856. The books show one visitor in 1860 and one in 1861, no others. Bishop O'Connell, aware that there was a problem, went to Downieville himself in mid-July, 1862, and stayed until August.[139] The Bishop then took over for Father Delahunty and took the only measure he had at his disposal to correct the matter. He suspended him from his duties.[140]

There have been, over the years, many stories about Bishop O'Connell's habit of suspending priests. It must be kept in mind that 1862 was more than half a century prior to the Code of Canon Law which has governed the church since 1918. Laws and their applications were not as clear-cut as they became after the publication of the Code.

Whenever Bishop O'Connell transferred a priest from one post to the next, he simply withdrew the priest's faculties (jurisdiction) and told him that the new faculties awaited him on his arrival at the new place. In that sense, it can be said that Bishop O'Connell suspended at one time or another every priest in his diocese except Father Dalton and Father Manogue, the only two whom he never moved.

However, suspension is normally, in the light of the Code, a punitive measure, and one author states that he doubts that Bishop O'Connell ever suspended anyone in this sense.[141] On the contrary, research confirms that he did so in the case of Father Delahunty, and in other instances where he deemed it necessary. It was only a temporary measure to impress on this otherwise good priest that he needed to reform his life. Bishop O'Connell sent Father Delahunty to live with Father Dalton during August, September, and October.[142] Since there was evidence of reform, he then gave him a new appointment as pastor of Carson City, Nevada,[143] where he served for some time and then returned to New York, the diocese from which he came.

The Bishop then had to send Father Morris to Downieville to replace Father Delahunty. He was no better off now than he had been before. With Fathers Blake and Delahunty gone from the local scene, Fathers Rigby and Callan simply filled gaps.

The experience with Father Delahunty sparked a flood of advice to All Hallows from the Bishop. Having been himself alone in Santa Inez, he knew what an oppressive thing loneliness could be, and his sympathetic heart understood but could not condone drinking as a means of solacing that loneliness. "Vae soli [woe to the man alone]," he wrote,

> still hangs over the lonely missioner, and I shall not die easy until, or unless I shall have seen each missioner in the Diocese mated. Some have asked me from time to time: Bishop what will you do with or where do you intend to station so many young priests? I have only to answer in the words of the aged Jacob to Joseph: I know, my son, I know.[144]

Ten years later, Bishop O'Connell reiterates the importance of his priests' being abstemious. One letter says: "I write in the hope that you will be able to supply me with one missioner at least every year whilst I live, but for heaven's sake, let him be whiskey-proof."[145]

And in another the same month he writes: "I must insist on

one or two conditions to be complied with by any missioner that may volunteer for Marysville, viz: total abstinence or strict temperance, and a knowledge of French."[146]

From this it must not be concluded that the Bishop was a rabid teetotaler. He was not. On his initial visit with Father O'Reilly in Weaverville, he told how his delighted host served champagne as a sign of his welcome for the Bishop.[147] In another letter, the Bishop mentions that a certain amount of alcohol was almost a necessity in the missions. And in a reminiscence of Bishop O'Connell by a resident of Marysville who was a boy during Bishop O'Connell's days, the following story is recalled:

> As a young boy I well remember Bishop Eugene O'Connell of the Catholic Church. At that time Marysville was the head of the Diocese; in later years it was moved to Sacramento. The Catholic church was only two blocks from my father's home, and father and the Bishop were good friends, and quite often father would invite the Bishop to take dinner with the family. The Bishop was rather small in stature, exceedingly affable, and had a wonderful fund of humor, and the family always enjoyed his visits. I also enjoyed seeing him come to dinner, but for perhaps a reprehensible reason. When he was present champagne was always served and when dinner was over and everyone retired to the parlor I would remain in the dining room, and before our Chinese cook, Jack, cleared off the table, I would watch my chance and empty any glasses which might have champagne left in them. When the Bishop would take his departure he would always place his hand on my head and say to me: "Always be a good boy, William"; and William would always feel a little guilty when he answered: "Yes, sir," with possibly a glass of champagne in his tummie which he had sneaked from the dinner table.[148]

So quite obviously, Bishop O'Connell was no "prude" but he saw a special danger in the use of drink, especially in the lonely outposts of his vicariate. Some years later he was able to report that with one or two exceptions all his priests were abstemious in the use of liquor, a fact for which he was very grateful.

Because of the setbacks encountered in 1862, Archbishop

THE REV. THOMAS J. DALTON, Founding Pastor of Grass Valley, 1855–1891
(Photo, courtesy of Historic Preservation Committee, Grass Valley)

Alemany decided to lend him one of his priests. One of the first priests to come to the archdiocese from the seminary at Carlow was Father Denis Dempsey. He was sent up to Marysville to assist Bishop O'Connell in January, 1863.

But again, Father Dalton in Grass Valley had family trouble:

> T'was only yesterday that I had to send Father Dempsey who is visiting me, to assist Father Dalton in his anguish after his brother Kit's tragic demise. A man named Con Reilly entered Kit Dalton's grocery and liquor store, and without any provocation on Kit's part, stabbed him seven times fatally, the poor fellow surviving only about an hour. Father Dalton heard his confession and anointed him. Isn't this lamentable? Father Rigby is going on, I hope, very well, in Father Blake's place, but until there are two priests in each Mission things can't be quite right. Vae soli, and that is the case with every one of my missioners.[149]

On February 26, 1863, the Bishop wrote again to All Hallows: "Oh then, dear Father, let my subjects smoke as much as they like, but let them avoid the dread drink."[150]

Fathers Callan and Griffin then were the regular assistants in Marysville. The Bishop, however, was away a good deal of the time between May and November on his pastoral visitation already described. Father Morris, with his grey horse Charley, left us an excellent picture of his first missionary journey in the parish of Downieville.[151] Leaving Downieville on September 28th, he was baptizing in the little church in La Porte on September 30, 1862. Two days later he was in Richmond, and the following day in Hopkins Creek. On October 5, he baptized a child in Whiskey Diggings and another in Gibsonville. The next day he was in Morristown and then back to Downieville.[152]

This narration of Bishop O'Connell's efforts to secure priests and the setbacks he incurred is only half the story. It is hard to realize that for each new priest named there was a large financial outlay. All through his years as ordinary, Bishop O'Connell paid not only the room, board, and tuition of his candidates, but also their passage to California. This is a story in itself.

On March 27, 1862, Bishop O'Connell wrote to Paris to thank M. Certes for the draft of $600 which he had received which, he said, nearly covered the expenses of the two missioners from Europe, Father Callan, and the second whom he was daily expecting, Father Manogue.[153] He later told that the bill he received from his agent, Father Quinn in New York, amounted to $395—nearly £80.[154] But on top of that he had to pay the medical bills and funeral expenses of a young, newly ordained Father Burke who would have been his first fruits from All Hallows:

> His death so soon after landing in San Francisco is not to be wondered at because, altho the climate in this country is an excellent preservative or antidote against consumption, yet, after the disease has once set in, California is the grave of consumptive persons.[155]

As if this were not enough, it cost Bishop O'Connell $400 taken from the Propagation funds to send Father Blake back to Dublin at the summons of his archbishop.[156]

Those setbacks made it very difficult for the Bishop to carry out his resolve to send £20 per year for the support of each of his students. In March and April, 1862, he had to write concerning one of his students:

> Mr. Clarke wrote asking for money for clothes, but I must refuse. If he knew how hard I find it to make up his annual pension and that of the other students he wouldn't ask. It shall be my utmost endeavor to repay the College as long as I live by sending £10 per month or more if I can. I am not conscious of having let a single month pass without sending you £10 at least.[157]

Later he recalls he had to skip the month in which he had to pay Father Burke's funeral bill.

This utter devotion to All Hallows and this sacrifice of all he had to ensure future priests for his vicariate was contagious. With delight he wrote in November, 1862:

> Father Callan has collected $150 during the past two months to pay for his passage across the sea, and he is determined to collect and organize a collection for All Hallows as long as he lives. When next I send an installment, I'll in-

clude Father Rigby's which he handed me the other day for All Hallows. Both he and Father Callan had hardly got a domicile when they thus affectionately remembered Alma Mater.[158]

On December 19, 1862, he sent Father Rigby's £2.[159] That this effort on the Bishop's part to support the seminarians for the vicariate was contagious is evident also in the burse which he sent on June 7, 1862, containing $50. The list contained six donations of $5.00 each, evidently from laymen, and $10 each from Father Dalton and Father Neal Gallagher, a graduate of Carlow.[160] Quite evidently, as fast as the money arrived from Paris, it was forwarded to All Hallows. That the Bishop achieved his goal is very evident from the testimony of the All Hallows treasurer Henry Bedford in a statement on May 10, 1866. He testified that in the period 1861–62–63, Bishop O'Connell sent a total of £580 to All Hallows for the support of twelve students.[161]

Nor was this pace to slacken, as the report shows, up to the time it was made in 1866. The effort to supply priests for his vicariate was the consuming passion of Bishop O'Connell's life. The year 1863 produced no new priests for the vicariate. Two came from All Hallows in early 1864: Dominic Monteverde, a native of Genoa, Italy, and John M. Nulty, a native of Navan, County Meath, Ireland. Dominic Monteverde left All Hallows in November, 1863, and came to San Francisco. On Sunday, January 31, 1864, Bishop Peter Losa, exiled bishop of Sonora, Mexico, gave the order of deacon to Dominic Monteverde in (Old) St. Mary's Cathedral at the request of Bishop O'Connell. Two weeks later, on Sunday, February 14, 1864, Archbishop Alemany ordained the young Italian deacon a priest of the vicariate of Marysville.[162] He was then assigned to Marysville as an assistant. Father John Nulty had been ordained in Ireland on October 4, 1863. He, too, left with young Monteverde on November 4, 1863, for California. He was in Marysville by January 7, 1864.[163]

Meanwhile, Archbishop Alemany loaned to Bishop O'Connell Father Denis Nugent, another All Hallows man ordained in 1862.[164] The Bishop had lost Father Griffin in the fall of 1863. When the Sisters of Mercy arrived in Grass Valley in August, 1863, the Bishop sent Father Griffin as an assistant to Father Dalton as he had promised to give the sisters a daily Mass as one of the conditions of their coming.[165] One more problem cropped up which caused another shift. Father Rigby had not proven satisfactory in Forest Hill. The loneliness had become too much, so that by June, 1863, the Bishop had replaced him by his own assistant Father Callan.[166] Father Rigby was sent as an assistant to Father Manogue, but after a few months evidently returned to his diocese of origin, New York.

The assistants now in Marysville were Fathers Monteverde and Nugent. The arrival of these new priests enabled the Bishop to make a few changes. As he had stated in an early letter, two of his original six priests were worn out, even at the time of his arrival. Father O'Reilly in Weaverville had traveled as much as 6,000 miles in one year on his rounds.[167] Father Crinion, up in Yreka, was suffering from rheumatism.[168] So the Bishop, in the spring of 1864, sent Father Nulty to replace Father O'Reilly after five years in that difficult and isolated mission. Intent on giving Father O'Reilly a completely different and possibly more healthful mission, he sent him to Nevada to found the parish of St. Patrick in Gold Hill, only two miles west of Virginia City. Father O'Reilly arrived in his new post on May 12, 1864.[169] Still concerned over the fact that the towns along the Pacific coast were left without a priest, the Bishop sent Father Crinion to establish a parish in Eureka.[170] The Bishop had no one to replace him in Yreka, so for the year he borrowed Father Guido Matassi, a Passionist priest.[171]

He could therefore report to Paris by March 10, 1864, that he had nine priests for a vicariate which stretched 480 miles north to south and 420 miles east to west. In this letter, he thanked the Society for the 10,000 francs and then informed them that since January the churches in Forest Hill and Shasta had been destroyed by violent winds and the churches in Nevada (City) and Downieville had burned to the ground.[172] His clergy and their stations by the end of March, 1864, were:

Marysville	— Frs. Monteverde and Nugent
Downieville	— Fr. Morris
Grass Valley	— Frs. Dalton and Griffin
Forest Hill	— Fr. Callan
Weaverville	— Fr. Nulty

Yreka	— Fr. Matassi, C.P.
Klamath	— Fr. Florian Schwenninger, OSB
Eureka	— Fr. Crinion
Virginia City	— Fr. Manogue
Gold Hill	— Fr. O'Reilly

The All Hallows report shows the bishop sent 12,850 francs to All Hallows for the support of his students during 1863 and another 9,175 during 1864.[173] Supplying good priests and supporting future missioners was indeed Bishop O'Connell's prime work as the bishop of the mines of California and Nevada.

Sources for Chapter VI

127. AAHC, letter of September 16, 1861.

128. AAHC, letter of January 28, 1862.

129. Baptismal Register, St. Joseph's, Marysville.

130. AAHC, letter of August 25, 1862.

131. AASF, "Libro Borrador," H–18.

132. AAHC, letter of March 28, 1862.

133. Walsh, *Hallowed Were*, p. 400.

134. Baptismal Register, St. Patrick's, Grass Valley.

135. AAHC, letter of April 23, 1862.

136. AAHC, letter of August 25, 1862.

137. AAHC, letter of December 19, 1862.

138. Baptismal Register, St. Joseph's, Forest Hill.

139. Baptismal Register, Immaculate Conception, Downieville.

140. AAHC, letter of August 25, 1862.

141. Walsh, *Hallowed Were*.

142. Baptismal Register, St. Patrick's, Grass Valley.

143. Gorman, *Seventy-Five Years*, p. 61.
144. AAHC, letter of May 4, 1868.
145. AAHC, letter of October 2, 1872.
146. AAHC, letter of October 31, 1872.
147. AAHC, letter of August 12, 1861.
148. Walsh, *Hallowed Were*, p. 397.
149. AAHC, letter of January 29, 1863.
150. AAHC, letter of February 26, 1863.
151. AAHC, letter of November 26, 1861.
152. Baptismal Register, Immaculate Conception, Downieville.
153. ASPF, letter of March 27, 1868.
154. AAHC, letter of September 26, 1862.
155. AAHC, letter of April 23, 1862.
156. AAHC, letter of April 14, 1863.
157. AAHC, letter of March 28, 1862.
158. AAHC, letter of November 27, 1862.
159. AAHC, letter of December 19, 1862.
160. *Catholic Directory*, Archdiocese of San Francisco, 1962.
161. ASPF, statement of May 10, 1866.
162. AASF, "Libro Borrador," H–20.
163. Baptismal Register, St. Joseph's, Marysville.
164. *Catholic Directory*, Archdiocese of San Francisco, 1962.
165. Archives of the Sisters of Mercy, Grass Valley.
166. Baptismal Register, St. Joseph's, Forest Hill.
167. ASPF, report of March 18, 1862, by Fr. P. O'Reilly.

168. AAHC, letter of November 27, 1862.

169. Baptismal Register, St. Patrick's, Gold Hill, Nevada.

170. Walsh, *Hallowed Were*, p. 270.

171. Ibid.

172. ASPF, report of March 10, 1864.

173. ASPF, statement of May 10, 1866.

Chapter VII

THE YEARS AS VICAR APOSTOLIC, 1861–1868

The year 1864 ended on a happy note for the Bishop. Father Dalton of Grass Valley had brought the Sisters of Mercy to that community in August, 1863, to staff his schools and to establish an orphanage for the children of the miners who were killed in the accidents which occurred so frequently throughout the vicariate. But the San Francisco community of sisters made it clear that it could not supply a new foundation permanently: the sisters were only on loan. Father Dalton left for Ireland on September 3, 1863, to recruit replacements for the San Francisco sisters. He was gone over a year. When he landed in San Francisco on October 24, 1864, he had with him three sisters of Mercy from Ireland and a deacon from All Hallows named Charles M. Lynch, a native of County Cavan.[174] He was only twenty-two years and five months old, but Bishop O'Connell had written to Rome on April 1, 1864, asking for a dispensation for him to be ordained at such an early age.[175] The dispensation was granted on June 13, 1864, and Charles Lynch was ordained a priest by Bishop Peter Losa, exiled bishop of Sonora, Mexico, in (Old) St. Mary's Cathedral on November 13, 1864.[176]

But again, Bishop O'Connell's joys were to be mixed with sorrow as Father Bernard Morris had requested permission to leave the vicariate. The bishop tells the story in his own words:

Fr Morris, whom I found here before me, has left me. Fr

THE REV. CHARLES M. LYNCH, 1842–1911
Pastor of Downieville, 1865–1877
Pastor of Eureka, California, 1877–1883
Pastor of Virginia City, Nevada, 1883–1894
Pastor of Grass Valley, 1894–1911
(Photo, courtesy of Historic Preservation Committee, Grass Valley)

Morris' health was constantly impaired. The same Fr Morris built the house in which I live in Marysville. May God reward him for his labors in raising the necessary funds.[177]

The Bishop was disturbed not only because Father Morris was leaving but also because he was such a good priest.

Father Morris, therefore, left Downieville after Christmas, 1864, and the newly ordained Father Lynch was sent to Downieville early in January, 1865.[178] Father Morris received a temporary appointment from Archbishop Alemany at St. Mary's Cathedral, but in April, 1865, he returned to Ireland.[179] Bishop O'Connell later heard that Father Morris had received an appointment as pastor of a parish in his home Diocese of Kilmore. He was indignant that the Irish bishop had made the appointment without any letters of recommendation or any formal papers or transfer from the Marysville vicariate.[180]

The year 1865 was brightened early in the year by the arrival of two vocations who were to give excellent service to the diocese, Father Vincent Riera, a Spaniard, and John Mary Mevel, a Frenchman. Father Riera's origin is unknown, but the coming of John Mary Mevel is recorded in detail. On July 10, 1865, Archbishop Alemany wrote to Bishop O'Connell that the student Mevel had arrived the previous day by steamer, that he had finished his course of studies, that he had all the necessary documents, and that he was being sent to the archdiocesan seminary until Bishop O'Connell sent necessary instructions. On July 21, 1865, the Archbishop examined young Mevel and deemed him ready for ordination. He wrote to Bishop O'Connell to say that he was going to confer the Minor Orders on him while awaiting further instructions. On July 22, the Archbishop conferred tonsure and the next day minor orders. Bishop O'Connell's letters came and young Mevel was ordained subdeacon on July 30 and deacon on August 6. The great day of ordination to the priesthood arrived August 10, 1865, on which date Archbishop Alemany ordained John Mary Mevel a priest of the vicariate of Marysville.[181]

Both began their services in Nevada, Father Riera at St. Mary's in Carson City, which had been without a priest for some time, the place being attended from Gold Hill; Father Mevel was sent to help Father O'Reilly at Gold Hill.[182] The Nevada mines were booming compared to a general slump on the California side

ST. ANTHONY'S CHURCH, Mendocino City.
Built by the Rev. Bernadine Sheehan in 1865.
(Photo, courtesy of Mendocino Historical Research, Inc.)

of the Sierras. The Bishop was anxious to increase the number of priests in the eastern portion of his vicariate. Suddenly, the Bishop received what he himself called "a windfall from Chicago."[183] A young man named Edward Kelly had arrived in San Francisco, already a deacon and with all the necessary documents permitting him to work in the vicariate. Archbishop Alemany ordained this young man a priest on July 16, 1865, in (Old) St. Mary's Cathedral.[184] The newly ordained Father Kelly remained with the Bishop in Marysville to replace Father Monteverde whom the Bishop now sent as an assistant to Father Manogue in Virginia City.[185] The Bishop was indeed impressed by Father Kelly whom he called "a most prepossessing young man."[186] The reports back from Father Monteverde told of a prosperous mining region in eastern Nevada which had no priest and which was 180 miles from Virginia City. What disturbed the Bishop most was the information that this community of Austin, which was fairly close to the Utah border, was being zealously proselytized by the Mormons. Therefore, in October, 1865, Bishop O'Connell created the new parish of Austin and sent Father Kelly to take care of it.[187]

Bishop O'Connell was blessed with two more new priests in the fall of the year, both from All Hallows, Father Patrick Farrelly from Old Castle in County Meath and Father Daniel Meagher from Cork. They were a blessing because two of the original priests were "caving in," to use the Bishop's own words, especially Father Crinion in Eureka, who was beset with rheumatism, and the faithful Benedictine, Father Florian Schwenninger up on the Klamath. The Bishop sent Father Farrelly to Yreka and attached to it Father Florian's old territory,[188] brought Father Florian to Marysville to replace Father Kelly, and then fulfilled a dream of three years' standing by creating a parish in Oroville.[189] The ailing Father Crinion was brought from the damp coast to the warm valley and became the first resident pastor of Oroville, thus lessening the burden on Marysville from which Oroville had been a mission. Finally, he sent Father Meagher to Gold Hill where he took over the reins as pastor on November 5, 1865.[190] Father O'Reilly was transferred from Gold Hill to Eureka, California, which he reached at the end of January, 1866.[191]

One final ambition of the Bishop's was realized that same year. There had come to his vicariate a very fine Franciscan priest named Bernadine Sheehan. Finally, in the fall of 1865, the Bishop assigned Father Bernadine to Mendocino City to take care of the coastal area of the vicariate.[192]

The report for 1865 shows thirteen parishes: nine in California—two on the coast, Eureka and Mendocino City; two in the northern portion of the vicariate, Weaverville and Yreka; five in the heart of the vicariate, Marysville, Oroville, Downieville, Forest Hill, and Grass Valley; and four in Nevada; and a total of sixteen priests.

Other matters occupied the Bishop's attention in 1865, especially at home in Marysville. Besides his indebtedness to All Hallows for the subsidy for his students and the passage money for the young priests who came to the vicariate, the Bishop was saddled with debts owed to Archbishop Alemany on three of the churches which had been transferred to the new vicariate.[193]

When Father Peter Magagnatto, the Passionist and first pastor of Marysville, built the church which was now Bishop O'Connell's cathedral, he left it heavily in debt. For this reason, the Bishop never really liked "Father Peter." The debt in November, 1862, was still $8,000.[194] Besides this, the new vicariate owed the mother archdiocese for the church in Grass Valley in the amount of $6,200, and there were debts on the uncompleted church in Shasta, a mission of the Weaverville parish.

Bishop O'Connell concentrated on the debt on the Marysville church so that at the end of 1864 he was able to report that he had paid it off.[195] It is doubtful that he ever had to assume a penny on the church debt in Grass Valley, as Father Dalton was well able to take care of his own problems and did so in due time. That the vicar apostolic of Marysville had this kind of confidence in Father Dalton is manifested in a letter which he wrote to Mother Baptist Russell in San Francisco regarding the coming of the Sisters of Mercy to Grass Valley:

> I beg you to take Father Dalton at his word and occupy his house forthwith. He can do no better at present, and the Church can and will pay her own debt in due time, without interfering in the least with your Sisters.[196]

What bothered Bishop O'Connell most was the $3,000 he owed on a stone foundation in Shasta.

In 1857, the pastor of Shasta, Father Raphael Rainaldi, a

ST. JOSEPH'S CHURCH, Marysville (Pro-Cathedral 1861–1884).
Built by the Rev. Peter Magagnotto in 1855, still in use.
(Photo, courtesty of Sisters of Notre Dame, Belmont, California)

man accustomed to the grand cathedrals and basilicas of Italy, decided to build in Shasta a much finer church than the little frame "Holy Cross" Church which served for many years. He laid the stone foundations (which still exist today) of a large church and had Archbishop Alemany up for the laying of the cornerstone on May 19, 1857.[197] But the gloom cast on the day by the rainy weather was to persevere through the whole scheme. Father Rainaldi and the architect got into some kind of litigation and the building proceeded no further. Meanwhile, the Archbishop was saddled with the bills, and when the new vicariate was created, these were passed on to the new vicar apostolic.

However, matters were even worse. It seems Father Rainaldi had contracted a personal loan from another priest for $500 at 18% annual interest. This, too, was being claimed from Bishop O'Connell, a matter which upset him very much. To use his own words:

> No sooner is one trouble at an end than another arises. There is a claim which Father Joseph Gallagher presses for a loan of $500 which he gave to the said Father Rainaldi. It does not appear from the parochial or pastoral register that Fr Rainaldi expended the $500 borrowed from Fr Joe on building churches. Poor Fr Rainaldi did not find it convenient to pay either principal or interest till the day of his death (inclusive) so that his debt, like a species of original sin, has fallen on me.[198]

These troubles were not the full extent of the concerns facing Bishop O'Connell in the mid-sixties. The condition of the church which was his cathedral was a sad one. As pastor of Marysville, he expressed it thus:

> I am in a nice fix, as I have been all along, between the old fabric called St. Joseph's Church—barn would have been a more appropriate title—and the heap of debt due on it to Archbishop Alemany, whom at length I have paid off.[199]

The church must have been barn-like, a very high building almost as long as it was wide, and with no tower to distinguish it. Therefore, in 1865 the Bishop began work on the church. He extended it by forty feet on the west side, thus adding the sacristies and sanctuary as well as additional seating capacity. He also finished the interior and added the tower.[200] This work is said to have cost $20,000. However, the net debt was just about the same as the original debt of 1861. Thus in his March, 1866, report to Paris, the Bishop informed M. Certes that he had to borrow $9,000. His original indebtedness five years previously had been $15,390. At the date of the writing of the report, his indebtedness was $15,455, plus $8,000 in the state of Nevada.[201] There seemed to be no progress in debt reduction, except that he now had a decent cathedral church.

History records that a boys' school was opened in the basement of the church in this same year. This problem of the Christian education of boys was always on Bishop O'Connell's mind. The sisters in his vicariate, the Notre Dame Sisters in Marysville, the Mercy Sisters in Grass Valley, and the newly arrived Sisters of Charity in Virginia City, were all limited to the education of girls and small boys. But that meant no possibility of a religiously oriented education for boys beyond a third-grade level. The problem was faced by the opening of schools in the Irish manner which were staffed by men or women who gave an education to the boys similar to what the sisters gave the girls in the convent school. Grass Valley had such a school all through the years until the sisters were finally permitted to teach older boys. Forest Hill and Gold Hill had such schools for years. This was the kind of school Bishop O'Connell opened in the church basement in 1865.

The concern of Bishop O'Connell for the Catholics living in Utah was not just a passing one. He did something about his concern. His first step was a clarification from Rome regarding the extent of his jurisdiction.

In a letter to Cardinal Barnabo, he states that in the apostolic letters given him, the boundary of the vicariate on the east was designated as the Colorado River, which actually does not appear between the 39th and 42nd degree of latitude. "Therefore I don't know how far the Vicariate extends to the East."[202] Evidently Rome responded that the Bishop's jurisdiction did include the area under concern. Therefore, Bishop O'Connell made the decision to send a resident priest to Salt Lake City. Father Ed Kelly of Austin had already visited this city on the occasion of a sick call he received in May, 1866, to attend the sick and dying soldiers at

Camp Douglas outside the city limits of Salt Lake City, some three hundred miles from Austin. On that occasion, Father Kelly visited the Mormon capital, was courteously received by Brigham Young, and offered the use of the Tabernacle which Father Kelly declined.[203]

Father Kelly himself told the rest of the story in a letter to the editor of *The Monitor*, in which he protested a statement in a previous edition:

> "There are only five Parishes (1868) established in Colorado territory, one each in Denver, Central, Trinidad, Conejas and Costella. In all of Utah there is none at present since Father Kelly was *forced to flee* from Salt Lake." Now it is not true that I was forced to flee. When by the advice of my Bishop, Dr. O'Connell, I first visited Salt Lake City in May, 1866, I was kindly received by Brigham Young who invited me to officiate in his place of worship. When it pleased my Bishop to send Father Monteverde as my successor in Austin, where I had resided since September 1865, and directed me to proceed to Utah as Pastor of Salt Lake City, I found no change in the kind treatment of Brigham Young and his people toward me. Since my departure the Mormons have not collected taxes on the Church property which I purchased during my stay among them.
>
> While assisting at the great Plenary Council of Baltimore, my Bishop sent me a letter to Salt Lake City, in which he intimated that as Utah and Colorado Territories were about to be erected into a new Diocese, so his jurisdiction over Utah would soon cease, and that I should fall back on Austin, Nevada. It was the letter of my Bishop, and nothing else that occasioned my departure on December 27, 1866.[204]

Thus Bishop O'Connell's efforts to serve the Catholics of this remote outpost were terminated when the vicariate apostolic of Colorado and Utah was erected by Rome as a result of the decision of bishops assembled at the Second Plenary Council of Baltimore in 1866. This Council was attended by the three California bishops. Thus Bishop O'Connell's pastoral visitation of his diocese was cut short in 1866 by this trip which consumed almost four months.

Archbishop Alemany, Bishop Amat, and Bishop O'Connell sailed on the steamer for Panama on August 18, 1866.²⁰⁵ Bishop O'Connell had appointed Father Dalton of Grass Valley as administrator in his absence.²⁰⁶ The Council opened in October, 1866. Since Bishop O'Connell was appointed one of the writers of Latin letters, he was kept busy during this Council. Among the many items on the agenda, the question of future dioceses came up. As we have seen, the Colorado-Utah area was included. Also included was the question of raising the Marysville vicariate to the status of a diocese. Evidently there was discussion about moving the see city from Marysville. Bishop O'Connell was in favor of Virginia City, Nevada. In fact, he had been badgering Cardinal Barnabo about this very matter.

> The Nevada portion of the Vicariate has 45,000 people and the California portion has 49,000. Virginia City has 20,000 with about one third Catholic. While you can scarsely find 1,000 Catholics in Marysville with one Church, whereas, Virginia City has three Churches and almost as many Catholics as the whole Diocese of Monterey and Los Angeles.

Three months later, December 21, 1864, he wrote:

> Virginia City, one hundred thirty five miles from here has 7,000 Catholics and three Churches. This city has one church and five hundred Catholics. Virginia City is constantly growing while Marysville diminishes. Should I continue to reside in Marysville?²⁰⁷

Evidently the commission charged with the formation of new dioceses thought otherwise and their decision on the see city did not agree with Bishop O'Connell's. The Apostolic Delegate seemed to feel that the nearby city of Grass Valley with its quartz mines gave more promise of stability. The decisions of the Second Plenary Council of Baltimore under the heading of Title XIII were sent to Rome.²⁰⁸ It as to take a full year before action came in response to the decision.

Bishop O'Connell began the return trip in company with his friend, the Archbishop, on November 1, 1866. They were in San Francisco on November 24.[209] On his arrival home, he found three new priests had arrived in October from All Hallows, Fathers Maurice Hickey, ordained on June 29, 1866, and his classmates Father William Clarke and Father Jeremiah O'Sullivan.[210]

This necessitated some moves in the vicariate. First of all, Father Jeremiah O'Sullivan was not well and it was thought best to keep him in Marysville. Similarly, Father Patrick O'Reilly had written that the Eureka climate was not only not beneficial to his health but was actually detrimental. Father O'Reilly sought for and obtained permission to take an extended trip.[211] He left Eureka at the end of the year and sailed for the Hawaiian Islands. The newly ordained Father Maurice Hickey was sent to Eureka in his place.[212] The third of the new trio from All Hallows, Father Clarke, was sent to Carson City to replace Father Riera who was involved in a move quite typical with Bishop O'Connell.[213]

The vicariate had four distinct areas and as a result four distinct climates. There was the cool coastal area, the hot Sacramento Valley area, the mountain parishes with their delightful weather except for the winter snows, and finally the dry, almost desert, lands of Nevada. Since the clergy had no vacations in the days of Bishop O'Connell, he provided them with a change of climate every couple of years. For example, we have seen the ailing Father O'Reilly transferred from the Nevada desert to the cool oceanside of Eureka; Father Crinion from the cool coast to the warm valley at Oroville; and now Father Riera from the Nevada town of Carson City to the coastal town of Mendocino City where he remained for three years. This pattern of changing the clergy to a totally different climate was fairly consistent with Bishop O'Connell. The few exceptions were mostly those priests who adjusted very well to or preferred the Nevada area. Some of them spent their whole lives in that state.

The year 1866 terminated with the arrival of a young priest who was to give sixty years of service to the church and who is considered the "character" of the diocese. Father Patrick O'Kane, as he was known the length and breadth of northern California and Nevada, arrived from All Hallows in February, 1866, and was

THE REV. PATRICK O'KANE, 1841–1926
(Photo, courtesy of Sisters of Mercy, Grass Valley)

ordained on February 24, 1866, at (Old) St. Mary's Cathedral by Bishop Thaddeus Amat of Monterey–Los Angeles.[214] The best way to describe Patrick O'Kane is through the words of Father Henry Walsh:

> He was one of those actors on the stage of life whose every word and movement intrigues, being flavored with the spice of the dramatic. To all outward appearances he was the antithesis of Bishop O'Connell, the latter being an individual of the nervous, wiry, ascetic type, while to Father O'Kane life was one long sweet summer day, and neither hurry nor worry nor the opinions and arguments of his fellow men could cause him to deviate one bit from the even tenor of his way. To his credit though, be it said that much as he might differ from the view of the Bishop, he never faltered in submitting to his commands with simple child-like obedience.[215]

At least fourteen times, Father O'Kane was moved by Bishop O'Connell, mostly because no pastor would put up with his eccentric ways. Bishop O'Connell seems to have solved the problem by making every pastor take his turn, including himself. He refers to Father O'Kane always with the epithet, "the absent minded,"[216] and on one occasion until he got used to this big good-natured man, he wrote: "Father O'Kane is no acquisition, he is too absent minded."[217] But the absent-minded priest from Kerry was to do much good and make many friends during his long life. He settled down eventually, long after Bishop O'Connell's time, in the village of Georgetown where he remained for twenty-five years. His first assignment was in the Bishop's house in Marysville; here he lived with the ailing Father Jeremiah O'Sullivan and Father Florian Schwenninger.

The year 1867 was to bring much sorrow to the vicar apostolic. The ailing pioneer missioner, Father Thomas Crinion, died on January 20, 1867, and was the first priest of the vicariate to be buried in the priests' plot in St. Joseph's Cemetery in Marysville.[218] His death was followed by a few days with the news that Father O'Reilly had died on shipboard en route from Honolulu to Valparaiso, Chile, and was buried at sea. Even the exact date of the death of this excellent pioneer priest is unknown. But there was still to be a third, on April 14, 1867, when his young and promising assistant went to an early grave: Father O'Sullivan was only twenty-five years of age. His funeral took place from St. Joseph's Church and he was buried in the same plot with Father Crinion.[219]

The last year of the vicariate, although it dawned on a sad note, had its cheerful side for Bishop O'Connell. The fruits of his recruitment program for that year were to be outstandingly fine men whose long service to the diocese would more than compensate for the losses. On June 11, 1867, in Dublin there were ordained three young priests for the vicariate, Father James J. Claire of County Kerry, Father Matthew Coleman, a native of Ardee, County Louth, and Father Thomas Grace from Wexford.[220] These three helped fulfill further ambitions of the Bishop in the matter of supplying priests. He had once previously mentioned that Red Bluff was a good-sized town without a priest. He created the parish of Red Bluff and sent Father Grace as its first pastor.[221] The parish of Grass Valley still covered an extensive area and so did Downieville. The Bishop carved out a large area from both of these and constituted Nevada City as a separate parish with Father Claire as the first pastor.[222] Father Coleman was sent to Weaverville to replace Father O'Kane.[223]

This is a story in itself which brings out the reaction of Bishop O'Connell to Father O'Kane. After a few weeks in Marysville at the end of 1866, the Bishop had exchanged Father Nulty and Father O'Kane. The parish of Weaverville should have been too large even for the strapping young O'Kane as it included the counties of Trinity, Shasta, and Tehama. When Father Grace arrived, the Bishop felt that Tehama and Shasta should have its own priest and leave Trinity County to Weaverville. He evidently communicated these intentions to Father O'Kane who immediately wrote back: "Bishop, this is a good mission for one." Bishop O'Connell concludes the story as follows:

> He couldn't convince the old Bishop that the three counties were only adequate to the support of one. The Vicar Apostolic lost no time in sending the first two available workmen to that extensive vineyard, Fathers Coleman and Grace, whilst O'Kane is transferred to a section of country near Marysville. This "good-enough-Parish-for-one" gentleman is

THE REV. THOMAS GRACE, 1841–1921
Founding Pastor of Red Bluff, California 1867–1868
Pastor of Carson City, Nevada, 1870–1871
(Built present St. Theresa's Church in 1871)
Assistant at Grass Valley, 1871–1874
Pastor of Marysville, California 1876–1880
Pastor of St. Rose, Sacramento, 1881–1886
Founding Pastor of Blessed Sacrament Cathedral, Sacramento, 1887–1896
Second Bishop of Sacramento, 1896–1921
(Photo, courtesy of Sisters of Mercy, Grass Valley)

now Pastor of Oroville, 29 miles north of Marysville, with the Missions of Cherokee, Chico (25 miles north of Oroville) and Colusa, the capitol of a county where there is only one Church and that the Catholic.²²⁴

So, obviously, the seminary professor made bishop was not going to tolerate any suggestions from the seminary student ordained priest!

But there is a much more interesting situation that occurred in 1867. All Hallows had written to the Bishop at the end of 1866 asking him to release one of his students. Lawrence Kennedy had distinguished himself scholastically during his years at All Hallows, and the authorities wanted to keep him and give him special training to become a professor. This posed a very great problem for Bishop O'Connell as he was torn between his love for All Hallows and its welfare and his own great need, especially for a theologian in the vicariate on whom he could rely for the solution of problems. He wrote in reply:

> I find it hard to refuse the request you make about Mr. Kennedy, yet the spiritual destitution of this Vicariate obliges me to claim him. The only Theologian I have, the only one I have to consult is Father Griffin. I wish it were in my power to do you this favor, but really well ordered charity forbids me.²²⁵

This first refusal did not stop the All Hallows authorities from trying again. In reply, the Bishop wrote:

> You know well the value and effect of persevering in your petition for Mr. Kennedy, and what can a poor debtor like me refuse his creditors? I may as well make a virtue out of necessity, for indeed I couldn't pay for his passage to Marysville.²²⁶

So the Bishop seemed to have lost. All Hallows then sent young Kennedy to Father Manogue's alma mater, St. Sulpice in Paris, but Lawrence Kennedy turned the tide. He evidently gave second thoughts to the matter, and on his own left Paris, returned to Ireland, and when the newly ordained Fathers Claire,

THE REV. LAWRENCE KENNEDY, 1842–1924
Ordained by Bishop O'Connell in Marysville, Nov. 1, 1867
Assistant at Grass Valley, 1868–1871
Pastor of Oroville, 1872–1874
Assistant at Eureka, California, 1875–1878
First Pastor of Ferndale, California, 1879–1892
Pastor of Eureka, California, 1893–1924
(Photo, courtesy of Sisters of Mercy, Grass Valley)

Coleman, and Grace left for Marysville in August, so did Kennedy. Bishop O'Connell was overjoyed and in quick succession ordained him a subdeacon, then a deacon in October, and finally a priest in Marysville on "All Hallows Day," November 1, 1867.[227] Just before Christmas, the Bishop wrote back to All Hallows:

> Father Kennedy resides with ourselves in Marysville. He is a remarkable young priest and well qualified to fill any department inside or outside the walls of a college. If however, he had a little more assurance and boldness, he would make a more favorable impression on the people of this country.[228]

The Bishop made a few more changes among the clergy. Father Mevel, who had been filling in for Father Crinion at Oroville during his last illness, was now displaced by Father O'Kane so he went to Forest Hill with a special assignment which will be taken up later.

The condition of the vicariate, therefore, at the end of 1867, the eve of its becoming a diocese, was as follows: there were the following parishes staffed by the following priests:

On the Pacific Coast:
    Eureka, California   Father Maurice Hickey
    Mendocino City   Father Vincent Riera

In the Northern portion:
    Yreka   Father Patrick Farrelly
    Weaverville   Father Matthew Coleman
    Red Bluff   Father Thomas Grace

In the Central portion:
    Oroville   Father Patrick O'Kane
    Marysville   Fathers Edward Kelly and Lawrence Kennedy
    Grass Valley   Fathers Thomas J. Dalton and John Griffin
    Nevada City   Father James J. Claire
    Downieville   Father Charles Lynch

THE REV. MATTHEW COLEMAN, 1844–1917
Assistant at Forest Hill, 1867
Pastor of Weaverville, 1867–1872
Pastor of Red Bluff, 1872–1874
Assistant at Virginia City, 1874–1878
Pastor of Smartsville, 1878–1887
Pastor of Woodland, 1887–1888
Pastor of Marysville, 1888–1917
(Photo, courtesy of Sisters of Mercy, Grass Valley)

Forest Hill	Fathers James Callan and J. M. Mevel
In Nevada:	
Virginia City	Fathers Patrick Manogue and John M. Nulty
Gold Hill	Father Daniel Meagher
Carson City	Father Wm. Clarke
Austin	Father Dominic Monteverde

The report to Paris written on December 27, 1867, thanked the Society for 9,000 francs and stated that all the money received from the Propagation of the Faith since 1861 had been spent in the education and travel expenses of seventeen missioners coming from All Hallows, two of whom had been sent back. The present debt there was $1,500.[229]

The vicariate in seven years had made remarkable progress despite the setbacks. In fifteen parishes there were nineteen priests instead of six, in seven years. The work of saving souls was progressing well in the vicariate of Marysville.

Sources for Chapter VII

174. Archives of the Sisters of Mercy, Grass Valley, "The Annals."

175. ASRC, Vol. 20, F66, letter of April 1, 1864.

176. AASF, "Libro Borrador," H–20.

177. AAHC, letter of October 29, 1868.

178. Baptismal Register, Immaculate Conception, Downieville.

179. AAHC, letter of June 22, 1866.

180. AAHC, letter of February 17, 1869.

181. AASF, "Libro Borrador," H–20, entries between July 10, 1865, and August 10, 1865.

182. Baptismal Registers, St. Patrick's, Gold Hill, and St. Mary's, Carson City.

183. AAHC, letter of June 2, 1869.

184. AASF, "Libro Borrador," H-20.
185. Baptismal Register, St. Joseph's, Marysville.
186. AAHC, letter of June 22, 1866.
187. Gorman, *Seventy-Five Years*, p. 88.
188. Walsh, *Hallowed Were*, p. 271.
189. Ibid., p. 291.
190. Baptismal Register, St. Patrick's, Gold Hill, opening statement.
191. Walsh, *Hallowed Were*, p. 292.
192. *Catholic Directory*, Archdiocese of San Francisco, 1962.
193. ASPF, letter of March 20, 1866.
194. AAHC, letter of November 27, 1862.
195. AAHC, letter of December 9, 1864.
196. Archives of the Sisters of Mercy, Grass Valley, "The Annals."
197. Walsh, *Hallowed Were*, p. 334.
198. AAHC, letter of December 9, 1864.
199. Ibid.
200. Thompson & West, *History of Yuba County*, p. 54.
201. ASPF, letter of March 20, 1866.
202. ASRC, letter of November 16, 1865.
203. AAHC, letter of June 22, 1866.
204. *The Monitor*, October 31, 1868.
205. Joseph W. Riordan, *The First Half Century of St. Ignatius Church and College* (San Francisco: H. S. Crocker Co., 1905), p. 146.
206. *Grass Valley Union*, September 27, 1866.
207. ASRC, letter of December 21, 1864.

208. Guilday, op. cit., p. 214.
209. Riordan, op. cit., p. 146.
210. Baptismal Register, St. Joseph's, Marysville, October, 1866.
211. Walsh, *Hallowed Were*, p. 292.
212. Ibid., p. 293.
213. Gorman, *Seventy-Five Years*, p. 61.
214. AASF, "Libro Borrador," H–20.
215. Walsh, *Hallowed Were*, p. 316.
216. AAHC, letter of May 4, 1868.
217. AAHC, letter of May 14, 1868.
218. Register of Deaths, St. Joseph's, Marysville, January 23, 1867.
219. Ibid., April 16, 1867.
220. *The Monitor*, July 27, 1867.
221. Walsh, *Hallowed Were*, p. 321.
222. Baptismal Register, St. Canice, Nevada City, October 22, 1867.
223. Baptismal Register, St. Patrick's, Weaverville, November, 1867.
224. AAHC, letter of May 4, 1868.
225. AAHC, letter of December 4, 1866.
226. AAHC, letter of February 25, 1867.
227. AAHC, letter of October 23, 1867.
228. AAHC, letter of December 17, 1867.
229. ASPF, letter of December 27, 1867.

Chapter VIII

EXTRAORDINARY CONCERNS

Bishop O'Connell had made remarkable efforts to supply priests and establish parishes to serve the scattered population of his vicariate. His duties required the annual round of visitations, confirmations, and other sacramental ministries throughout his enormous territory. He had great cares as pastor of Marysville and the ever-present financial problems he faced. Over and above all this, Bishop O'Connell's apostolic zeal for the welfare of the people under his charge led him to many other concerns about which he did more than worry.

The status of religion throughout his vicariate disturbed him. Because most of the sheep of this zealous shepherd were people who had come either for the gold or the silver which abounded in the soil, they were very materialistic. There had to be extraordinary means to emphasize the spiritual side of man's life. Bishop O'Connell felt that "missions" were the best means available to call men back to a sense of the supernatural. Therefore, almost immediately on his assuming jurisdiction over his vast vicariate, he began to call upon religious orders to give missions in the various parishes.

He began with an appeal to the Jesuits in San Francisco who sent a missionary who was to become a famous preacher before his death in 1889, the Reverend James Bouchard, S.J. Father Nicholas Congiato, superior of the San Francisco Jesuit community, in a report to the Superior General wrote: "I mentioned above

Two outstanding missionaries who gave many missions throughout the Grass Valley diocese THE REV. JAMES BOUCHARD, S.J., and THE REV. PATRICK HENNEBERRY, C.PP.S. (Photos, courtesy of University of San Francisco and Society of Precious Blood, Ohio)

how Fr Bouchard has gone through the entire Vicariate of Marysville giving missions to the inexpressible joy and consolation of Monsignor O'Connell who is all taken up by the good Father."[230]

The first mission that Father Bouchard gave in the vicariate was in the parish of Grass Valley for Father Dalton, and also in its mission church, Sts. Peter and Paul in Nevada City. The local newspaper announced the event as follows:

> A revival is going on in the Catholic Church which commenced last Sunday and will last till Thursday next. A Missionary has been sent here by the Catholic Bishop, who is represented to us by those who have heard him as an eloquent divine. His success is great among members of the Catholic Church.[231]

Father Bouchard was back again in Grass Valley for a mission in 1864. He was in Nevada State in June, 1865, and conducted a mission in Austin even though there was no church. He had come by stage, accompanied by Father Manogue of Virginia City. Bradford's Hall was used by the two priests as the center for the mission where they were available each morning from 6:30 A.M. until 9 A.M. and again in the evening from 7 to 8:30 P.M. On June 20, 1865, they returned to Virginia City and Father Bouchard opened a mission at Gold Hill.[232]

The year 1866 saw Father Bouchard in Downieville and Marysville and many other places in Sierra, Nevada, and Yuba counties. It is safe to state that Father Bouchard returned to Bishop O'Connell's territory almost every year as long as Bishop O'Connell was the ordinary of the diocese. He also preached on several special occasions, such as the dedication of the new church in Yreka in 1867, the new churches in Chico and in Oroville, and for the reopening of St. Mary's in the Mountains in Virginia City in 1877.[233]

The Jesuit Father Bouchard was not the only celebrated missionary to stir up the faith in the parishes and mission stations of the Marysville vicariate. Another well-known missionary of those days was the Irish-born Father Patrick Henneberry of the Precious Blood order. He came to California in 1864, and between that year and 1877, when he began giving missions in Australia, Father Henneberry's fame as a preacher rivaled that of Father Bouchard.[234]

Bishop O'Connell's concern for his flock was not limited to the English-speaking. His care extended also to those who spoke many foreign tongues. Even though he was himself fluent in Spanish, he still brought in Spanish-speaking missionaries. As early as September, 1861, he had Father Antonio Gomerly working in the vicariate. Bishop Pedro Losa, the exiled bishop of Sonora, Mexico, was also a visitor and served the Spanish-speaking peoples of the mining regions both in the vicariate and in the archdiocese.[235]

The finest acquisition at this time was made by Archbishop Alemany who received into the Archdiocese of San Francisco a young seminarian from the Diocese of Guadalajara in Mexico, named Luciano Osuna. Negotiations with the bishop of Guardalajara for a Spanish-speaking student to work among the Indians in California had gone on during 1862. Luciano Osuna, who spoke both Spanish and English, arrived in San Francisco in December, 1862. Since the Mexican bishop of Sonora, Peter Losa, was a guest in San Francisco at the time, Archbishop Alemany deputed him to give the tonsure and minor orders to Luciano Osuna on New Year's Day, 1863. On January 4, 1863, and two days later, the young man received the subdeaconate and deaconate. Archbishop Alemany ordained him a priest on January 11, 1863.[236] Eleven days later he wrote to Bishop O'Connell to tell him that this young priest was ready to depart on his mission to the Indians, most of whom were located in Bishop O'Connell's vicariate. Father Osuna served the vicariate for fifteen years.

For the French-speaking, the Bishop showed extraordinary interest. Evidently the French who came west seeking gold and silver did not have much concern for religion. In spite of his efforts to provide them with the services of the church, he was disappointed in their response. He remarked on one occasion: "Pere Mevel can preach intelligently in English and the French wont come to hear him in their own language."[237] In October, 1862, he obtained the services of a Father A. Y. Poulin to give missions among the French. He was delighted when Father J. M. Mevel came to the vicariate in 1865.

On November 27, 1862, the Bishop had written to All Hallows as follows:

We have enough to do (here in Marysville) bétween the

GERMAN CHURCH in Marysville

Situated at the corner of 8th & F Streets.
Built by the Rev. John Meiler in 1874.
Dedicated to the Immaculate Conception on May 6, 1874.
Ceased as a parish in 1884.
Dismantled and moved by railroad car to Williams by
the Rev. Michael Walrath in 1892.
Reconstructed as Church of the Annunciation, Williams, 1893.
(Photo, courtesy of Marysville City Library)

Irish, and Mexicans and Germans. Very few French-men or Americans trouble us in the tribunal of penance or on their deathbed; but I wish, dear Father, and beg of you to impress on my ecclesiastical students with you at All Hallows the necessity of learning French and German and Spanish. There are many good holy souls who stand in need of priests who can speak their own language.[238]

We also recall his insistence on two conditions to be complied with by any who might volunteer for service in the Marysville vicariate: strict temperance and a knowledge of French, "an expedite knowledge so that they can hear confessions in French, and in German if possible, because the language of Bismark and Luther is spoken by many Catholics throughout the country."[239]

The Bishop's concern for the German-speaking met with a more encouraging response. He even established a German parish in Marysville. The first of the German-speaking priests to come to the vicariate was a Father Joseph Reindl in the fall of 1862, and in 1864 a Jesuit Father G. Laufhuber came for a while.[240] Like so many of the missionaries of those days, these special priests moved from place to place doing what they could for those who wanted to avail themselves of the comforts of religion, moving on to the next place a few days later.

The first German-speaking priest the Bishop was able to get on a permanent basis was Father Julius Herde in January, 1871.[241] This priest began to organize the Germans in the Marysville area, and Bishop O'Connell gave their efforts parochial status under the title of St. Teresa's parish. Father Herde served the community for two years but, on December 16, 1872, he was recalled by Archbishop Alemany and appointed pastor of San Andreas. Two years later he became pastor of St. Boniface Church in San Francisco.[242]

Father Herde was succeeded by Father John Meiler, who then took up the work of his predecessor and proceeded to build a church in Marysville on the corner of F and 8th streets. The cost was $4,000 and the church was dedicated on May 6, 1874, under the title of The Immaculate Conception.[243]

During these pioneering days, changes of names occurred frequently, both in the names of churches and in the names of some of the clergy. When Father Dalton built the second church in Nevada (City), he named it Sts. Peter and Paul, the first church having been called St. Peter's. When the second church burned in the great fire of 1863, it was Father Griffin of Grass Valley who built the new one. Since Father Griffin came from Kilkenny where the patron saint is St. Canice, he named the new church St. Canice.

Archbishop Alemany had blessed the church in Goodyears Bar on September 30, 1855, under the title of Immaculate Conception,[244] and the church in Downieville on June 22, 1856, under the title of The Assumption, but the Downieville church burned down in the spring of 1858. It was, therefore, Father Thomas Dalton who built the present church in 1858 and he chose to name it Immaculate Conception. Meanwhile the Goodyears Bar church disappeared from the scene.

Similarly, everything Father Manogue built was named after the Blessed Mother. Therefore, the second church built in Carson City was named by him St. Mary's.[245] It was Father Grace who, when he built the present church in that city in 1871, named it St. Theresa's. Likewise, the first church in Smartsville was St. Rose and the present one is The Immaculate Conception.[246]

We also note some changes among the names of the clergy. The well-known Father Patrick O'Kane was known in All Hallows as Patrick Keane.[247] Shortly after his arrival in the vicariate, we find him signing himself as Patrick O'Keane, eventually and permanently as O'Kane. Father Patrick Farrelly started out as Farley; Father John Nulty for a while called himself McNulty, but eventually resumed the simpler form.[248]

Most puzzling of all was the change of names involving Father Sheridan. The All Hallows records show that John F. Sheridan was ordained from there for Marysville on June 24, 1875. The Marysville register shows him signing himself as John Sheridan during the year or so that he was an assistant in that parish. But from the time he became pastor of Mendocino City in 1877, he seems to be listed as James D. Sheridan. When he was transferred in 1883 as pastor of Eureka in California, Bishop O'Connell, in a letter to Rome, refers to him as John Daniel Sheridan. Yet the *Catholic Directories* and local papers over those years always listed him as James D. Sheridan, so that what seems on the surface to be two individuals is actually one and the same

An artist's sketch of Passionist church at Divide, made with the help of a magnifying glass from an old photo of Divide showing the church in the background. Immaculate Conception Church was established as a parish in December, 1863. It ceased in 1865. The living quarters at the rear was the Passionist Monastery which housed the eight Italian priests who formed the community until their departure in 1865.

(Photo, courtesy of St. Mary's in the Mountains, Virginia City)

person. This drastic change in first and middle names is indeed puzzling.

Beginning in 1874, the German parish in Marysville was Immaculate Conception with Father Meiler as pastor. He served for seven years and was succeeded in 1879 by Father L. Buholzer who remained until the parish ceased to exist in 1884, shortly before the retirement of Bishop O'Connell.[249]

The Italians were also a concern of Bishop O'Connell. We are already aware of the Bishop's opinion of his predecessor, Father Peter Magagnotto, an opinion which he formed because of the huge debt Father Peter left behind him on St. Joseph's Church. Father Peter was a member of the Passionist Congregation and a letter from Bishop O'Connell to All Hallows tells how this Congregation came to the vicariate: "He purposes to bring over a colony of Passionist priests and plant them in this Vicariate."[250] However, Bishop O'Connell, in his desperation for priests, approved the idea and actually wrote to Paris asking for assistance to help Father Magagnotto build a monastery for the seven priests he did bring over from Italy.[251]

Father Peter had been pastor of St. Francis Church in San Francisco and Vicar General to Archbishop Alemany. When Bishop O'Connell approved of Father Peter's plan, the latter resigned his pastorate at St. Francis. An amusing tribute was presented to him as a going-away present from his appreciative parishioners in the form of "an elegant gold snuff box."[252]

Father Peter sailed for Italy on the *Golden Age* in August of 1862.[253] It took him ten months to make the trip, recruit candidates for a monastery and return to the vicariate. It seems strange but true that Father Magagnotto decided to establish his monastery just west of Virginia City on the divide that separates that community from Gold Hill. Father Peter and Father Angelo Lugero arrived in Virginia City in September, 1863.[254] Two others, Father Hyacinth and Father Guido Matassi, were given assignments by Bishop O'Connell. The other four were sent to the Dominicans at Benicia to learn English. They were Fathers Amadeo Garabaldi, John Gismondi, Ildephonso Obach, and John Philip Baudinelli, who was later better known as Father Philippus.[255] Within six months, Father Peter had gotten himself again heavily in debt by constructing a combination wooden building consisting of a two-storied church with a three-story living quarters attached at the rear to serve as a monastery. By December, 1863, this wooden church was officially constituted a parish under the title of The Immaculate Conception. The eight priests moved in and began to live the religious life according to the Passionist rule. Thus, the first religious monastery of men had been founded in the vicariate.

Bishop O'Connell's one and only visit to the Divide parish took place on July 31, 1865. On that occasion, he gave confirmation to eight boys and twelve girls. This visit may have sealed the fate of the enterprise for, by September, the community had been moved by the provincial to Mexico.[256]

This sudden demise of the monastery had many causes, a few of which are known. Among the unknown, however, is the question of why, with so many priests in the area, did Bishop O'Connell create the parish of Gold Hill just a mile away to the west in May, 1864, with Father O'Reilly as pastor? One is reminded of a pincer movement: an Irish parish on the west, an Irish parish on the east, and the Italian parish in the center.

It is true that there were difficulties, especially on the part of Father Angelo Lugero. Actually the three parishes were so close together that the question of jurisdiction could easily be confused. Evidently, Father Angelo baptized infants and married couples from either of the other two parishes, whoever came to him. This did not sit well with the neighboring pastors who evidently complained to the Bishop. The Bishop, in turn, called these matters to the attention of Father Angelo. Then came the explosion!

On the following Sunday, Father Lugero denounced Bishop O'Connell in no uncertain terms in the church at Divide. This brought the whole matter out into the open and therefore, on the two following Sundays, Bishop O'Connell very forthrightly preached against the abuses, reminding the people of parish boundaries and of the obligation to receive the sacraments in their proper parish. But at no time did Bishop O'Connell mention Father Angelo's name.

The uproar which resulted from Father Angelo's denunciation caused some of the leading Irish parishioners to write to Rome in defense of Bishop O'Connell. The letter was as follows:

> The undersigned testify that we were present in St. Patrick's Church, Gold Hill, on Sept. 17, 1865 when Bishop

GOLD HILL, Nevada, in 1878, with St. Patrick's Church in right foreground.
ST. PATRICK'S CHURCH, Gold Hill, built by the Rev. Daniel Meagher in 1867.
(Photos, courtesy of Nevada Historical Society, Reno)

O'Connell spoke about certain abuses. We testify that no priest was denounced or name mentioned by his Lordship. What he said was in self defense and to vindicate himself from aspersions publicly cast upon him by Rev. Angelo Lugero (Passionist), who on the Sunday preceding uncharitably denounced the Bishop in the Passionist Church.

We admire the piety and the zeal of the Bishop in rectifying abuses, but were scandalized and disedified at the pride and disobedience of Rev. Angelo Lugero.

> Signed:
> Thomas A. Carroll
> J. P. Flannery
> Michael Fitzpatrick
> Michael Sullivan
> [one other signature, undecipherable][257]

An identical letter was written by the Virginia City parishioners, stating that they were present in St. Mary's Church on Sunday, Sept. 24, 1865, etc. This letter was signed by:

> John Mallon
> John McCarthy
> E. W. Keyes
> James Kelly
> P. S. O'Reilly
> Michael Lynch
> M. O'Connor
> Patrick Coyle
> James Delaney
> [two others unreadable][258]

The war was on! Bishop O'Connell, when the law was on his side, could be tenacious. The documentation shows too that he could carry on quite a battle, even over a trivial matter. Evidently Rome asked for an explanation, which he sent. But, on May 4, 1866, long after the Passionists had departed, he sent a more detailed explanation.

Card. Barnabo:

In my vindication, sent a few weeks ago I erred in saying that the child baptized by Fr Angelo Lugero, on which occasion $10.00 was gained, had been baptized by the same Angelo in a neighboring Parish. The fact is not so, although the mother of the child vehemently desired and asked that Fr Angelo baptize the child in his own private house. But whatever Fr Angelo and the mother of the child wanted I did not consent. Finally I assented to the wishes of both in this way: Fr Angelo could baptize the child in his own Church, retaining nothing from it because the child belonged to a neighboring Parish. But, in spite of this agreement, Fr Angelo Lugero not only retained the $10.00 given on the occasion of the Baptism (as is evident from the written statement of the Sponsor which I sent to your Eminence) but also even gave the child a non-Christian name, "Oscar." The names of those whom Fr Angelo married in the middle of the night on June 20th last year are Michael McLoughlin and Mary Buckley without publishing any Banns and without consulting me even though I was living in the same city.

True it is indeed that one of these parties resided near the limits of the Passionist Parish. But besides the above named parties, there are those whom the Passionist Fathers joined in marriage even tho neither party belonged to their Parish.[259]

When the community left the Divide, the property was put up for sale. The debt on the property in August, 1864, had been $16,000.[260] The property consisted of a lot, 121 feet on Ridge street by 376 feet on E Street. The church and dwelling was 100' x 40' and contained the church itself, with a classroom and kitchen underneath with the three-story residence attached to it. The disposition of the property is not known.

Meanwhile, during their stay, the Passionists had given missions to the Italians throughout the vicariate. Bishop O'Connell invited them to return in 1877 and this time three, including Father Philippus, were sent. They gave missions in such places as Marysville, Colusa, Willows, Yreka, Fort Jones, Oroville, Chico,

Red Bluff, Nevada City, Smartsville, Colfax, Forest Hill, and Carson City. During eight months, a total of thirty-one missions and six retreats were given by this zealous mission band who were able to handle five or six languages.[261]

It should be quite obvious from the above that the welfare of all, no matter the language, no matter the status, was the concern of Bishop O'Connell all through his years as bishop.

Perhaps the best example of the largeness of heart of Bishop O'Connell was his concern for the people working on the building of the transcontinental railroad. This undertaking had begun in 1864 on the California side and, by June, 1865, the track-laying had reached to the boundaries of the Marysville vicariate, and by September they were laying track in Colfax, a mission of the Forest Hill parish. From this point on, construction would be much slower as they were approaching the forbidding Sierra mountains. Secondly, as winter approached there would also be the heavy snows. To complicate matters more, the predominantly Irish crew went on a wage strike. Superintendent Crocker responded by bringing in a trainload of Chinese. Wages were $26.00 a month, an appealing wage scale for the Chinese who flocked to the scene of construction. The winter of 1865 was an especially severe one: snow lay in 20-foot depths on the level, but the workers pushed on. The tunnel at the summit took a year to build, partly due to the difficulties of the terrain encountered, partly due to the fact that the Civil War created a scarcity of powder and raised the price beyond all expectation. The pace of construction increased once the summit was conquered.[262] However, the whole process was beset with many accidents and, since the Irish were in command of the important jobs, the presence of a priest was needed when these accidents occurred. Furthermore, the crews were scattered in camps all along the right of way, making the ministration of a priest difficult unless there was one priest free for this apostolate.

Bishop O'Connell solved this problem by creating a special parish, the Railroad Line parish. The first pastor of this unique parish was the French missioner, Father J. M. Mevel. We have seen how he served as an assistant to the ailing Father Crinion in Oroville in 1866 and how Father O'Kane had been sent to Oroville in 1867. This freed Father Mevel, and the Bishop sent him to Forest Hill to be "Pastor of the Railroad Line."[263] From this point, Father Mevel was able to serve the railroad line as it pushed from Colfax to Dutch Flat, then from Dutch Flat to Alta, then to Cisco, and, at the end of 1867, from Cisco to the summit. Early in 1868, construction was completed from the summit to Truckee. Thus we find Father Mevel moving from Forest Hill as his area of concern crossed the summit. His last ministrations in Forest Hill are recorded in June, 1868. Thus began the parish of Truckee. Although all records of this parish are lost, we know it existed because, in his report to the *National Catholic Directory* for 1870, published in 1871, the Bishop listed it as: "Truckee and line of Railroad to Toano: J. M. Mevel, Pastor."[264]

Bishop O'Connell was enthusiastic in his praise of Father Mevel:

> Father Mevel is Pastor of the line of railroad along which so many accidents happen almost daily and so many lives are lost. And Father Mevel's forte and specialty (as the Americans say) is to assist the sick and dying at all costs and all hazards. He is at present collecting subscriptions for a Church in honor of St. Louis.[265]

In another place, we get a glimpse of how Father Mevel solved his problem of having no church or chapel; the account also reveals Bishop O'Connell's concern for the letter of the law.

> Father Mevel—the great difficulty is to restrain him from erecting an altar in private houses, as they used to of old in Ireland. Hence, we had to make a Diocesan regulation prohibiting priests to say Masses in private houses not ten miles distant from a Church.[266]

By the winter of 1868, the line had been pushed halfway across the Nevada desert toward the meeting point with the Union Pacific, just west of Ogden, Utah. Thus the spring of 1869 found Father Mevel working in the Reno area. Again all records of that parish have been lost. The earliest account we have is a notice in the *Nevada State Journal* of January 28, 1871, announcing that Father Mevel would say Mass in the schoolhouse at 10:00 A.M. the following morning.[267] At the beginning of November, 1871, the ladies held a fair for three evenings at the local theater for the

ST. CANICE CHURCH, Nevada City, California. Built by the Rev. John Griffin in 1864,
and still in use as a parish church.
(Photo, courtesy of Historic Preservation Committee, Grass Valley)

ST. PATRICK'S RECTORY, Grass Valley.
One of few good rectories in the early days.
(Photo, courtesy of Historic Preservation Committee, Grass Valley)

benefit of the church. Just how long Father Mevel remained in this difficult pastorate is not known. There is no evidence of him anywhere after 1879. There is some evidence that when he left the Grass Valley diocese, he went to Haiti. He served well and goes down in history as the founder of both the Truckee and the Reno parishes.

The successor to Father Mevel on the California side of the railroad was Father Daniel Meagher, who evidently cared for the Railroad Line parish from Nevada City during 1873–74. During those years, Father Meagher had as an assistant Father Charles Becker. So in 1874, Father Becker became the pastor of Truckee.[268] The great missionary and successor of Father Mevel in the Nevada portion of the railroad line was Father William Moloney, who for thirteen years traveled the length and breadth of the little towns strung out along the railroad line: Lovelock, Winnemucca, Battle Mountain, Carlin, Elko.[269]

To complete the list of special concerns of Bishop O'Connell during these years, we must shift our attention to entirely different questions which preoccupied him, questions which he repeatedly submitted to Rome and which Rome declined to answer, hoping that the Bishop would solve them himself. Since he could not, they only served to increase his inner turmoil.

The first question which perplexed him was the question of the Mass obligation on certain feasts which had bound Californians when that territory was under Mexican rule, feasts which were not celebrated the same way under American rule. In the days of Mexican rule, the Catholics were obliged to observe the feasts of:

St. John the Baptist   Immaculate Conception
Sts. Peter & Paul   Our Lady of Guadalupe
Mary, Refuge of Sinners

The first time Bishop O'Connell asked if these feasts still carried Mass obligation was on August 29, 1865. A second request has no date on it. The third time, July 31, 1870, he asks point-blank that these feasts be abolished in his diocese.[270] It must have been granted as there are no more requests after that date.

Another concern for his people which the Bishop evidently favored but in which he did not know the extent of his jurisdiction was the matter of miners being dispensed from the meatless Friday obligation. As early as November 20, 1867, the first case was submitted to Rome for an answer which was never given. Again on March 7, 1869, the Bishop asked, "Can I dispense the miners and permit them to eat meat on Fridays?" In 1870, while in Rome, he asked plainly—". . . permission for the miners to eat meat every day, because many miners, especially the Irish who number about 3,000, are having scruples." He extended the request to include Lent—". . . whether these workers on account of the heavy labor which they do day and night in the bowels of the earth, may eat meat daily in Lent, especially if they cannot do their work otherwise."

How this problem was resolved we do not know. Evidently some decision was made for there were no more requests on this matter after 1870. It appears that Rome would have preferred that the Bishop solve some of these problems himself, but it was not in the nature of Eugene O'Connell to presume anything. His concern was the careful spiritual care of his priests and people in express accordance with the intention of Rome. Distance, the newness and boldness of the pioneer territory, unforeseen problems—these only served to increase Bishop O'Connell's solicitude and desire for approval on the decisions he was required to make, decisions which he often postponed for an exasperatingly long time, awaiting such approval from Rome.

Sources for Chapter VIII

230. John B. McGloin, *Eloquent Indian, Life of James Bouchard* (Stanford, California: Stanford University Press, 1949), p. 197.

231. Ibid., p. 186.

232. Ibid., p. 209.

233. Ibid., p. 368.

234. Ibid., p. 193.

235. Baptismal Register, St. Joseph's, Marysville, 1861.

236. AASF, "Libro Borrador," H-18, entries for January, 1863.

237. AAHC, letter of October 29, 1868.
238. AAHC, letter of November 27, 1862.
239. AAHC, letter of October 31, 1872.
240. Baptismal Register, St. Joseph's, Marysville, May, 1862.
241. Ibid., January 2, 1871.
242. *Catholic Directory*, Archdiocese of San Francisco, 1962.
243. Thompson & West, *History of Yuba County*.
244. AASF, "Libro Borrador," H–20.
245. Baptismal Register, St. Mary's, Carson City.
246. *National Catholic Directory*, 1870, p. 193.
247. AAHC, Student Register, entry #744.
248. AAHC, letter of June 22, 1866.
249. Thompson & West, *History of Yuba County*.
250. AAHC, letter of August 25, 1862.
251. ASPF, letter of November 1, 1863.
252. *Marysville Appeal*, August 13, 1862.
253. Ibid.
254. Gorman, *Seventy-Five Years*, p. 54.
255. Ibid.
256. Walsh, *Hallowed Were*, p. 203.
257. ASRC, Vol. 21, F938, letter of April 19, 1866.
258. ASRC, Vol. 21, F939, letter of April 19, 1866.
259. ASRC, Vol. 21, F937, letter of May 4, 1866.
260. ASRC, Vol. 20, F950, letter of August 10, 1864.
261. Walsh, *Hallowed Were*, p. 493.

262. *The Last Spike Is Driven* (Western Railroader Booklet, 350 S), p. 5.
263. Baptismal Register, St. Joseph's, Forest Hill, February 2, 1867.
264. *National Catholic Directory*, 1871.
265. AAHC, letter of May 4, 1869.
266. AAHC, letter of October 29, 1868.
267. *Nevada State Journal*, January 28, 1871.
268. *National Catholic Directory*, 1875.
269. Walsh, *Hallowed Were*, p. 207.
270. ASRC, letter of July 31, 1870.

Chapter IX

YEARS OF MAJOR DECISIONS, 1868–1871

On March 3, 1868, the vicariate of Marysville was raised by Rome to the status of a diocese; the episcopal see was to be Grass Valley.[271] Eugene O'Connell was no longer vicar apostolic of Marysville; he was now first bishop of the Diocese of Grass Valley. The letters from Rome reached him some time in April and his reaction to the change of the see to Grass Valley was anything but favorable. For the next two years, his correspondence with Rome reveals why he resented the change to Grass Valley.

Tradition has always maintained that Bishop O'Connell never occupied his see or cathedral because Father Dalton would not let him, or because Bishop O'Connell was afraid to occupy that church. But this is unfair to both venerable clergymen and the letters of Bishop O'Connell prove it untrue. For one thing, occupation of St. Patrick's Cathedral in Grass Valley would not have affected Father Dalton's position as pastor. As a matter of fact, one of the first things that resulted from the change was that Bishop O'Connell had to give up his own position as pastor of St. Joseph's in Marysville. He was now pastor of the whole diocese. He therefore appointed Father Edward Kelly as pastor of St. Joseph's in Marysville.[272] The real reason why Bishop O'Connell did not take possession of his new cathedral was simply that he did not want to. The first indication is found in a letter (undated) addressed to Rome in which the Bishop says:

Whether I dare to ask this last! namely, to keep my residence or Episcopal See in Marysville which much more deserves the dignity rather than the town called Grass Valley. Truly the transfer from the city of Marysville to Grass Valley is going from the greater to the lesser in every sense, as I have already informed your Eminence and the Baltimore Fathers.[273]

Again on July 31, 1870, he writes to Father Simeoni, secretary to the prefect of Propaganda, in which he asks for:

The privilege of staying in Marysville rather than in Grass Valley for the reasons already given and which daily acquire more force, viz., the growth of Marysville and the decline of Grass Valley, so that, humanly speaking, the one must increase and the other decrease because the mines are dying out.[274]

This letter is signed: "Eugene O'Connell, Bishop of Marysville," evidence of the tenacity of the former vicar apostolic when he made up his mind on something! It was fully three years before Eugene O'Connell began to sign himself Bishop of Grass Valley. The final reference to the matter is found as a postscript in a letter addressed to Father Simeoni on April 21, 1871:

I cannot live in the town of Grass Valley, nevertheless the shadow of that place extends to this whole Diocese. Remarkable thing indeed. The Archbishop has not yet transferred me there. Signed,

> E. O'Connell
> Bishop of Marysville
> or Grass Valley[275]

Evidently the matter just resolved itself. Whether there was any formal response from Rome is unknown. Meanwhile, until it was settled, the Archbishop did nothing about installing Bishop O'Connell in his new cathedral. He mentions this in a letter to All Hallows:

Your letter came yesterday, the anniversary of my translation from Marysville to Grass Valley, a translation which hasn't taken place as yet. I still encumber the ground in Marysville and am likely to cumber it till the final translation of my remains to the Grass Valley Cathedral and thus the translation shall not always be a fiction of law.[276]

There is a humorous side to this story. Evidently when the decree came from Rome, it was addressed to the Rt. Rev. Daniel O'Connell. Bishop O'Connell responded to this in the following words, tongue in cheek, but at the same time very sincere:

The Apostolic Bull erecting the Vicariate of Marysville into the Diocese of Grass Valley is directed to a certain Rev. Daniel O'Connell, and therefore, it seems that I (Eugene) am no longer to be the Bishop either of Flaviopolis (his Titular See) or of Marysville. My Metropolitan dares not transfer me to the City (or rather village) of Grass Valley. What, therefore, am I to do? Gladly would I cede my right if I have any and my Episocpacy in favor of Daniel O'Connell and I ask that the Holy See excuse me from it. Meanwhile I stay in Marysville waiting the disposition of the Holy See, hoping that another may receive my Episcopacy.[277]

This letter was answered by Rome promptly on October 1, 1868. Evidently Rome was satisfied with Eugene. Eventually Bishop O'Connell performed one other necessary task which was required because of the change of status. He appointed Father Dalton of Grass Valley his Vicar General for California and Father Manogue of Virginia City as Vicar General for Nevada. Thus, in his absences, there was someone in each major portion of the diocese who had jurisdiction by law and who would give dispensations for marriages.[278]

The new bishop of Grass Valley carried on his usual work in 1868. He welcomed to the diocese in the fall two from All Hallows, Father Thomas Pettit and Father James Rooney, both of whom had been ordained on June 24, 1868.[279] Quite naturally this necessitated some changes. As mentioned already, Father Kelly was the new pastor of Marysville; the newly ordained

THE REV. THOMAS J. PETTIT, 1844–1884
Assistant at Forest Hill, 1868
Pastor of Oroville, 1868–1872
Pastor of Mendocino City, 1873–1877
Pastor of Reno, Nevada, 1877–1879
Pastor of Forest Hill, 1879–1881
Pastor of Willows, 1881–1884
(Photo, courtesy of Mendocino Historical Research, Inc.)

Father Rooney, and Father James Callan, who was brought from Forest Hill, were his assistants.[280]

Father Daniel Meagher was changed from Gold Hill to Forest Hill, and Father Clarke came from Carson City to be the new pastor of Gold Hill. Of course, any set of changes could not omit Father O'Kane. He left Oroville to succeed Father Grace in Red Bluff, while Father Grace went as pastor to Eureka, California. Father Kennedy, the Bishop's valuable assistant in Marysville, was sent as an assistant to Father Dalton in Grass Valley.[281]

For the two priests Bishop O'Connell gained in the fall of 1868, he had to lose two about the same time. The two he lost were Father Griffin and Father Hickey. He tells the story himself about both of them. On October 29, 1868, the Bishop's letter to All Hallows states:

> Father Griffin is at present in the Archdiocese of San Francisco. However his health was partly the cause of his departure. I said partly, because the primary cause was his wish to see a little more of the world of men and manners. He told me that his term of five years had expired and therefore he was free to leave. I couldn't see it in that light, but I let him go quietly.[282]

Father Griffin left early in March, 1868. The people of Grass Valley, in appreciation for the five years of dedicated service given them by Father Griffin, held a reception and presented him with a burse in the amount of $800. Father Griffin gave half of the amount to the newly established orphanage. He had acted as pastor of Grass Valley during the year-long absence of Father Dalton; he had built the new St. Canice Church in Nevada (City), and now his parting gift endeared him even more in the hearts of the Grass Valley parish.[283]

He was appointed an assistant at St. Mary's Cathedral from March till October, at which time the Archbishop appointed him first resident pastor of "San Leandro and Haywards." However, his stay was short and by July, 1869, he was back at the cathedral for a very brief period. He left for the eastern part of the United States; but within three years, John Griffin was dead, a victim of tuberculosis. He died in Holyoke, Massachusetts, on May 2, 1872.[284]

The departure of Father Hickey was due to a certain incompatibility between the Bishop and himself. When first appointed to Eureka, he had given great promise. When Bishop O'Connell made his visitation to Eureka in 1867, he was deeply impressed by the fine class prepared for confirmation and by the lovely parish house in which he found Father Hickey residing.[285] But the rift between them developed soon after:

> If you saw the letters which Fr Hickey wrote in reply to civil questions which I asked him, as I ask other Pastors, and as I am obliged to do, you would feel for both of us. Father Hickey told me it wasn't expedient to answer all my letters.[286]

To give a possible explanation for Father Hickey's reaction, it might be pointed out that many pastors were to grow weary of the Bishop's constant series of questions about matters which were often trivial, just as the prefect of Propaganda seemed to grow weary and therefore often did not respond. Bishop O'Connell could accept this from his superiors, but certainly not from his inferiors. Whether Father Hickey made the move by "asking out" or whether the Bishop dismissed him is not known. Father Hickey transferred to the archdiocese and was assigned to the cathedral and then as an assistant at St. Peter's in San Francisco.[287] However, within two years he had left the archdiocese. He eventually served long and well in Brooklyn, New York.[288] Of the three young priests who came in 1866, one was dead, one had departed, and only one was left, Father William Clarke.

The gaps created by the departure of these two were filled at once. Father Patrick Henneberry, the Precious Blood missionary, had asked to make a foundation in the diocese. Bishop O'Connell suggested he locate in the parish of Eureka; the vacancy in Carson City was filled by Father William Gleeson.[289] Here again, Bishop O'Connell was destined for another clash. Father Gleeson was almost forty years old, a veteran of fifteen years in the missions in India and of a chaplaincy to the military in Turkey, and had served in Scotland. Bishop O'Connell received the request from All Hallows to accept Father Gleeson into the diocese. Being somewhat tired of priests who did not stay on the mission of their adoption, Bishop O'Connell seemed reluctant to accept him. He responded as follows:

He did not promise, in the event of my adopting or accepting him, to remain with me forever, but only for a few years, and "perhaps" he said, "forever". I referred him to you, and told him I would abide by your arrangement, should you deem him a fit subject and ship him along with the forthcoming missioners. On reflection, I considered that this was running too great a risk, because he may change his mind and after a little while leave me still more in your debt. If then, my dear Father Fortune, you approve of, and can prevail on him to promise to remain with me, I am quite satisfied to adopt him.[290]

Father Gleeson did indeed arrive with Fathers Pettit and Rooney and was duly appointed to Carson City in place of Father Clarke. There seemed to be some clash in the beginning between himself and his neighbors in Gold Hill and Virginia City. Then things went well for awhile, but when both Father Clarke and Father Rooney became ill in Gold Hill in the spring of 1869 and Bishop O'Connell wrote and asked Father Gleeson to attend Gold Hill during their illness, he refused unless he was appointed pastor of Gold Hill. The results of this attitude brought immediate response from Bishop O'Connell.

The moment our "bird of passage" made a dictator of himself in this and many other respects, I withdrew his faculties, and left the rover free to be off to the east or the west. Really, my dear Father, eight years of experience had taught me that every student ought to be obliged to live and die in the mission of his adoption.[291]

Father Gleeson went to the archdiocese, became a professor at St. Mary's College, wrote a history of the Catholic church in California in 1879, and was the founding pastor of St. Anthony's parish in Oakland, where he served for thirty-two years.

The year 1868 found Bishop O'Connell busy at his usual round of visitations. In May, he made the Grass Valley–Nevada City circuit. In June and July, he was north again to Weaverville and Yreka. On August 9, 1868, he was in San Francisco serving as co-consecrator for Bishop Louis Lootens, the newly appointed vicar apostolic of Idaho.[292] By August 16, he was in Virginia City for the laying of the cornerstone of Father Manogue's new

VIRGINIA CITY, Nevada, in 1865.
With Episcopal Church, Fr. Manogue's first church, and the Methodist Church
(Photo, courtesy of California State Library, Sacramento)

church. In September, he was in Downieville.[293]

The year 1869 was a memorable one for Bishop O'Connell. In February, he was in Grass Valley for a profession and confirmation.[294] In early May, he received word that the pastor of Mendocino City, Father Vincent Riera, who had left in February to see if a warmer climate might restore his health, had died in Loretto, Lower California, on April 22, 1869. He too was a victim of tuberculosis.[295] Word also came from Italy of the death of his own predecessor, Father Peter Magagnotto, on November 17, 1868.[296]

Another chief concern of the Bishop at this time was his worry concerning his expenses for attending the Vatican Council called by Pope Pius IX. Although the Bishop did not make any special effort to gather funds, the word got out and his people rallied to assist him. Eventually a diocesan-wide collection was taken up for this purpose.[297]

The Marysville people were taken somewhat by surprise when it was found out that the Bishop was leaving for Rome. A hurried collection was taken up and he was presented with a purse. He evidently left Marysville shortly after having confirmation there on May 16, 1869, and he headed for Nevada where he spent August and September. A correspondent from Virginia City to *The San Francisco Monitor* tells the story:

> Our good Bishop has favored us with his presence for one month prior to his departure for Rome. On the day of departure Father Manogue presented him with a purse of $1200.00, a subscription by some of the leaders of St. Mary's. The St. Vincent de Paul Society gave him $200 and the children of St. Mary's School gave him $100.00. Likewise the people of Gold Hill through their Pastor Father Clarke gave him $800.00. And the people of Austin, Nevada gave him $300.00.[298]

The trip to Rome would have one major change since the last time the California prelates traveled east. They were to cross the continent by railroad. Archbishop Alemany left San Francisco accompanied by Bishop Amat of Monterey on the Central Pacific Railroad. When the train pulled into the Reno station on October 7, 1869, Bishop O'Connell was waiting on the platform.[299] The

ST. THERESA'S CHURCH, Carson City, Nevada

Built by Father Thomas Grace in 1870 at a cost of $5,000. It has been extensively renovated and improved, and still

three prelates then journeyed to New York where they boarded a ship for Europe.

Interestingly enough, Bishop O'Connell dropped in the mail a series of clerical changes just as he boarded the train, an old trick of many bishops in former times because with the Bishop gone there was no recourse except go to one's new assignments. This list is the only one ever published in *The Monitor* for the Grass Valley diocese.

It should be noted first that there were four new arrivals included. Father William Moloney, who was a former student in All Hallows but who had gone home sick in 1861, had arrived in the diocese on April 18, 1869.[300] The second priest was Father Luke Tormey, the only one ordained from All Hallows for Grass Valley on June 24, 1869.[301] The third and fourth were from an eastern diocese, Father Charles F. Becker and Father Stephen Kearney. With these in mind the list of changes was as follows:

Father Callan new Pastor of Marysville
Father Stephen J. Kearney and Father Charles F. Becker assistants at Marysville
Father Kelly back to Austin, Nevada
Father Moloney from assistant in Marysville to Pastor of Downieville. [This was a temporary assignment as Father Lynch was suffering from severe rheumatism. Father Lynch was also assigned to St. Joseph's in Marysville.]
Father James Rooney from assistant at Austin to assistant at Gold Hill.
Father Luke Tormey, assistant to Father Claire at Nevada City.
Father Thomas Grace from Pastor of Eureka to Pastor of Carson City.
Father Patrick Henneberry, Pastor of Eureka, California.[302]

Surprisingly, Father O'Kane was not included. He remained on in Red Bluff.

On his arrival in Rome, Bishop O'Connell lodged at the Basilica of St. Clement with his old friend and former superior Dr. Moriarty, who was now the bishop of Kerry. Since the Holy Father received the American bishops in groups, Bishop O'Connell was included in one of these audiences at the end of November. Most of the bishops brought some kind of gift from their home dioceses for the Holy Father. It was Eugene O'Connell's that caused the greatest stir. As bishop of the Mines of California and Nevada, he brought ingots and nuggets of silver and gold. However, one ingot of silver, sent by an Irish immigrant Denis J. Oliver of the Grass Valley diocese, weighed 350 pounds and had to be carried into the audience chamber by six papal guards. It was estimated to have been worth 1,000 pounds sterling.[303] A pre-synodal session was held in the Sistine Chapel on December 2, 1869, but the grand opening was held in St. Peter's in the right apse on December 8, 1869. This first session lasted without a break from 10 A.M. until almost 4 P.M. The ceremonies had included Mass, a sermon, an act of obedience to the Holy Father, prayers and an exhortation by Pius IX, and then the business session. In attendance at this opening session were 698 Fathers, forty-five of them being from the United States.[304]

The sessions continued through the chilly winter months into the beautiful springtime of the year and then on through the hot summer until September 1, 1870, when the last general congregation was held. By that time, the number of Council Fathers had dwindled to almost half the original number. The impending war hung heavy over the gathering as the bishops departed from Rome. On October 20, Pope Pius IX formally dissolved the Council.[305]

These long months in Rome, difficult as they may have been from the weather, his own poverty, the long weary sessions—eighty-nine in all—the interminable speeches which numbered in the hundreds, the stubbornness of some of the Council Fathers, in spite of all this, Bishop O'Connell's letters from the center of Christendom show that he enjoyed being there. This humble man whose three largest churches would fit all together inside any one of the major basilicas was surrounded by ageless buildings of grandeur. This simple bishop whose concerns were the ministrations of baptism, confirmation, marriage, etc., to people who labored in the earth to extract silver and gold was surrounded by brilliant minds speaking in the Latin he knew so well. This was a feast for the intelligence of a man who was starved for such company. He was in Rome for Holy Week and Easter, and yet at one juncture he wrote:

> The Pope ought to walk into the Council Hall and discharge us in globo. I believe that the great majority of us would be

THE REV. JAMES J. HYNES, 1847–1899
Founding Pastor of St. Brendan's, Eureka, Nevada, 1872–1876
Founding Pastor of Chico, California, 1878–1887
Pastor of Woodland, California, 1888–1899
(Photo, courtesy of Sisters of Mercy, Grass Valley)

serving the interests of religion as effectually and a small minority far more effectually, dispersed throughout their respective Dioceses, than here all gathered together in Council.[306]

When the final votes on papal infallibility were tallied, Eugene O'Connell, bishop of Grass Valley in California, had voted "Placet" along with 432 others, as opposed to 2 "non placets."[307] He was present on that memorable July 18, 1870, when Pius IX solemnly declared the doctrine for belief by the Universal Church.

That evening, a reception was held at the Irish College to honor Cardinal Cullen for his admirable role in the Council as an Irishman. Present were thirty-one Irish-born bishops, Bishop O'Connell being the only American bishop among them.[308]

What joy filled his heart on the day he left for Ireland. What must have been his feelings during those two weeks he spent in his beloved All Hallows. There is no record, so one can only guess. But that joy was terminated on October 11, 1870, when he sailed for home.[309]

His next letter, written the day after he got home in Grass Valley, stated: "After some 6,000 miles of travel over sea and land I arrived safely, thank God, in Grass Valley, yesterday the feast of St. Cecelia" (November 22, 1870).[310]

In spite of the fact that Bishop O'Connell was gone from his diocese more than one year, he kept up a correspondence with his Vicars General and continued his rule over the diocese. Therefore, we find as many changes of clergy in that period as at any other time.

For one thing, he created three new parishes in that year: Crescent City and Colusa in California, and Hamilton in Nevada.[311] But that was to bring to a close the era of rapid expansion. He was almost at the end of his first ten years. In the next ten, he created only four more in California and two more in Nevada. This final year in the first decade of his administration was also the last time he received into the diocese more than two priests per year. The new arrivals were Fathers James J. Hynes, whom he sent as an assistant to Gold Hill, and Father Andrew O'Donnell, whom he sent as assistant to Forest Hill. These two were ordained from All Hallows on June 24, 1870.[312] The third was

Father Leon Haupts whose origin is unknown but who came to the diocese in 1870.

Father Callan evidently got permission to go home to Ireland for a visit. Bishop O'Connell did not favor such trips but found it hard to resist the request of Father Callan, who seems to have been among those whom the Bishop most admired and respected. Therefore Father Moloney was transferred from Downieville to Marysville as pastor.[313] Father Lynch, meanwhile, had recovered his health sufficiently to return to his mountain parish of Downieville. These changes took place immediately on the return of Bishop O'Connell to the diocese. Meanwhile, that intrepid Nevada missionary Father Dominic Monteverde had found a new and fertile field for his missionary labors. While pastor of Austin, he had discovered that White Pine County had several new mining camps and had no priest. So in March, 1869, he had moved from Austin to Hamilton where he established a new parish and proceeded to build a church.[314] The White Pine County parish became the most easterly and most distant of the parishes in the diocese. It was, in turn, visited by Bishop O'Connell in 1872. When Father Monteverde moved from Austin, the Bishop sent back there its former pastor, the ever-obedient Father Edward Kelly.

At this juncture, it should be mentioned that the Archdiocese, just south of the line which separated it from the Grass Valley diocese, had one lone parish in eastern Nevada named Pioche in Lincoln County. It became a parish under Father Lawrence Scanlan of the archdiocese in the same 1870. However, it was usually listed under the Grass Valley diocese since it was more accessible to Bishop O'Connell than to Archbishop Alemany.[315] However, the two bishops shared jurisdiction in several other areas also.

Bishop O'Connell had always been concerned about the most northerly of the coastal towns, Crescent City. Until this time it had been taken care of by the priest in Eureka. Finally, with the arrival of Father Leon Haupts, Bishop O'Connell was able to separate that area from Eureka and appoint Father Haupts as the founding pastor.[316] At the same time, he separated Colusa–Grand Island from the Oroville parish and transferred Father Becker from Marysville to Grand Island and Colusa as the first resident pastor.[317] Eureka remained in the care of the Precious Blood

IMMACULATE CONCEPTION CHURCH, Colusa, California

Built in 1867, without tower, for $2,700; dedicated by Bishop O'Connell, December 8, 1867. Rectory built by Father Ed Kelly in 1872. Tower of church and addition to rectory added by Father M. Walrath in 1878. The church was replaced by a new one in April 1881: the present Our Lady of Lourdes.

CRESCENT CITY'S SECOND CHURCH: ST. JOSEPH'S
Built by Father Michael Walrath in 1874. Photo shows it in the last moments of its existence as it burned to the ground in the early 1900s.
(Photo, courtesy of Del Norte Historical Society)

fathers, but Father Henneberry gave the care of the parish over to Father Dickman who became the new Eureka pastor. The other Marysville assistant, Father James Rooney, was sent to fill the vacancy in Mendocino City which was caused by the death of Father Riera.[318] With the creation of these three new parishes, Bishop O'Connell began to take a second look at his program. He had pretty well developed all the areas that troubled him originally as being priestless. He had poured all the diocesan resources into paying for the education and transportation of missioners for the diocese. In general, he had pretty well fulfilled his goal. Of course, there were still some areas to be developed, but he now had second thoughts about continuing on this same course any longer.

While he was in Rome, one of his Vicars General—he doesn't say which one—wrote and made a great plea for some of the diocesan resources to be put into the education of children rather than more priests at such a rapid rate. This letter made an impression on Bishop O'Connell. As a result, a big decision was made by him in this regard. He wrote it to Father Fortune, the president of All Hallows:

Rome, May 25, 1870

My dear Fr Fortune:

I fear that the note which I addressed some weeks ago, in reply to your kind letter, never reached you and that consequently you may be under the impression that I paid no attention to your favor. However I beg to assure you, it is not my fault if my note "failed to connect" as the Americans say. I must now repeat that the last allocation from the Assoc. in Paris is in all probability the last which I can apply to All Hallows in consequence of the far more urgent need we have of teachers for the children in the Diocese of G V than of priests to administer the Sacraments etc to the adults. Hence I was compelled, however reluctantly, to request of you to educate only as many Missioners for me as I am able to pay for in future. The last letter which my V.G. wrote to me only confirms my resolution to provide what alas I have failed to do—teachers for the children who are in imminent danger of losing their faith or morals in non Catholic schools. Now my dear Fr F you must not be displeased with me, nor suppose for a moment that the diminution or reduction of the number of my subjects in All Hallows is owing to any other cause but the paramount duty of providing for the lambs as well as for the sheep entrusted to my care.[319]

From 1871, and for the second decade of Bishop O'Connell's years as bishop of Grass Valley, the supply of priests was sharply reduced—one or two per year, enough to take care of replacements caused by sickness or death, as even the number of priests leaving the diocese became, happily, less. There was a second reason, not mentioned in his letters, but which accounted for the reduction in the number of priests. The economic condition of the whole mining industry was in a slump. There was very little growth during the second decade, therefore very little need for expansion.

Sources for Chapter IX

271. The Rev. Donald C. Shearer, *Pontificia Americana, A Documentary History of the Catholic Church in the United States, 1784–1884* (Washington, D.C.: Catholic University of America, 1933), No. 126.

272. *The Monitor*, October 31, 1868.

273. ASRC, Vol. 23, F436, undated letter.

274. ASRC, Vol. 23, F430, letter of July 31, 1870.

275. ASRC, Vol. 23, F1057, letter of April 21, 1871.

276. AAHC, letter of March 23, 1871.

277. ASRC, Vol. 22, F436, letter of September 1, 1868.

278. *The Monitor*, October 2, 1869.

279. Ibid., August 1, 1868.

280. Baptismal Register, St. Joseph's, Marysville.

281. Baptismal Register, St. Patrick's, Grass Valley.

282. AAHC, letter of October 29, 1868.

283. Archives of the Sisters of Mercy, Grass Valley, "The Annals."

284. Wm. Abeloe, *Our First Century* (San Leandro, California: St. Leander's Church, 1964), p. 27.

285. Walsh, *Hallowed Were*, p. 293.

286. AAHC, letter of May, 1868.

287. *The Monitor*, February 25, 1871.

288. Ibid., January 23, 1889.

289. AAHC, letter of October 29, 1868.

290. AAHC, letter of May 14, 1868.

291. AAHC, letter of June 2, 1869.

292. *The Monitor*, August 1, 1868.

293. Baptismal Register, Immaculate Conception, Downieville.

294. Archives of the Sisters of Mercy, Grass Valley, "The Annals."

295. *The Monitor*, July 24, 1869.

296. Ibid., January 16, 1869.

297. ASRC, letter of December 28, 1869.

298. *The Monitor*, October 23, 1869.

299. Ibid.

300. Baptismal, Register, St. Joseph's, Marysville.

301. *The Monitor*, July 31, 1869.

302. Ibid., October 2, 1869.

303. James J. Hennessy, *The First Council of the Vatican* (New York: Herder & Herder, 1963), p. 32.

304. Ibid., p. 38.

305. Walsh, *Hallowed Were*, p. 427.

306. AAHC, letter of May 31, 1870.
307. Walsh, *Hallowed Were*, p. *423*.
308. Hennessy, op. cit., p. 283.
309. Walsh, *Hallowed Were*, p. 428.
310. AAHC, letter of November 22, 1870.
311. Gorman, *Seventy-Five Years*, p. 100.
312. AAHC, Student Register.
313. Baptismal Register, Immaculate Conception, Downieville.
314. AAHC, letter of October 29, 1868.
315. *National Catholic Directory*, 1873, p. 200.
316. Walsh, *Hallowed Were*, p. 278.
317. *National Catholic Directory*, 1871.
318. Walsh, *Hallowed Were*, p. 409.
319. AAHC, letter of May 25, 1870.

Chapter X

THE CARE OF THE INDIANS

Bishop O'Connell could certainly rest his conscience that he had populated his diocese with priests in all the major population centers. He certainly had no reason to reproach himself in regard to his efforts for the various national groups in his diocese. But he did find one more group to challenge his zeal, namely the Indians who lived in his vast diocese, those in the Mendocino-Lake section of the California portion, and those who lived in the Nevada portion. It was just about this time when he could feel somewhat satisfied that he had taken care of the other groups that mention of the Indians becomes frequent in his correspondence.

Father Manogue had from the start been concerned about the Indians living in the confines of his parish and there are tales about his success among them.[320] The first mention that Bishop O'Connell makes of this special apostolate is in a letter written shortly after arriving in Rome in December, 1869, addressed to M. Certes at Paris. It is a lengthy description made by the Bishop himself:

> There are two reservations in which the American Government keeps the Indians which are without Chaplains to teach Christian Doctrine. In those Reservations are kept and fed about 1500 Indians. In vain have I asked a stipend or alms from the same Government so I can provide missionaries for the instruction of the Indians. Finally I implored a Mexican Archbishop to send me one priest who in

the Spanish language (because many of the Indians speak that language) teaches them the mysteries of the Faith. The Most Rev. Archbishop consented and so at least one Chaplain for the Indians has been found. But what can only one do among so many Indians scattered all over California and the neighboring State of Nevada, speaking different languages. Therefore thru the depths of the Mercy of God will you not increase your allocation and grant my Diocese as much as the Monterey Diocese? If you do not believe me, consult my Metropolitan, the Archbishop of San Francisco, who will inform you of my destitution and my need. I ask you for the Indians because I cannot provide Chaplains for two Reservations unless you help me.[321]

But Bishop O'Connell did not confine his pleas only to M. Certes. He attempted to interest the Cardinal Prefect of Propaganda, hoping he would intercede in the situation. In two of his letters while in Rome he mentions the matter:

I don't know what to do to get Missionaries for the Indians. I get help for the education and transportation of priests for the farmers and miners from the Society for the Propagation of the Faith in Paris; I have one lone Missioner sent by the Archbishop of Guadalajara, but what is this among so many?[322]

In another letter he complains:

What about the Indians? The Council of Baltimore in 1852, approved by the Holy See, gave the care of the Indians to the Jesuits. I have again and again asked the Provincial, Father Soprana [Felix Sopranis] who lives in San Francisco, to send one or two missionaries to the Indians in my vineyard but in spite of his promise, no missionary has appeared among my Indians. I admit and say with a most grateful heart there has never been a lack of Missionaries of those who preach missions to the poor and rich throughout my Diocese, but there is no one for the poor Indians.[323]

Finally, on July 22, 1870, he addressed a direct request to Cardinal Barnabo asking him to intercede on his behalf with the

Society in Paris for the Indians. "I have only one Mexican priest and I can't send any more because I don't have the money."[324]

We recall that as early as 1863 Bishop O'Connell had the services of Father Luciano Osuna, evidently at first for the Spanish-speaking people of the whole vicariate. But Father Osuna began to confine himself more and more to the Spanish-speaking Indians of Mendocino, Lake, and Sonoma counties. Since the line separating the Diocese of Grass Valley and the Archdiocese of San Francisco ran through Mendocino and Lake, Father Osuna shared jurisdiction in both dioceses and reported to both bishops. But his ordinary was Bishop O'Connell. The Round Valley Reservation was entirely in the Grass Valley diocese. When Father Riera left Mendocino City in February, 1869, for the trip from which he never returned and in the intervening space until the Bishop sent Father Rooney, it was Father Osuna who took care of Mendocino. But his principal work was among the Indians.

Father Osuna must have been an extraordinary man, identifying with the Indians to a degree not quite acceptable to established society but nonetheless exercising a noteworthy influence over them. His manner of life is best described by himself:

> I have been with the Indians most of the time, they are sick and hungry and so I am hungry with them. We have no place where to live, nothing to do to work for our living. They had good crops but we have nothing to eat.
> The Indians are starving in both respects, in the body and in the soul. We must do something, otherwise our charity will not reach them. I do not see any other way to help them but to get a place and there under the priest's care, they will work for their living, for soul and body. I spoke to a man in Lake Co. and he will let me have a place for very little if I only pay the taxes of the place this year. As winter is nigh, we must take hold of every chance, lest by neglect some of these little ones may perish, obliged to pass the winter with the rain upon their heads and with empty stomachs; and what is worse without the shelter of Religion. I hope, Bishop, that you will agree with my views, and for your part you will do all that is in your power to do so, to raise all kinds of help in provisions, in money, in clothing, in blankets, and so forth. That is the way to put money in

the bank of heaven and on the last day we will avoid that terrible sentence of our Lord: "You saw me hungry and naked and did not recognize me." I hope all the Catholics will join in our work. Whatever is to be sent must be sent to me at Cloverdale, in care of Matalang. Letters to be directed to Kelseyville, in care of Pete Clark.[325]

Evidently Father Luciano carried on his apostolate among the Indians without too much interference for the first ten years of his missionary endeavors among them. The largest concentration of Indians seems to have been at the Round Valley Reservation in Mendocino County. That reservation in 1871 was given over to the administration of a Methodist minister named Gibson who became the first Indian agent.[326] He was succeeded two years later by J. L. Burchard, another Methodist minister who, like Pharoah of old, "knew not Joseph"—in this case, Luciano—and who evidently reacted very unfavorably to Father Osuna's free and easy ways. It is obvious from reading the voluminous records of the trouble which occurred between Father Luciano and the Indian agent that Father Osuna acted imprudently and that Mr. Burchard was jealous of Father Luciano's influence over the Indians and somewhat prejudiced also.

According to letters written to Archbishop Alemany, Father Osuna bought ten acres of land in Sunol which was intended to be his headquarters. The Archbishop had sent him a plan for a simple house measuring 30 feet by 20 feet. It was estimated to cost about $500.[327] In the late summer, it is possible to trace this missionary's journeys from Knights Ferry to Mokelumne to Stockton. By the beginning of November, 1873, he was in Ukiah.[328] From there he intended to visit the Round Valley Reservation near Covelo before the winter rains set in. This visit was to have unexpected results.

Before telling the story, it might be useful to know that Father Osuna was very much pro-Indian and a champion of their rights. On one occasion he wrote: "Every day I am convinced more of the necessity of caring for the Indians, much more because the Indians have become the prey of all and they have no one to offer a friendly hand."[329] During his troubles with the Indian agent, part of the reason why the agent wanted to rid himself of the priest was because he championed the rights of the In-

ROUND VALLEY, CALIFORNIA, in 1858, from the southwest
The Indian reservation included the north end of the valley
(Photo, courtesy of Smithsonian Institution, National Anthropological Archives,
Bureau of American Ethnology Collection, Washington, D.C.)

dians. For example, Joel Vance, one of the employees of the reservation, testified that on one occasion when he was riding along with an Indian named Andreas and Father Luciano, these two began to talk in Spanish, not knowing that Mr. Vance understood Spanish. Father Osuna was advising Andreas that he ought to leave the reservation as he could make more money off the farmers and do better by himself than if he stayed on the reservation.[330]

Father Luciano was so much part of the Indian way of life that he taught the men even in the "sweat houses" where they spent the night, thus keeping them awake, according to his accusers, and preventing them from doing their best work on the following day.[331] He also challenged the right of the Protestant authorities to teach religion. All of these did not sit well with the Methodist authorities of the reservation. With this in mind, we can understand the events which took place on the day of his arrival at the Round Valley Reservation during the first week of November, 1873.

As was his custom, Father Luciano went straight to the Indian camp without bothering with permissions or any other formalities. His presence was announced to Mr. Burchard who ordered Father Luciano to be brought to his office. The agent explained that the rules and regulations of the superintendent of Indian Affairs required that any white man, other than the employees of the agency, had to have permission to visit in the camps. Father Osuna evidently responded in an independent manner that since he was a priest, these rules and regulations did not apply to him and that he had the right to go where he pleased in order to teach the people. He evidently pointed out to Mr. Burchard that he had been coming and going for ten years and that no one, not even General Grant, could stop him.[332]

Mr. Burchard then informed Father Luciano that he had to leave the reservation and not return. He then took Father Osuna by the arm and led him outside. But the obstinate missionary immediately returned and was again led outside. By this time, tempers were rising on both sides. Father Luciano returned again, this time flourishing his fists and shouting, "You want to fight, do you?" It was now the agent who lost his control and, taking up his cane, he struck Father Luciano across the shoulders two or three times. Once again the priest was led out, this time outside the camp.³³³ But in a few days Father Luciano returned, in the same manner, just slipping into the Indian camp without any permission. Again he was discovered and brought to the agent's office.

This time the agent decided he had better turn the offending priest over to the civil authorities, but since there was no sheriff in Mendocino County, he took him to the military authorities at Camp Wright. The commanding officer, C. Woodruff, testified that when brought before him, Father Luciano was "clothed in some of the habiliments of a priest, but his appearance generally would scarcely do credit to the Church he represents, for a more dirty, ragged specimen of humanity is rarely seen on the public highway."³³⁴

Mr. Burchard described Father Luciano in these words: "He was barefooted, unwashed, uncombed, torn robe, cow manure and mud between his toes and on his feet."³³⁵ Hardly likely to make a good impression on anyone! The commander of the army post tried to urge Father Luciano to stay away from the reservation. This was the most he could do. But in a few days he was back again. This time Mr. Burchard locked the priest up and sent for the commanding officer. Again persuasion was tried and Father Luciano was sent out of the reservation. Two or three days later he was found again in the Indian camp. This time, Mr. Burchard sent him to Ukiah, sixty miles away on horseback under escort, to the justice of the peace, Mr. Harrison, evidently a very fair man who reported the matter to Archbishop Alemany, stating that on April 21, 1874, he had examined Father Luciano on a charge of insanity but had dismissed the case. However, he advised the Archbishop to take some kind of action, as Father Luciano "follows his mission among those particular Indians by your order and will not abandon it without your sanction. I am satisfied serious personal trouble will result to him if he persists in what he believes to be a conscientious attention to his duties there."³³⁶ He urged the Archbishop to prevent further trouble,

> ... as Mr. Burchard's position affords him advantages, he seems disposed to avail himself of it. I am satisfied from observation as well as from what I have heard, Mr. Burchard will enlist all the Protestant prejudices of his community against Father Luciano and thereby render a continued

sojourn in the neighborhood of the reservation one uncomfortable for the Father. Here and elsewhere, Father Luciano is very much esteemed. His present personal condition of dress etc. might not commend him to strangers.[337]

Bishop O'Connell's description of Father Osuna in a letter to John Gilmary Shea on August 27, 1874, is perhaps the best:

> In order to gain over the Indians to Christianity Padre Osuna conforms to their mode of living. He goes without shoes and wears sandals, therefore he is insane! He eats, drinks and sleeps after the fashion of the Indians therefore he is insane! I wonder what our feather bed Officer would say if he saw St. John the Baptist in the desert or on the banks of the Jordan. No doubt he would pronounce him insane and a fit subject for Stockton lunatic asylum.[338]

Even all this did not deter Father Osuna from pursuing what he considered to be his right as well as his duty. He was soon back in the camp again. This time it was about nine o'clock at night when he was apprehended. Since Father Osuna seemed not to have any fixed residence of his own, he evidently was welcomed into the cabins of the Indians wherever he went. On this occasion, he had evidently already retired for the night and when he was arrested he was found in his night attire. This caused the employees of the agent to make scoffing remarks. Father Osuna often referred to the Indians as his children. One of the agency employees remarked that maybe some of them were! This caused great laughter among the bystanders.[339] Once again he was put off the reservation. Finally, on October 1, 1874, Father Osuna, perhaps at the advice of either of the bishops, went formally and asked permission to conduct religious services and to teach the Indians. It so happened that on that date, since two high-ranking clergymen of the Methodist church were present, Mr. Burchard referred Father Luciano to them. These two men refused the permission. Father Luciano did not return to the reservation after that date.[340]

Bishop O'Connell and the Archbishop now took the matter to higher authorities. For one thing, Father Luciano swore out on May 18, 1875, an affidavit of the treatment he had received and this was forwarded to Washington which then on June 4, 1875, ordered an investigation. Meanwhile, the two bishops formally submitted a request that the government grant permission to them to build a Catholic chapel and rectory on the reservation. This request, sent in on February 20, 1875, included the idea that such a mission would be not only for the Indians on the reservation but also for all those "now wandering outside the reservation."[341] The office of the Catholic Commissioner for Indian Missions, Charles Ewing, presented this request on April 5, 1875. It was turned down on May 14, 1875, as impossible. The upshot of the whole case was that the Archbishop bought 160 acres of land at Big Valley in Lake County for $5,000 in 1875, and a rectory, barns, and other outbuildings were erected.[342] This was the beginning of St. Turibius Indian Mission. On this ranch there were many Indian cabins built, as well as a schoolhouse. There more than 100 Indians were employed on the ranch, which became self-supporting. Father Luciano administered it until 1879, when he returned to Mexico and was replaced by a Franciscan priest, Father Bonaventure Fox, who stayed about two years. He was replaced by Father Dominic Governo for two years when the Holy Cross Fathers came.[343]

Thus Bishop O'Connell's appeal for funds to send missionaries to the Indians was not heeded, and were it not for his friend the Archbishop, the whole apostolate would have come to nothing.

Bishop O'Connell tells of his visits to these Indian parishioners during his years as their bishop. On one occasion, June 24, 1869, he was deeply impressed when he witnessed Father Osuna baptizing twenty-four Indians.[344] On August 9, 1874, he gave confirmation in Lakeport in the little church built in 1870. There is evidence that he also confirmed in the church in Kelseyville built in 1871, although that church was over the line in the Archdiocese of San Francisco.

There were Indians also in the northernmost portion of the Diocese of Grass Valley. In 1873, Bishop O'Connell assigned Father Michael Walrath to Crescent City. Evidently he was told to give concern to the Indians because in September, 1875, he wrote a rather complete report on this subject to Bishop O'Connell:

There are 300 Indians living 12 miles from here and in the 2 counties under my direction there are 3,000. The Government has kept 700 on a reserve under Methodist control. I can't do anything for them but the others are free and are scattered all over the 2 county territory. When I first went among the Indians with bell and crucifix to preach the Gospel, they listened with a mixture of curiosity and anxiety, fearing that I might be bringing them more suffering. On the first Sunday of the month, I dedicated a chapel to St. Michael. They now understand that my mission among them is honest and disinterested, and that I am working for their good, and they are full of confidence. They go in numbers to the chapel and you should see with what respect and attention they listen to the word of God. What pleasure to give to these starving souls the bread of life of which they have never heard, and I don't doubt that I shall soon be able to baptize most of the neighboring Indians. Thirty have already asked for baptism. Religion will influence them and soon they will be quite different. The plan that I have thought up is to help them to legally acquire a home so that they may not be dispossessed; after that, I could teach them agriculture and crafts. For the moment, what they have the most need of is a school and I hope that your Lordship will help me to obtain the money necessary to its construction as you have done for the chapel. I can't find much money here and there isn't a priest closer than 100 miles.[345]

Writing to the Society for the Propagation of the Faith in 1879 begging for aid for the Dominican Sisters in Reno, Bishop O'Connell tells something about the work among the Indians in the Reno area:

> The Sisters of St. Dominic also have a little school for Indian boys and girls. Reno is a central depot, surrounded by 4,000 Indians. My greatest desire is to educate a certain number of the most intelligent children taken from the Washoe, the Piute and the Shosone tribes, and to send them in a few years amongst their respective tribes in order

to teach and propagate amongst their heathen brethren the consoling doctrines of the Gospel of Christ. It is time indeed, messieurs, that those ignorant and too long forsaken inhabitants of the plains and deserts should be taught the mysteries of our holy Religion. But how can the Dominican Sisters contend successfully against the Protestant emissaries who receive all the money they need from the American Bible Societies? How can they continue to instruct the poor Indians whose salvation we so ardently desire if you in your well known generosity do not come to their assistance?[346]

The Bishop then asked for 25,000 francs. What response he got to this plea is not known.

It should be quite obvious from these letters that Bishop O'Connell's concern for the Indians was as great as his concern for the miners or the farmers. But his success was quite limited because of his inability to move the Society for the Propagation of the Faith, on whom he had to depend mostly for his support. Whatever was done for California's native population was done by individual priests, and whatever help was given came from Archbishop Alemany. In this area, Eugene O'Connell would consider himself a failure.

Sources for Chapter X

320. Sister Fredrick Ann Hehr, O.P., "History of the Catholic Church in Virginia City, Nevada," master's thesis, University of San Francisco, 1969, pp. 48ff.

321. ASPF, letter of December 28, 1869, from Rome.

322. ASRC, Vol. 23, F436, undated letter.

323. ASRC, Vol. 23, F438, undated letter.

324. ASRC, Vol. 23, F441, July 22, 1870.

325. AALA, letter of August 29, 1872, from Cloverdale, California.

326. AALA, report of May, 1875, on Round Valley Reservation.

327. AALA, letter to Archbishop Alemany from Sunol, June 17, 1873.

328. AALA, letter from Ukiah, November 2, 1873.

329. AALA, letter from Sunol, June 17, 1873.

330. AALA, sworn testimony of Joel Vance, June 16, 1875.

331. AALA, sworn testimony of James R. Brown, June 15, 1875.

332. AALA, letter of J. L. Burchard to Commission of Indian Affairs, April 10, 1874.

333. AALA, sworn testimony of J. L. Burchard.

334. AALA, report of commanding officer to Archbishop Alemany, March 30, 1874.

335. AALA, sworn testimony of J. L. Burchard, June 15, 1875.

336. AALA, report of R. Harrison, county judge, to Archbishop Alemany, April 21, 1874.

337. AALA, letter of R. Harrison, county judge, to Archbishop Alemany, May 12, 1874.

338. Archives of Archdiocese of Philadelphia, letter to John Gilmary Shea, August 27, 1874.

339. AALA, sworn testimony of James T. Brown, June 15, 1875.

340. AALA, sworn testimony of Luciano Osuna, May 18, 1875.

341. AALA, joint letter of the two bishops to Washington, D.C., February 20, 1875.

342. *History of Napa and Lake Counties* (San Francisco: Slocum, Bowen & Co., 1881), p. 184.

343. *Catholic Directory*, Archdiocese of San Francisco, 1962.

344. ASPF, letter of December 28, 1869, from Rome.

345. ASPF, letter of Fr. M. Walrath to Bishop O'Connell, September 29, 1875.

346. AALA, letter of Bishop O'Connell to the Society for the Propagation of the Faith, October 17, 1879.

Chapter XI

THE BUSY YEARS, 1871–1876

When the year 1871 dawned, Eugene O'Connell was completing ten years as shepherd of the diocese of northern California and Nevada. Since he had to renew his faculties which were granted by Rome for five years at a time, he had to send a report which showed in those first ten years how he had used these permissions.

> Ten years have passed since I came to this Diocese of Marysville or Grass Valley, and therefore I must give an accounting of my stewardship.
>
> Dispensations granted to Catholics contracting marriages with non-Catholics number about 397 of which 95 were to non-baptized persons. [In a postscript he changed the total to 404.]
>
> In this Diocese there are five convents of nuns in which 401 girls are enrolled, among whom are some non-Catholics; but for boys not even one College is found in the Diocese of Grass Valley. Why this state of affairs? Because of the lack of resources which scarcely suffice to educate Missioners in Europe and transport them here. Workers are indeed scarce in this Diocese and in order that several studying in All Hallows, Dublin, can be maintained cost $23,541, the greatest part of which came from the Society for the Propagation of the Faith in Paris. The Catholic population is 14,000 people.[347]

What he did not mention in this report was that he had been able to develop the diocese from six parishes and seven priests to twenty-two parishes with twenty-eight priests. Parishes and priests in mid-1871 were as follows:

On the Coast:	Crescent City	Fr Leon Haupts
	Eureka	Fr B. O. Dickman, C.PP.S.
	Rohnerville	Fr Patrick Henneberry, C.PP.S.
	Mendocino (City)	Fr James Rooney
		Fr Luciano Osuna
In the North:	Yreka	Fr Patrick Farrelly
	Weaverville	Fr Matthew Coleman
	Red Bluff	Fr Stephen Kearney
	Colusa	Fr Charles Becker
In the Center:	Oroville	Fr Thomas Pettit
	Marysville,	Fr Wm. Moloney
	St. Joseph's	Fr Andrew O'Donnell
	Marysville,	
	Immaculate Conception	Fr Julius Herde
	Grass Valley	Fr Thomas Dalton
		Fr Lawrence Kennedy
	Nevada (City)	Fr James J. Claire
	Downieville	Fr Charles Lynch
	Forest Hill	Fr Daniel Meagher
	Truckee	Fr J. M. Mevel
In Nevada:	Virginia City	Fr Patrick Manogue
		Fr John M. Nulty
	Gold Hill	Fr William Clarke
	Carson City	Fr Thomas Grace
	Austin	Fr Dominic Monteverde
	Hamilton	Fr Patrick O'Kane
	Pioche	Fr Lawrence Scanlan

Father James Callan was still on vacation in Ireland and the assignment of Father Luke Tormey in this year has eluded the researcher.

There are several items in both the report and the listing that have not been previously mentioned. First, there were now five establishments of sisters. Besides the Notre Dame Sisters in Marysville, the Sisters of Mercy in Grass Valley, and the Daughters of Charity in Virginia City, two more were founded at this time. Father Farrelly in Yreka had been working to obtain sisters for the far-flung county of Siskiyou. He first had a promise of sisters from Canada, but by the time this hard-working priest

ST. JOSEPH'S CHURCH, Yreka, California

Built by the Rev. James Callan in 1876 after a fire on July 4, 1871, destroyed Father Farrelly's 1866 church named SS Peter and Paul. This fourth church, enlarged and remodeled in 1956, has served the Yreka parish to the present time.
(Photo, taken in 1900, courtesy of St. Joseph's Church, Yreka, California)

had the convent ready, the sisters wrote that they could not come. Since Bishop O'Connell was away at the Vatican Council, Father Farrelly appealed to him to stop off in Montreal on his way home and bring these sisters with him.[348] Instead, the Bishop appealed to the Sisters of Mercy in Manchester, New Hampshire, who early in 1871 sent Mother Camilius McGarr and two novices to make the foundation in Yreka. Father Farrelly purchased the residence of F. J. King at the corner of Butte and 4th streets.[349] To this original house, which was 36 x 50 feet, a wing was added (20 x 48 feet) and a large yard was included in the property. The total cost of the grounds and building was $7,500. The sisters opened their school in February, 1871, with only five students, but in the years that followed, the enrollment increased to as many as 85 pupils. It seemed that the foundation was doomed from the start, as on July 4, 1871, the lovely little brick Sts. Peter and Paul Church which had been built by Father Farrelly in 1866 burned to the ground, together with his rectory. The loss was estimated at $4,000.[350] But Father Farrelly was not to be stopped in his zeal. He undertook the building of Yreka's third church, St. Joseph's, in 1876. This was the reason why, in his report to Paris in January, 1873, Bishop O'Connell stated that there was a $9,000 debt on the Yreka foundation.[351] What he did not tell was that he had taken $6,000 which had been given to him for his trip to the Vatican Council and had given it to the Yreka sisters.[352] Financial troubles continued to beset the community of St. Joseph in Yreka till, in 1876, some of the sisters, feeling that the end was inevitable, transferred to Rio Vista in the San Francisco archdiocese. However, the remaining sisters struggled on until finally in 1883 they too gave up and transferred the community of sisters to Red Bluff.[353]

Before telling of the fifth foundation of sisters, it is necessary to review the coming of the second religious congregation of men into the diocese. The famed missionary Father Patrick Henneberry of the Precious Blood fathers had approached Bishop O'Connell in 1868 regarding the founding of a house of the order in the diocese. Bishop O'Connell was not only willing to see a foundation made, but also offered to turn over the Eureka parish to the community. He therefore appointed Father Henneberry the pastor of Eureka, California, in November, 1868. Father Henneberry left for Ohio in the spring of 1869 to make arrangements for the founding of a monastery. He returned on June 21, 1869, accompanied by two more priests, Fathers Bernard Dickman and Anthony Guggenberger, and a seminarian, Godfrey Schlachter.[354] Father Henneberry proceeded to purchase for $1,750 a whole block of property where the Eureka Inn now stands, bounded by 7th and 8th streets from F to G.[355] He next constructed a substantial wooden building, and the community of three priests, three brothers, and seven seminarians took up residence in it. The priests served the nearby towns of Rohnerville, Ferndale, Table Bluff, and Arcata. However, the income from these towns was insufficient to support the monastery. Father Henneberry determined to open a residential school for boys which should provide the needed income. Accordingly, he purchased a 160-acre tract of land for $6,500 for the new college in Ferndale, eighteen miles below Eureka, but found during the wintertime that this land flooded. Therefore, in the spring it was put up for sale and a search for a new site was undertaken. An ideal site was selected in Rohnerville, seven miles east of Ferndale. The owner, James Degnan, donated thirty acres, twelve of which were flat, the remainder on a lovely bluff overlooking the countryside.[356] Father Henneberry let the contract for the new building in 1869, borrowing heavily, oftentimes at exorbitant rates of interest.

The new building, consisting of two floors and an attic floor, was 170 feet long and 46 feet deep. However, the central portion was deeper than the two ends. A corridor 8 feet wide ran 120 feet, almost the length of the building. There were 62 doors, 97 windows, and 8 skylights. Built of wood and plastered interiorly, the building contained many fireplaces, needed because of the damp climate in the entire Humboldt area. Nine carpenters, three painters, and two bricklayers, as well as a laborer, were kept busy all through 1870 and most of 1871 until the building was completed in September, 1871.[357] The new school was widely advertised, and when classes began on January 16, 1872, there were one hundred students, both boarders and day pupils.[358]

When the college opened, the community of priests, brothers, and seminarians moved from Eureka to the new building. Father Henneberry resigned as pastor of Eureka and was appointed superior of the new college. Father Dickman was appointed the new pastor of Eureka. The major superiors sent additional personnel from Ohio in the persons of Fathers Thomas O'Neill, who became the assistant at Eureka, and Joseph Uphaus, who went to the college, and Father Daniel F. Dade came from Visalia in California.[359] But, encouraging as things seemed in 1873, the following year was filled with tragedy. Father Dade died on April 2, 1874. Father Guggenberger left the community, went to Buffalo, New York, and joined the Jesuits. Several of the seminarians became discouraged and left. One of them, William Walrath, later went to India as a Jesuit missionary; the seminarian Lawler later entered the Dominicans and was known as Father Sadoc Lawler. The only priest left with the small community in 1874 was Father Thomas O'Neill, along with three seminarians and a total of eighteen students.[360] The college limped along, laden with debt and too far-removed from the centers of population to attract sufficient students to make it self-sustaining. At this time, Bishop O'Connell came to the rescue of the financially burdened community by sending the well-known scholar Father Lawrence Kennedy to teach at St. Joseph's. He remained with the Precious Blood community until the school closed in 1879, when he became the founding pastor of Ferndale.

When the Precious Blood community moved from their building in Eureka to the new college in Rohnerville, the new Eureka pastor, Father Dickman, contacted Father William Quinn, pastor of St. Peter's Church in New York, about the possibility of getting sisters for the vacant building. It is not known for sure, but it is quite likely that this was the same Father Quinn who often acted as agent for Bishop O'Connell in arranging for the transportation of his priests from New York to California, the same Father Quinn to whom he was so often in debt.

Father Quinn approached the Sisters of Mercy at St. Catherine's Convent in New York City. These agreed to send sisters if a formal request came from Bishop O'Connell.[361] In due time the Bishop sent the request, and the sisters were selected for the foundation. The two professed sisters had both been born and raised in England. Two novices were included in the group, and one postulant. The two remaining sisters were both professed Sisters of Charity who had entered the New York Mercy House when their Halifax Convent had dissolved. Mother Gertrude Ledwith was the founding superior. The sisters left New York on April 12, 1871, and arrived in Eureka in May, 1871.[362] In reports

ST. JOSEPH'S COLLEGE, ROHNERVILLE, CALIFORNIA.
Built by Father Patrick Henneberry C.PP.S. in 1871. It served from January 16, 1872, to September 17, 1879, and again for a brief period from 1886–1889 when it closed.
(Photo, courtesy of the Humboldt *Beacon* (July 30, 1953 issue) and Fortuna Advance)

to Paris in 1873, Bishop O'Connell forwarded the sad financial conditions of both of the Eureka foundations. Sisters M. Gertrude stated that there was a $6,000 debt on the house; $1,000 spent for improvements; "there are 60 pupils most of whom pay nothing and there are ten orphans for whom no aid is provided."[363]

Whether any help was given directly by the Propagation of the Faith in response to these appeals from Eureka is not known. It is known that Bishop O'Connell received a draft for 18,400 francs on July 22, 1873, and since he had already reduced his allotments to All Hallows, evidently some of the amount was sent to both of these foundations.[364] This allocation of approximately $3,700 would certainly have to be spread thinly by the hard-pressed bishop. In 1874, the records show he received 16,000 francs in two installments, 4,000 and 12,000. This amounted to $3,200.[365]

Many things transpired to make his burden seem heavier. Not only had he expanded his diocese with new parishes, convents, and schools, all of which needed help, but he was also faced with a great economic slump related to the gold mines. The opening of the Comstock in the late 1860s had drained off a great deal of the California miners, and things were slow in the western side of the Sierras. On top of that, Paris began to reduce his allocation. Bishop O'Connell quickly took his benefactors to task.

> The Diocese of Grass Valley is larger than San Francisco or even Monterey in the same province. I have contributed more to the Society for the Propagation of the Faith from my Diocesans, poor as they are, than the other two Dioceses in the Province.[366]

Three years later, in a more diplomatic manner, Father Manogue, writing for the Bishop, puts across the same idea in these words:

> Our Diocese is very extensive; the people are scattered and dispersed over an enormous extent of territory. What is still worse, they are poor; for the most part working in the mines, and consequently unable to contribute much to our assistance. The adjoining Dioceses are more concentrated, possess populous cities, many rich Catholics, while at the

same time all the various crops, not excepting vineyards, render them both prosperous and desirable. In this connection I would respectfully call your attention to the proportion of the sums subscribed to the Association and the distribution in turn awarded by the same. Situated as we are we do all in our power in this respect. Last year our contribution amounted to $800 (4,000 francs). I do not mention this matter to injure others, but merely suggest it for our own interest. Good Bishop O'Connell is doing all he can to meet the needs of his Diocese, but the greatest zeal, without means, is often paralyzed.[367]

This evident lack of understanding on the part of the Society in Paris disturbed Bishop O'Connell so much that he appealed to Propaganda in Rome in February, 1872.

The distress in which we live in this part of Calif. compels me to beg you to help us and to kindly grant the same privilege to this Diocese as the others have—i.e. to keep back at least a part of the offerings of the faithful for the Propagation of the Faith and to apply them to the urgent needs of this Diocese, in which not even one orphanage for boys has been erected. The S.P.F. in Paris which annually sends many thousand francs to my fellow Bishops—e.g. The Bishop of Monterey and LA., the AB of Oregon and his suffragans gives us nothing as if we were not poor. But I don't know whether a Cathedral Church can be found like that of G.V. which is unable to sustain its own Bishop. Would that this were the only need in which we labor. Would that we could build Xtra schools in which the bread of sound doctrine would be broken for our children. But still I don't envy the annual allocation granted from the Parisian Society to the rest of the Bishops. Rather I marvel more that the Director of the same Society in North America exacts from me, much less expects the offerings of the people of my Diocese for SPF. especially after Monsieur Certes, sect. of SPF had assured me 2 yrs ago that with safe conscience I could keep the offerings of this kind providing I give an accounting, as I have already done, of what was retained.[368]

It should be quite clear from the above that one of the regular annual collections in the Diocese of Grass Valley was that for the missions. The other seems to have been the one for the Holy Father. Here the great loyalty and personal devotion of the Bishop to the Holy See seems to have been contagious. First reference to this collection is found in a letter to Rome on November 16, 1865:

> Mindful of the words of our Lord: "It is more blessed to give than to receive," and mindful of the trials and distress which have come upon our beloved Holy Father, the sheep and the lambs, scattered far and wide throughout the Vicariate of Marysville, gladly offer this small gift of $200 to the Sovereign Pontiff, Pius IX. Small as it is, it comes from a great and willing heart. May the Most Holy Father accept our small gift and pray for their Shepherd and us sinners.[369]

Similar amounts and even much larger amounts found their way each year to Rome. In 1868 the amount was $360; in 1871 the collection totaled $658; and in 1872 the amount from just three parishes was $332.[370] Therefore, Bishop O'Connell requested Apostolic Blessings for the three pastors, Fathers Thomas Dalton of Grass Valley, William Clarke of Gold Hill, and Edward Kelly of Marysville. One month later he forwarded $500 from Virginia City, asking for a Papal Blessing for Father Manogue and his people.

> Would that the Sovereign Pontiff could see the Church built by the same Pastor on the steep side of a mountain with so much difficulty, and likewise an orphanage built in the distress of the times and already filled with the unfortunate ones.[371]

On the same date the Bishop requested

> ... an Apostolic Blessing for Father James J. Claire, Pastor of the Church of St. Canice in Nevada City, and the flock committed to his care who have given $40 to the Sovereign Pontiff. Although the flock is small (they consist of only 90

Catholics) and the Pastor is in poor circumstances yet they give the indicated amount most lovingly and with a big heart and a willing spirit.[372]

Even while plagued with so many financial troubles, Bishop O'Connell's greatest struggles were with his own indecisions. In 1865 a decree had been issued at Rome against "Secret Societies." The interpretation of this decree was to cause Eugene O'Connell some trouble-filled hours, all the more because one of the Irish societies seemed to him to fall under the ban. He himself had a branch of the Ancient Order of Hibernians in St. Joseph's Parish in Marysville, established in May, 1869.[373] This organization, like so many others of its day, although not a secret society did have secret pass words and other "lodge secrets." Bishop O'Connell could not bring himself to an interpretation of this matter. He first held back on publishing the decree. Then his conscience bothered him on that point so he wrote to Cardinal Barnabo while he was in Rome in 1870: "Let your Eminence state whether it is licit for me any longer to refrain from publishing the decree 'Contra Fenianos' in my Diocese on account of the grave evils which seem to follow its promulgation."[374] As usual, Rome avoided replying to Bishop O'Connell, hoping he would make up his own scrupulous mind.

Later on, Bishop O'Connell began to think the decree applied also to labor organizations of miners whose members bound themselves by an oath unless they got a fixed daily wage. His scruples about the Ancient Order of Hibernians came in 1872 after he had finally published the decree.

> In regard to the Society known as the A.O.H. I don't know what I must do. In the Metropolitan Diocese of San Francisco, the Sacraments of Penance and Holy Eucharist are not denied to those and such like. I struggle to know whether secret words and signs as well as the oath by which members of this kind of Society are bound stand in the way of administering the Sacraments to them. Often my companions assure me that it is allowed regardless of the oath. Meanwhile no one is admitted into the A.O.H. who is non-Catholic or who ever gave his name to any of the Societies condemned by the Church. Please tell me how I must act towards Societies of this kind.[375]

One month later, the Bishop forwarded to Rome a leaflet describing the A.O.H. Whether Rome ever answered him is unknown. However, a loyal member of the A.O.H. in Stockton, Thomas C. Mallon, sent a letter of complaint to Rome on March 23, 1873, because of Bishop O'Connell's strict interpretation. This must certainly have caused Eugene O'Connell great internal pain because he was being torn between his two great loves, obedience to the church and his love for Ireland and all things Irish. It seems safe to say that his stand on this matter as well as his long procrastination began a wave of antagonistic feeling against him which was to increase as the years progressed. Mr. Mallon's letter refers to this as "a bitter and unfriendly feeling now exists among Catholics."[376]

Regardless of the problems which faced him from finances, from scruples, or from any other source, his devotion to his pastoral apostolate kept Bishop O'Connell constantly traveling during the months when he could. With twenty-two parishes to cover, he now began a program of visiting all every two years, the exception being the parishes of Nevada, because by now he had grown accustomed to spending the hot summer months of July and August each year in Nevada. Therefore, each year between 1871 and 1876 found Bishop O'Connell in Nevada. In 1872, he was in Forest Hill, Iowa Hill, and Colfax in August on a confirmation tour.[377] He was in Nevada in September. In 1873, he was in Nevada in June and in Weaverville and Yreka in July. August 3 found Bishop O'Connell in Los Angeles as a co-consecrator of Bishop Francis Mora, the new coadjutor to Bishop Amat of Monterey.[378] On his return, he headed for Downieville with its many missions in which he gave confirmation at the end of September and the beginning of October.[379]

In 1874, Archbishop Alemany held a Provincial Council starting April 26. The four bishops were in attendance with their Vicars General and their advisers. Bishop O'Connell was the secretary for this Council, probably because the proceedings had to be translated into Latin and sent to Rome.[380] On June 14, Bishop O'Connell blessed a new church erected in Graniteville by the pastor of Nevada City.[381] In July of this year he was back for his visitation in Nevada, and by August 9 he was in Lakeport, Lake County, for confirmation.

In 1875, the year he turned sixty years old on June 15, the pace was as arduous as ever. He was in Yreka in June, in San

ST. AUGUSTINE'S CHURCH, Austin, Nevada.
Built by the Rev. Dominic Monteverde, 1867.
(Photo, courtesy of St. Mary's in the Mountains, Virginia City)

EUREKA, NEVADA, WITH ST. BRENDAN'S CHURCH.
Built by the Rev. James J. Hynes, 1874.
(Photo, courtesy of Nevada Historical Society, Reno)

Francisco to celebrate Archbishop Alemany's Silver Jubilee as a bishop on July 29, in Nevada in August and September.[382] On August 28, he presided at the laying of the cornerstone of the new Sisters Hospital in Virginia City. This year found him adding a new Nevada parish in his visitation, that of Eureka, Nevada.[383]

This pace was to continue only one more year, as there was evidence that Eugene O'Connell's health was beginning to weaken under the strain. We in the 1970s are prone to forget that the life expectancy in the 1870s was not what it is today. By the standards of those days, sixty years of age was considered old. The first reference Eugene O'Connell made to this fact occurred in a letter in 1872 in which he asked Father John Simeoni to intercede to have Nevada cut off from his diocese into a separate vicariate "because I haven't the strength to visit the whole of this Diocese."[384] That same year, when sending Father Manogue's donation to the Holy Father, Bishop O'Connell concluded the letter by saying: "Most Rev. Father I commend myself, already growing old and needing a Coadjutor, to your prayers."[385]

When writing to Rome to get approval for the Provincial Council of 1874, Archbishop Alemany refers to Bishop O'Connell in these words: "The Bishop of Grass Valley has often asked that a coadjutor be given him, which, considering his age, his health and his many labors covering vast distances, seems to me to be highly recommended."[386]

On October 13, 1873, in a letter to John Gilmary Shea, Bishop O'Connell makes the statement: "Hence when obliged to go eastward for the benefit of my feeble health, I shall be happy to join you in the recitation of the Rosary according to the old form."[387]

According to this testimony, Eugene O'Connell was beginning to wear out after fifteen years as bishop of the enormous diocese that was his. However, the schedule he maintained in 1876 gives no indication of any wearing out. In February, he attended a religious profession in the Presentation Convent in San Francisco.[388] In July, he presided at the commencement exercises at Notre Dame in Marysville. In August, he was in Nevada, making the usual rounds of confirmations in Carson City, Gold Hill, and Virginia City. In September, he was confirming in the Forest Hill missions of Iowa Hill and Colfax.[389] At the beginning of October, he was in Downieville and its missions. But on Oc-

THE RT. REV. EUGENE O'CONNELL, taken in 1876, at age 61.
(Photo, courtesy of Historic Preservation Committee, Grass Valley)

The new "St. Francis Church" dedicated on Oct. 14, 1876, on the occasion of the Centennial of Mission Dolores. Bishop O'Connell celebrated the dedication Mass.

(Photo, courtesy of Mission Dolores, San Francisco)

THE REV. DANIEL O'SULLIVAN, 1846–1928
Founding Pastor of Smartsville, 1872–1878
Assistant at Virginia City, 1878–1881
Second Pastor of Virginia City, 1881–1883
Pastor of Mendocino, 1883–1887
Founding Pastor of Redwood City, California, 1887–1895
Pastor of All Hallows, San Francisco, 1898–1928
(Photo, courtesy of St. Mary's in the Mountains, Virginia City)

tober 14, he was celebrant of the Mass at Mission Dolores commemorating the centennial of that mission, and he took part with Archbishop Alemany in the dedication of the new church, "St. Francis," erected to take the place of the Mission. The program of the day was a long, exhausting one, but Bishop O'Connell stood it well enough to be in Colusa for confirmation on the following Sunday.[390]

There are indications, however, that all was not well in the winter between 1876 and 1877 as quite a number of letters are written from Oakland, the place of residence of his brother. Likewise, the year 1877 is almost devoid of confirmations with the exception of a "close to home" tour in April which included Oroville and its mission, Cherokee Flat.[391]

It is obvious that from that time Bishop O'Connell began to show signs of age and the decline began to set in. It was still to be some five years before Rome would be able to find him a coadjutor. He carried on, meanwhile, to the best of his ability, but this most active part of his missionary career was over.

During this period, from 1871 to 1876, the Bishop welcomed into the diocese eight new priests. The year 1871 saw the ordination of the last two from All Hallows. From that time on there would be only one per year. The newly ordained on June 24, 1871, were James Hunt and Daniel O'Sullivan. When they arrived in October, 1871, the Bishop made a few changes. He sent the newly ordained Father O'Sullivan to Crescent City to replace Father Haupts, who went to Gold Hill where he remained as an assistant until January, 1877.[392] Father Grace was transferred from Carson City to assistant at Grass Valley, replacing Father Kennedy who returned to Marysville as an assistant. Father Luke Tormey became the new pastor of Carson City, beginning a career of fifteen years as pastor of that community and joining the ranks of the "unsuspended." One more change involved the replacement of the ever-moving Father Patrick O'Kane from Hamilton, Nevada, and his replacement for a few months by Father James Hynes, who had been assistant in Gold Hill. In October, 1871, the Bishop had to replace Father Rooney, who was totally unable to assume the burdens of being pastor. From the start, this delicate young man had given evidence of being supersensitive and unable to take the hard knocks of daily life as a priest. In October, 1871, Bishop O'Connell sent him as an assis-

IMMACULATE CONCEPTION, Smartsville, California
Built by Father Daniel O'Sullivan in 1872
(Photo, courtesy of Historic Preservation Committee)

tant to Father Claire in Nevada City.[393] It seems that Father Callan returned from his visit in Ireland that month, so he was appointed the new pastor of Mendocino City in place of Father Rooney.

Early in March, 1873, a new priest came to the diocese, evidently not a graduate of All Hallows, Father Joseph Coffey. He was temporarily assigned to St. Joseph's in Marysville, but in June, 1873, he was sent as pastor of Crescent City. Since this was an extra priest, it gave the Bishop an opportunity to erect another parish. He took the longtime mission of Marysville, Smartsville, and erected it as a parish with the young Father Daniel O'Sullivan as first pastor.[394] There was a change in the pastor of St. Joseph's, Marysville. Father Farrelly was brought from Yreka in April, 1872, and Father Moloney went to Austin, Nevada, to replace Father Monteverde who now went to Pioche to replace Father Scanlan whom the Archbishop had appointed pastor of Petaluma in California. Bishop O'Connell was afraid at that time that he was going to lose Father Monteverde. This good priest was tired, very tired, from his nine years of missionary work, most of it in Nevada. He wanted a year off to spend in a monastery or house of prayer, and then permission to find a new field of endeavor. Bishop O'Connell's letter to Rome is pathetic.

> A certain well deserving priest in this Diocese whose name is Dominic Monteverde pitiably seeks to go out and thru my intercession begs the Holy See that he be allowed to go out of the Diocese and be discharged from it after so many exhausting labors and the building of four churches during a ministry of nine years. To my question of where he wishes to go, he answered that he has no particular place in mind, but that he be allowed at least a year to rest from his labors in some religious house and after that to go wherever the spirit leads him. If I may ask one thing, I ask this of the Holy See, that the aforesaid Rev. Dominic Monteverde not be permitted to leave at the present time for our workers are few and the harvest is great. However whatever the Holy Father decides, I will willingly accept.[395]

Perhaps Father Monteverde got some time off, but he built a fifth church in Belmont, Nevada, in 1874 and continued to work

BELMONT, NEVADA, IN THE 1890s. Catholic church on extreme left built f $3,000 by the Rev. Dominic Monteverde in 1874; moved to Monument, Nevad around 1900.
(Photo, courtesy of Nevada Historical Society, Reno)

in that state until 1883 when he did get permission to leave and went to Brooklyn, New York. He became pastor there of Holy Rosary parish, and died in Baltimore, Maryland, on January 2, 1898, at the age of sixty-one.[396] He goes down in history with Father Patrick Manogue as one of the great founders of the Catholic church in the state of Nevada.

Sources for Chapter XI

347. ASRC, Vol. 23, F1111, May 29, 1871.

348. ASRC, Vol. 23, F264, May 3, 1870.

349. Walsh, *Hallowed Were*, p. 271.

350. *History of Siskiyou County* (Oakland, California: D. J. Stewart & Co., 1881).

351. AALA, Manogue to Society for the Propagation of the Faith, January 18, 1873.

352. ASPF, letter of July 20, 1874.

353. Archives of the Sisters of Mercy, Burlingame, California.

354. Walsh, *Hallowed Were*, p. 295.

355. Pamela Renner, "History of Catholic Activity in Rohnerville," Dissertation for Senior History Seminar, Humboldt State University, Arcata, California, December, 1967, pp. 58ff.

356. Walsh, *Hallowed Were*, p. 296.

357. Renner, op. cit., pp. 58ff.

358. *Nuntius Aulae*, Publication of the Precious Blood Fathers, Carthagena, Ohio, Vol. 17: 178.

359. Walsh, *Hallowed Were*, p. 296.

360. ASRC, Vol. 25, F607, report of August 25, 1874, from Archbishop Alemany.

361. Archives of the Sisters of Mercy, Burlingame, California. Biographical data on Sister M. Gertrude Ledwith.

362. Ibid., "Eureka 1871–1901."

363. ASPF, report of November 8, 1873, on three convents.

364. ASPF, letter of appreciation from Patrick J. O'Connell, September 18, 1873.

365. ASPF, letter of July 20, 1874.

366. ASPF, letter while in Rome, December 28, 1869.

367. AALA, Manogue to M. Certes, January 18, 1873.

368. ASRC, Vol. 171, F221.

369. ASRC, Vol. 20, F1667.

370. ASRC, Vol. 22, F436; Vol. 24, F363.

37.1 ASRC, Vol. 24, F386.

372. ASRC, Vol. 24, F392.

373. Thompson & West, *History of Yuba County*.

374. ASRC, Vol. 23, F438.

375. ASRC, Vol. 24, F363.

376. ASRC, Vol. 24, F772.

377. Baptismal Record, St. Joseph's, Forest Hill.

378. Code, op. cit., p. 207.

379. Baptismal Record, Immaculate Conception, Downieville.

380. *The Monitor*, May 2, 1874.

381. Ibid., June 27, 1874.

382. Ibid., July 29, 1875.

383. Gorman, *Seventy-Five Years*, p. 92.

384. ASRC, Vol. 172, F633.

385. ASRC, Vol. 24, F386.

386. ASRC, Vol. 1004, F807.

387. Archives of Archdiocese of Philadelphia, letter to John Gilmary Shea, October 13, 1873.

388. *The Monitor*, February 19, 1876.

389. Baptismal Register, St. Joseph's, Forest Hill.

390. *The Monitor*, October 21, 1876.

391. Confirmation Register, St. Joseph's, Marysville.

392. Walsh, *Hallowed Were*, p. 278.

393. Baptismal Register, St. Canice, Nevada City.

394. Baptismal Register, Immaculate Conception, Smartsville.

395. ASRC, Vol. 24, F440.

396. *National Catholic Directory*, 1899.

Chapter XII

ADMINISTRATOR OF AFFAIRS

It may not seem necessary at this juncture to give special attention to Bishop O'Connell's administration because his success or lack of it should be quite clear from what has already been revealed during his fifteen years as bishop. Yet it is in the area of administration that he has been most criticized and therefore it is necessary to go into the matter in detail and to make an evaluation.

It is necessary first to tell something about the only priest ordained for the diocese in 1874, Father Joseph Phelan. He is the one who gives us some insight into Bishop O'Connell's administration. When Father Phelan was ordained at All Hallows in June 24, 1874, he was already thirty-five years old. Like his predecessor, Patrick Manogue, Joseph Phelan, born in Rathdowney, Queens County, Ireland, had emigrated to the United States when only eighteen years old and took up mining outside Nevada City and in Cherokee, both of which were in the Grass Valley parish in 1857. Nine years later, probably due to the influence of Father Dalton, Joseph Phelan left the mines, spent one year as a student at St. Mary's College, then located in Oakland, transferred to Mt. Mellary in Ireland for three more years of college, and then entered All Hallows for his theology. When he arrived back as a priest at the scene of his former mining labors, Bishop O'Connell assigned him as assistant at Grass Valley, changing Father Grace from there to become pastor of St. Joseph's, Marys-

THE REV. JOSEPH PHELAN, 1839–1903
Pastor of Austin, Nevada, 1876–1894
Chaplain to St. Vincent's Boys Home, San Rafael, Calif., 1894–1903

ville. Father Phelan stayed two years in Grass Valley and then was appointed Pastor of Austin, Nevada, on September 19, 1876. With this move, Father Phelan joined the ranks with Father Dalton, Father Manogue, and Father Luke Tormey of the "unsuspended." He kept his post in Austin for eighteen years until 1894, when he joined the archdiocese of San Francisco and was appointed chaplain to the Christian Brothers and the orphan boys at St. Vincent's in San Rafael. There, to while away his time, and fancying himself somewhat of a poet, Father Phelan wrote his *Poetical Works and Biographical Remarks of Rev. Joseph Phelan*, which he published in 1902.[397] As a work of poetry it was so poor that Archbishop Riordan was embarrassed to have it circulated and he bought up as many copies as he could get his hands on, thus making it very much sought after. It is a book of versification rather than poetry, but the sentiments expressed are from the heart of a deeply sincere man. His poem on "Eugene O'Connell," written in 1900, gives us a good insight into a man whom Father Joseph Phelan deeply admired and revered.

When one talks about a bishop as an administrator today, one thinks of a Chancery Office, of management of finances, building programs, and very involved business affairs that go with the management of a diocese in the complicated world of the 1970s. But the bishop of Grass Valley had no Chancery Office; his finances, we have seen, were very limited; and whatever building was done was the work of individual priests and religious communities in which Bishop O'Connell's permission was usually his only contribution or involvement. So we certainly cannot evaluate his administration from the twentieth-century point of view.

As a first clue, when Archbishop Alemany asked Rome in 1859 to divide his diocese and create a see to the north, he asked for the recommendations of several bishops. One of the replies which went to Rome and was included in the presentation to the cardinals of Propaganda Fidei was a letter from Bishop Thaddeus Amat of Monterey. It was Amat who recommended that the new see be a vicariate rather than a diocese. When speaking about the three candidates for bishop, his evaluation of Eugene O'Connell included the following remarks:

> I have been assured that he has no talent for governing and that it would be unfortunate for him and his Diocese if he

were made Bishop, while he does much good where he is and will do so everywhere else as long as he depends on someone else.[398]

In spite of this warning, Eugene O'Connell had been chosen as bishop. Now, fifteen years later, it is time to see if Bishop Amat was correct or not.

The fact that there are no archives surviving from the twenty-three years of Bishop O'Connell's term as ordinary certainly would indicate some kind of ineptitude for administration in these days. But considering the general attitude of those times regarding record-keeping, Eugene O'Connell was no different from his contemporaries. However, there are indications that he was careless about such matters. It is a fact that he had no Chancery, nor even an Office, just his two rooms in the Marysville rectory. Yet he did manage to lose important documents. He was forced to confess to this in a letter to Rome:

> Please excuse me if I make one request, a copy of the Faculties which the Sovereign Pontiff granted me several years ago, but alas, I don't know where I put them, not on account of carelessness but from too much fear that they perish. Without a doubt they are somewhere but after diligent search they have not yet appeared and I can't find them. If therefore this one time you pardon me, I promise in the future to take care to avoid the least fault in safeguarding this precious document.[399]

However, there were similar instances of misplacing forms sent him for reports to the Society for the Propagation of the Faith, and invariably his reports were incomplete because he had not gotten one in turn from some parish or convent for inclusion in his report.

Worst of all was his carelessness in regard to the reports to the *National Catholic Directory*. An original set of statistics sent in 1866 went unchanged through 1870, even though the number of parishes and priests increased each year. Oftentimes he merely sent in the list of appointments he had made the previous year, leaving it to the editors to change and delete. Thus we often find a priest named in two places at the same time, his former assignment and his new one. A classic example occurred in 1876 when Bishop O'Connell simply cut out the pages of the previous *Directory*, wrote in a few corrections and mailed them on to one of the religious houses in his diocese for them to add their statistics and then mail in to Sadlier Brothers. Needless to say, the publishers never received them.[400]

The indications, therefore, that Eugene O'Connell kept no records to hand down to posterity seem well founded. However, it is not unheard of that boxes of letters and other (to us) valuable materials may have been found among the Bishop's possessions and simply burned as useless by someone else who had no appreciation of their value. In either case, there were no records left from his administration and there are indications of carelessness in this regard.

Certainly there is no reason to criticize him for his handling of finances. He had a purpose in mind, namely to populate the diocese with priests, and every cent he got he devoted to the education and transportation of priests to California and Nevada. Likewise, he managed to have sufficient funds to pay for his extensive travels throughout his diocese. Furthermore, he left no indebtedness, as Bishop O'Connell followed a "pay as you go" policy. If there was any weakness in regard to his handling of money, it would be his adamant stand on the question of usury—or borrowing of money at interest.

The Catholic church in the last century had taken a very severe attitude on the whole question of the morality of earning money as profit from lending money. Eugene O'Connell, as one might expect by now, held a rigoristic interpretation on this question. On assuming his duties as bishop, he was appalled at the free-and-easy attitude he found in the West regarding the whole question of being in debt.[401] He found that everywhere parishes and clergy had debts. His attitude toward Father Peter Magagnotto was based on the fact that this priest borrowed money readily and ran up large debts. This was scandalous in the mind of Eugene O'Connell. His attitude in this matter was to change over the years, so that eventually he himself borrowed to pay for the enlarging of the Marysville cathedral, but his troubles with religious congregations were often centered on the fact that they ran up debts for which they could not pay. How Eugene O'Connell settled this whole question of usury in his own mind is not known. One thing is certain: he would never have varied one iota from his original position unless someone had convinced him that paying reasonable interest for borrowing money was not morally wrong.

Bishop O'Connell likewise was no Father Manogue. His Vicar General for Nevada had wealthy friends, and an appeal from him met with a most generous response from his hearers. Bishop O'Connell seems to have had no talent for getting money in generous amounts from affluent benefactors. In his letters to All Hallows, he sent donations from lay persons in his diocese. He spoke of the generosity of Judge and Mrs. Ord, Charles Smith of San Francisco, Anthony Fenstegge of Marysville, Ed McLaughlin of Grass Valley, and Mr. and Mrs. Eugene Kelly,[402] but none of them even began to approximate the kind of money that Father Manogue was able to generate, or Father Dalton in Grass Valley. But it is obvious by now that Bishop O'Connell did manage well the money that he did acquire. He was fortunate in having as his agent for the business transactions his brother Patrick, who was a merchant in Oakland. Patrick owned the Oakland Dry Goods House, 1092 Broadway near 10th Street. He or his partner, P. A. Murphy, took complete care of Bishop O'Connell's monetary transactions, either to All Hallows or to Rome or to Paris, including all acknowledgments for monies "received." Thanks to them, this area of Bishop O'Connell's responsibility was well administered.[403]

We note that Bishop Amat did not say Eugene O'Connell was inept in financial administration. He said: "He has no talent for governing." It was in the area of human relations that Bishop O'Connell was lacking. It has already been pointed out that to the seminary professor made bishop, his clergy always remained his seminarians ordained priests. This attitude toward his priests was partly the cause of his unpopularity among the clergy. For one thing, Bishop O'Connell wrote very freely about his priests to All Hallows. He had a habit of characterizing each of them with a one-word epithet, such as "O'Kane, the absent-minded," and there is reason to suspect that many of the priests had friends among the All Hallows faculty who relayed back to the priests what the Bishop had said about them. We have abundant examples of this:

> Kelly, the windfall from Chicago
> Gleeson, the bird of passage
> Hickey, the exquisite
> Grace, the preacher par excellence
> Claire, the debtor
> Rooney, the eccentric
> Pettit, the equestrian

Yet at the same time it is very noticeable that there is no criticism of Manogue, Dalton, Tormey, or Phelan—the ones he never or seldom moved. There is actual praise for Lynch, Farrelly, and Meagher as "good men and true," and Griffin and O'Reilly were "two of most obedient and satisfactory missioners."[404]

This seminary mentality, which Bishop O'Connell never lost in regard to his former students, showed up each year when, on his visitations, he inspected the baptismal and marriage registers. It was almost as if he were examining their themes or test papers, because corrections and comments were made in the margin, many of which provide us today with a good laugh. If the books were well kept, Bishop O'Connell wrote: "I have this day inspected this book and have found in it nothing meriting censure." But when he found something that he disapproved of, the notation included the corrections to be made. Some of these notations are worthy of mention. For example, he insisted that the fact that the parents were married be mentioned in the baptismal entries. This is a common correction in several parishes, although oftentimes it applies to the same pastor as he moved from parish to parish. A few classical examples are worth noting. In the Nevada City baptismal register is to be found a running commentary between the Bishop and Father Becker. It seems that Father Becker had performed a marriage at Moore's Flat and had omitted publishing the banns of that marriage. He entered in the record the fact of the omission. Bishop O'Connell came along on a visitation on November 16, 1869, and at the end of the record in question wrote three words: "By what right?" The pastor noticed it and wrote, "By right of the Pastor," and initialed FCB. Bishop

O'Connell discovered the notation and wrote a classical remark which ended all discussion:

> The Pastor had no right: therefore he usurped the jurisdiction of the Bishop.
> Signed: E. O'Connell, Grass Valley

That ended that running commentary.[405]

In August, 1879, Bishop O'Connell was on a visitation in Downieville. Father Andrew O'Donnell was the pastor at that time, a priest for whom writing in Latin was evidently difficult. On page 191 of the baptismal register, Father O'Donnell had evidently entered the baptism of a child born out of wedlock, and had made the notation "illegitimate." Because his Latin construction was clumsy, Bishop O'Connell wrote: "Who is illegitimate, John Brown or his parents?" On the following page he wrote, "O what primitive Latin!" Then the Bishop suggested a couple of alternatives for the clumsy construction used by the pastor. Finally, on page 193, the Bishop, having finished examining the "student's paper," writes out his commentary: "Today I examined this Baptismal book and I found nothing meriting censure except scarcely intelligible Latin in some places."[406]

How the clergy reacted to these corrections is not known, but since they do indicate that Bishop O'Connell never changed his seminary professor attitude towards his priests, it could easily be concluded that these entries were the subject of conversation and at times of dissatisfaction among the clergy.

Likewise, the Bishop's inability to make decisions without writing first to Rome must have been very hard on the clergy. Bishop Amat was most correct in stating that Eugene O'Connell would have to depend on someone else. That someone else was Cardinal Barnabo and later on Cardinal Simeone. Both tried to force Bishop O'Connell to make his own decisions by not answering his every question, but since he could not, the delays must have been most aggravating. Only the more important matters have been mentioned so far. But there were dozens of questions for them to settle, such as permission to have the Blessed Sacrament in newly erected religious houses; whether he could use non-wax candles since wax ones were hard to get; whether Laymen could transport the Holy Oils on account of the vast dis-

ORPHANAGE OF SISTERS OF MERCY, Grass Valley, California, in the 1870s
Built by the Rev. Thomas J. Dalton in 1865
Declared Historical Monument in 1972

BRANCH HOUSE for Boy orphans
Built by Mother Baptist Mogan on Pleasant St. in 1872
(Photos, courtesy of Historic Preservation Committee, Grass Valley)

tances; the number of candles to be used in ceremonies; and others of a trivial nature which Rome would have preferred that the Bishop decide for himself but which he just would not do.

However, the most serious charge against his administration was his lack of tact. Father Joseph Phelan summarizes this in the words: "In business matters he had no tact."[407] We have a few examples of this. For example, when Father Farrelly wrote to Bishop O'Connell in Rome about the decision of the Montreal sisters not to come to Yreka, Eugene O'Connell wrote: "I have written them a threatening letter." How could one who is begging possibly write a threatening letter to someone he is trying to entice? Yet Bishop O'Connell did.

In 1869, because he was obsessed by the debt on the Grass Valley orphanage, Bishop O'Connell decided to sell the orphanage to the state for a military barracks. He did not reckon with Father Dalton in making this decision, and the Bishop quickly learned who was "the boss" in Grass Valley. Father Dalton very quickly raised the needed money and got the orphanage out of debt.

The classic example of tactlessness occurred in February, 1872, when Mother Baptist Mogan of Grass Valley received the following letter from Bishop O'Connell:

> Having convened my Council, they concluded to remove all the female orphans to Virginia City to the Sisters of Charity, and convert the present Grass Valley asylum into a refuge for the male portion of the destitute children of this Diocese, and you and your Sisters can take charge of them or quit.

We can be sure that the decision of the Council was a prudent one, but the manner in which Bishop O'Connell communicated this to Mother Baptist Mogan certainly was not. However, this nun was like Father Dalton, unflinching in her determination. She replied as follows:

> In reply to your proposal, I will only say this, that as for me I can disencumber your Diocese whenever I please [she was only on loan from the San Francisco Community], whereas the Sisters who have been professed under your authority

cannot. If you wish, a lot has been purchased on Pleasant street, that would be very appropriate for a male orphan asylum. A suitable building that would answer your design could be got up without great expense. I can have it done if you give the necessary assistance.[408]

Thus the boys' orphanage in Grass Valley was born. A less strong person would have been badly hurt by Bishop O'Connell's tactless way of putting things. Mother Baptist Mogan was a giant in those days, well able to rise above the tactless ways of someone in authority.

Bishop O'Connell also had a tenacity which made him very righteous when the law was on his side. He could "ride someone into the ground" if they were not observing a law and he got wind of it. The best example of this was the case of Mother Dolores of the Dominican Sisters in Reno. This event took place near the end of his days, but gives an example of what is meant. The Dominican Sisters in those days were somewhat cloistered, monastic, required to stay very much at home in their convent. Mother Dolores was a pioneer missionary, well respected by clergy and laity, who found it necessary for the survival of her struggling community of nuns and their school to visit the towns, make known the story of their school in Reno, and even beg for funds to support the struggling institution. Somehow Bishop O'Connell learned of this and ordered Mother Dolores to get back in her convent and stay there.[409] Strictly speaking, the Bishop was within his rights to do this. There was no allowance, however, on his part for the extraordinary circumstances which necessitated Mother Dolores's departure from the usual practice of cloistered religious. The ensuing struggle provoked the lasting antipathy of several priests who were involved in the case of these sisters.

Probably most damaging to Bishop O'Connell's rule was his inability to make up his mind, his constant postponement of decisions awaiting an answer from Rome, which seldom came. We can be sure that many of his clergy had to make decisions for themselves, hoping Bishop O'Connell would not find out, knowing that if he did they might incur his displeasure.

The most severe criticism of Bishop O'Connell is found in a letter from a disgruntled priest who wrote an anonymous letter to

Rome in 1876. First of all, the letter should be discredited because it was anonymous. It was signed "Sacerdos Regularis," a religious order priest. Secondly, it should be discredited because it is full of exaggerations. In the light of these two facts the accusation reads:

> Rt. Rev. O'Connell is the Bishop of this Diocese, a pious man but most imprudent, whose administration does grave harm to religion. Annually many lose their faith on account of his insane manner of governing and his insatiable avarice.[410]

It should be quite clear by now that if Eugene O'Connell could be found guilty of anything it certainly was not avarice. In the light of this, we question his "insane manner of governing." However, there is reason to presume that there was some basis even for the exaggerated accusation.

Finally, we should note that by the end of fifteen years as bishop, the diocese was rather well-populated with priests, and since in the more populated areas there was easier communication between them, the opportunity to talk about the Bishop and to compare notes was much greater than in the early years. Therefore, any dissatisfaction with Bishop O'Connell's decisions could be spread more easily and gather some momentum. Bishop O'Connell had this to face in his declining years.

From the above can be deduced whether or not Bishop O'Connell's administration was the disaster predicted by Bishop Amat or not. Judged in the light of his own priorities—to populate his diocese with parishes and priests and to provide for the spiritual needs of his people—Bishop O'Connell was a great success. If viewed from a more modern viewpoint as a manager of personnel, a decision-maker, then much was to be desired in his administration. But for the times in which he lived, his priorities seem to have had real validity and to have brought great benefit to the church.

Sources for Chapter XII

397. John T. Dwyer, *One Hundred Years an Orphan* (Fresno, California: Academy Library Guild, 1955).

398. AALA, Amat to Barnabo, July 9, 1860.

399. ASRC, Vol. 24, F85.

400. Archives of the Archdiocese of Philadelphia, letter of November 10, 1876.

401. AAHC, letters of July 16, 1861, and August 25, 1862.

402. AAHC, letter of March 5, 1868.

403. ASRC, Vol. 24, F177 and F417.

404. AAHC, letter of August 25, 1862.

405. Baptismal Register, St. Canice, Nevada City.

406. Baptismal Register, Immaculate Conception, Downieville.

407. Joseph Phelan, *The Poetical Works and Biographical Remarks of* . . . (San Francisco: Commercial Publishing Co., 1902).

408. Archives of the Sisters of Mercy, Grass Valley, California.

409. ASRC, Vol. 38, F527.

410. ASRC, Vol. 27, F576.

Chapter XIII

THE DIFFICULT YEARS, 1874–1881

It would seem that the early years, when Bishop O'Connell had few priests, thousands of miles to travel under primitive conditions, and great financial needs, would have been termed the difficult years. But the prelate was a much younger man in those days, in the full possession of great stamina, not yet tired, and burning with zeal. He was now an old man, by the standards of the times, and his problems were many, though of a different nature; as usual there were good things mixed with the bad.

On September 24, 1873, Bishop O'Connell had the joy of ordaining the first fruits of the little seminary in Rohnerville. When the Precious Blood fathers opened the college there in 1871, one of the first students was William Walrath. His younger brother Michael followed him in the fall of 1871. The brothers were natives of Prussia who fled to London in 1865. The brother William migrated to Ohio in 1866 and Michael followed him in 1867. He entered the seminary in Cincinnati and then followed his brother again in September, 1871, to Rohnerville. There Michael taught in the boys' school and pursued his own studies for the priesthood at the same time. It was this same Michael Walrath who was ordained a priest in St. Joseph's, Marysville, on September 24, 1873, by Bishop O'Connell.[411] In November, Father Walrath was appointed pastor of Crescent City in place of Father Joseph Coffey who went to Colusa.

The only other additions to the clergy besides Father Wal-

THE REV. MICHAEL WALRATH, 1849–1917
Graduate of Rohnerville College
Ordained by Bishop O'Connell in Marysville, Sept. 4, 1873
Pastor of Crescent City, California, 1873–1876
Pastor of Weaverville, California, 1877–1879
Pastor of Colusa, California, 1879–1912
Pastor of Woodland, California, 1912–1917
(Photo, courtesy of Sisters of Mercy, Grass Valley)

rath in 1873 and Father Joseph Phelan in 1874 were Father James Hegarty at the end of 1874 and Father John D. Sheridan from All Hallows in 1875. Father Hegarty came from Milwaukee because of his health and was assigned by Bishop O'Connell to Colusa for two years.[412] Father Sheridan was ordained at All Hallows on June 24, 1875. He was in Marysville in October, 1875, and was kept there at St. Joseph's as an assistant to Father Grace. There were no additions to the clergy in 1876.

In attempting to show the status of the diocese in 1876 and the location of the priests, it is difficult to know what month to choose because there were transfers at different times throughout the year. However, it is safe to say that by November, 1876, the diocesan roster, if there ever was one, would have appeared as follows:[413]

On the Coast:	Crescent City	James J. Claire
	Eureka	John M. Nulty
	Rohnerville	Joseph Uphaus, C.PP.S.
		Lawrence Kennedy
	Mendocino City	Thomas Pettit
In the North:	Yreka	James J. Callan
	Weaverville	Michael Walrath
	Red Bluff	Patrick Farrelly
In the Valley:	Oroville	(Suppressed as parish in 1874; again a mission of Marysville)
	Marysville, St. Joseph's	Thomas Grace James J. Hynes John D. Sheridan
	Marysville, Immaculate Conception	John Meiler
	Colusa	Andrew O'Donnell
	Smartsville	Daniel O'Sullivan
In the Mountains:	Grass Valley	Thomas J. Dalton and James Hunt
	Nevada City	Daniel Meagher P. O'Kane, assistant since 1874
	Downieville	Charles Lynch

In Nevada State:	Forest Hill	William Moloney
	Truckee	Charles Becker
	Virginia City	Patrick Manogue
		Matthew Coleman
	Gold Hill	William Clarke and
		Leon Haupts, since 1871
	Carson City	Luke Tormey
	Austin	Joseph Phelan
	Eureka	Dominic Monteverde until 1883
	Hamilton	(Ceased to be a parish in 1872)
	Reno	J. M. Mevel

The diocese seems to have lost two priests in 1876. The well-known missionary Father Edward Kelly entered a monastery after thirteen years of devoted service to the diocese. Likewise, ill health took its toll on the nervous system of Father James Rooney who had to be hospitalized because of a nervous breakdown in that year. This means there were twenty-two parishes, twenty-eight priests, ten schools, and five convents of sisters, two orphanages, one Catholic hospital in Virginia City, one college for boys in Rohnerville which was not doing very well because of its remote location.

The year 1877 was to bring sorrow to Bishop O'Connell because the "good man and true," Patrick Farrelly of Red Bluff, died on January 17, 1877. He was described as a man of culture, an accomplished musician, with an extensive knowledge of philosophy and theology. Father Farrelly was only forty-three years old. He was buried in St. Joseph's Cemetery on January 19, 1877, the fourth to be buried in the priest's plot in Marysville.[414] He was replaced in the fall of the year by the arrival of Father Patrick Kirley, a priest who had been a missionary in Alaska.[415]

There were two disasters in these years also, and one near disaster. The first and third involved the Notre Dame Sisters in Marysville. That city had all through its existence been subject to floods in the winter and in the spring because it is located at the confluence of two major rivers: the Feather and the Yuba. The winter floods were caused by heavy rains, the spring floods by fast-melting snow in the mountains which fed these rivers. When

NOTRE DAME ACADEMY, Marysville, established in 1855
(Photo, courtesy of Sisters of Notre Dame, Belmont, California)

Bishop O'Connell first went to Marysville, he wrote about the terrible floods in December, 1861, which broke off all communication with his priests; and in December, 1861, he mentioned the problems that occurred when couples who wanted to get married could not get to the priest for weeks on end on account of the floods. Now, on January 19, 1875, there was another which did severe damage to the Notre Dame Sisters' convent. There was four feet of water in the convent, a wall collapsed, and pianos and furniture were damaged. This flood brought to a head the growing discontent of the Notre Dame Sisters who found the Marysville climate very difficult.

The Superior General, Mother Constantine at Namur in Belgium, after several communications with the sisters both in the Marysville and the San Jose houses, made the decision in October, 1875, that the Marysville convent should be closed, the property sold, and the sisters sent to other houses of the order in more healthy areas of California. Shortly after this stunning news was received by Bishop O'Connell, Mother Constantine died and the decision was suspended. But since the new Superior General, Mother Aloysius, continued to receive reports regarding the debility of the sisters in Marysville who were severely affected by the floods in the winter, the heat in the summer, and the mosquitoes which bred in the swamps left from the flood waters, the same new Mother General renewed the orders in late August, 1876. Bishop O'Connell was distraught at the idea. He could see nothing but triumph for the anti-Catholic forces and a definite setback for the advancement of Catholic education in the diocese. On September 6, 1876, he wrote a letter of protest to the Superior General in an attempt to override the decision. In part, he wrote:

> It is noted that the chief reason given why the Sisters must leave Marysville is the intemperate weather. I confess indeed that the heat for the space of about three months is great, so that some are sick with fever and for a while must take to bed. But having learned from experience I doubt whether the heat and the floods in the city of Marysville exceed either the heat and the periodic fevers in the city of Rome and in other places where Missionaries and Sisters labor with zeal for souls rather than for the sake of their

health. If some Sisters in the Convent are ill, the illness is to be attributed not only to the inclement weather but also to their labors in the schools and to other causes as is apparent in the testimony of former Superiors and likewise of Doctors who ministered to them, and also of seventeen or eighteen Sisters living there who with one or two exceptions have enjoyed sufficiently good health.

To the suppression of a Community which has labored faithfully for nearly 25 years in my Diocese and has produced much fruit, I cannot acquiesce on account of the scandal which would follow not only to the faithful but also to the non-Catholics of California whose daughters have for so many years been educated in the Sisters' Academy.[416]

The Mother General, on October 13, 1876, appealed to Propaganda Fidei for approval of her decision and, to strengthen her appeal, she asked the bishop of Namur to intercede on her behalf.[417] His letter of November 23, 1876, also reached Propaganda Fidei. Evidently this time Cardinal Barnabo sided with the distraught bishop of Grass Valley because the closing of the convent was delayed.

The year 1875, which witnessed the flood that provoked this great scare, also witnessed a fire which brought great sorrow to the diocese. Fires were a frequent concern in the fifteen years of Bishop O'Connell's incumbency. Fires had damaged or destroyed many churches in his diocese over the years. Fires were common in the whole mining country, destructive fires which raced through the wooden structures which composed most of the mining towns. Scarcity of water was the real cause of the extent of these fires which raced unchecked and leveled many blocks at a time. It was because of these fires that the more substantial buildings were built of brick.

Brick buildings with their iron shutters on the outside of the windows gave some assurance of protection from the destructive fires. If the roof was kept watered down during such a fire, the whole building could be saved. The entire diocese possessed only four churches of this category: Marysville, Grass Valley, Austin, and Virginia City. The church in Virginia City was the most beautiful of them all. Yet the news was received in Marysville on Tuesday afternoon, October 26, 1875, that this church too had become the victim of such a fire. The fire broke out on A Street about 6 o'clock in the morning. A high wind was blowing at the time so that the fire spread with incredible rapidity. Even though every piece of equipment was employed, both from Virginia City and from nearby Gold Hill, all efforts were in vain. The fire spread from A Street to B Street. The high wind in turn carried cinders to C Street. Almost everything went. The brick International Hotel, the railroad depot, and the hoist and buildings of the Consolidated Virginia Mine which employed so many of the residents. The distress of the people was frightful; as many attempted to save from their homes some of their possessions, children became separated from parents, and the sick were carried out on the cold, wind-swept streets on mattresses.

Flying embers landed on the steeple of the beautiful Church of St. Mary's in the Mountains. Because of the wind and the inadequacy of the equipment to reach so high, the steeple was permitted to burn. An engine stood by and water was pumped as high as could be reached. Finally, the steeple fire seemed to be under control and the engine was called away to a more urgent scene.

By 10:15 A.M. the danger to the church seemed past. But an unseen ember had fallen on the roof and was soon consuming the shingles. The engine could not be recalled. Destruction appeared inevitable. During the anxious moments while the steeple burned, townspeople and children were removing everything possible from the church to the safety of the convent three blocks farther down the hill. The beautiful paintings brought by Father Manogue on his return from Europe were saved. The statues, the altar decorations, everything was removed from the $80,000 building. Father Coleman was the only one home at the time. He did what he could and then stood with the others and watched St. Mary's burn. The nearby Episcopal church, built of wood, was consumed in a flash. By sunset that night, a visit to the church site revealed the four brick walls still standing, some of the minarets still in place, a portion of the spire still burning. Gazing into the basement, which once had been the residence of the priests, smoking embers were all that was left of the beautiful altar, the recently purchased pipe organ, the pews which Sunday after Sunday had held the devout Catholics of Virginia City.[418] Father Manogue was homeless, together with so many of his

The famed "ST. MARY'S IN THE MOUNTAINS," Virginia City, Nevada. Built by the Rev. Patrick Manogue in 1868. Burned in the great fire of October 26, 1875. Rebuilt in 1877, and still in use as a parish church.

Rear view of ST. MARY'S HOSPITAL on Union Street, Virginia City. Opened in 1876 at a cost of $45,000 and closed in 1897. The building still stands.

(Photos, courtesy of St. Mary's in the Mountains, Virginia City, Nevada)

people. His insurance covered only $30,000 of the immense loss. Luckily, the orphanage, the convent, and the school, and the newly built and not yet completed hospital had not suffered in the fire.

A false rumor had been circulated that the church had been dynamited, a story which persists to this day. It is true that in some instances buildings were dynamited in an attempt to check the spread of the fire, but St. Mary's Church was not. When Father Manogue rebuilt, the same walls were used; however, they were removed to the top of the window level so that the new church would have gothic-shaped windows. The walls of the present St. Mary's, therefore, are the original ones except the portion above the top of the windows.

The years between 1874 and 1878 brought further distress to the aging bishop. In 1874, he received 16,000 francs from the Society for the Propagation of the Faith. In 1875, the amount was cut to 14,000. Further reductions came in 1876 when he received only 9,200. The last allotment which came in 1877 was for only 6,000 francs. Nothing at all was sent in 1878. This was understandable. The Society had been supporting Bishop O'Connell now for seventeen years. There was growth in the missions throughout the world, and Paris had to be concerned about the worldwide needs of the church. Although he could understand all this, yet his financial distress was not alleviated by such action on the part of Paris. In his concern, Bishop O'Connell wrote at the end of 1878:

> Would you have the kindness to inform me why I have lost my title to the usual allocation from the Propagation of the Faith? This year I have received nothing. Perhaps you have the idea that I have been enriched by the "Pious Fund"?[419]

The "Pious Fund" was an endowment started in Spain by generous benefactors in 1697, the interest of which was to be used to support the Missions of Upper and Lower California. Over the years, the capital amounted to more than two million dollars. The administration of these monies passed from the control of Spain to that of Mexico when that country won its independence. At the time of the suppression of the Jesuits, who were the predecessors of the Franciscans in the work of the Missions, the Mexican government confiscated all Jesuit holdings, which of course included the Pious Fund. When, in turn, that government became anti-Catholic and secularized the Missions, confiscating the Mission properties and selling them to the highest bidder, the properties and money of the Pious Fund were confiscated. A decree on October 24, 1842, transferred the Pious Fund to the Mexican treasury, yet with the promise that the interest would continue to be paid to the missions.

From the time of the transfer of Upper California to the United States in 1848, the Mexican government ceased to pay its portion of the interest from the Pious Fund. The new American bishop of Monterey, Joseph S. Alemany, worked for what rightfully belonged to the church from the first days of his arrival in California. When the so-called Mixed Commission was established by the Treaty of 1869 to handle claims of American citizens against Mexico and of Mexican citizens against the United States which had arisen between February 2, 1848, and February 1, 1869, the three California bishops filed a claim for the 21-year interest from the Pious Fund. This was judged to amount to $904,700.79 or $43,080.99 per year. On March 7, 1877, judgment was made which awarded this sum of money to the American church in California, to be divided as follows:

$26,000 to the heirs of Jose Antonio Aguirre in payment for a loan made in 1842.
$24,000 to the archbishop of Oregon City (now Portland) for missions in his province, especially Idaho.
$40,000 to be divided between the Jesuits and the Franciscans.
$116,388 to the missions of Utah and the sum of
$232,776 to each of the three California bishops.[420]

Thus Bishop O'Connell's share in the award was rather substantial. This might have had something to do with the decision of the Society for the Propagation of the Faith to eliminate the subsidy for the Grass Valley diocese. Suspecting this, Bishop O'Connell wrote to M. Certes:

> Perhaps you have the idea that I have been enriched by the Pious Fund. But as a matter of fact, the portion of the Pious Fund allotted to my Diocese is entirely for the Indians of

Reno, Lake County and Del Norte and for the Sisters who teach this generation born in paganism.[421]

So, at last, Bishop O'Connell's concern for the care of the Indians was met. This explains how the bishops were able to build and support the Mission of St. Turibius in Lake County as an answer to the adverse results of the Osuna versus Burchard controversy in the Round Valley Reservation.

This, however, did not relieve Bishop O'Connell's general financial circumstances. In a sort of desperate last appeal to the Society for the Propagation of the Faith in 1879, he wrote as follows:

> The good and charitable works to be accomplished in my extensive Diocese increase every year, and the means to sustain them becomes smaller.
> The boarding school and the two orphan asylums for boys and girls kept at Grass Valley by the zealous Sisters of Mercy:
> The Convents at Eureka, Humboldt County and at Yreka, of the same Congregation of Mercy:
> The Convent of the Sisters of Notre Dame at Marysville:
> The Orphan Asylum and the Hospital conducted by good Sisters of Charity in Virginia City, State of Nevada, are all, as well as many of the Churches in my Diocese, involved in debt:
> I have felt myself obliged to erect in Reno a Convent directed by the Sisters of St. Dominic. They have good schools for girls and boys until they attain their twelfth year. The Dominican Sisters were obliged to borrow several thousand dollars in order to build their Convent which is far from being finished. I beg of you then, Gentlemen, to appropriate to the Sisters at Reno 25,000 francs.[422]

We recall that as pastor, the faithful Father John Mary Mevel wrote a letter to Paris from Reno on November 5, 1879, adding his own plea to that of the Bishop. What response was made to this request is unknown. There had been a disastrous fire in Reno on March 2, 1879, in which Father Mevel lost his

SECOND CATHOLIC CHURCH in Reno, Nevada
Built by the Rev. James J. Callan in 1879; destroyed by fire in 1905
(Photo, courtesy of Nevada Historical Society, Reno)

church. This seems to have not only wiped out this zealous missionary's work but also terminated his stay as pastor of Reno. He left the diocese at that time and went to Haiti. Nothing more is known of him.

The new pastor of Reno and the builder of the second church was Father James J. Callan, whose moves certainly portray Bishop O'Connell's format of giving climatic changes to his priests—from Forest Hill to Marysville, to Mendocino, to Yreka, to Reno; mountains to valley; valley to coast; coast to mountains; mountains to desert. Father Callan secured a new site for the church, moving from the original Fourth and Center to Sixth and Lake Streets.[423]

It is time now to take a look at the location of the various priests in the diocese, and 1878 appears to be a good year because it seems to have ended Bishop O'Connell's habit of moving his priests so frequently. It is from this year that we begin to see some stability.

It should be pointed out at the outset that there were three new priests in 1878. It is not known from where Bishop O'Connell got Father Thomas Lynn, but in April, 1878, he was assigned as assistant in Grass Valley. It was to be an unhappy arrangement, as the Bishop was forced to dismiss him from the diocese after Christmas in 1879. Father Michael Walsh was ordained from All Hallows on June 24, 1878; Father Thomas Nugent from St. Vincent's Seminary in Latrobe, Pennsylvania, on July 11, 1878.

When these arrived in late September, 1878, Father Walsh was assigned as an assistant to Father Grace in Marysville and co-assistant with Father O'Kane, and Father Nugent was sent as an assistant to Father Manogue in Virginia City. Besides losing Father Mevel from the diocese, the Bishop also lost Father Becker. Research has failed to turn up evidence of his whereabouts in 1879.

The diocesan roster, therefore, in 1878, should have appeared as follows:

Marysville:	St. Joseph's—Father Grace, Pastor; Fathers O'Kane and Walsh, Assistant Pastors. Immaculate Conception—Father John Meiler.
Oroville:	A mission of Marysville; parish had been suppressed since 1874.

THE REV. JOHN D. SHERIDAN, 1850–1893
Pastor of Mendocino City, 1877–1883
Pastor of Eureka, California, 1883–1893
Built present St. Bernard's Church in 1886
(Photo, courtesy of Mendocino Historical Research, Inc.)

Red Bluff:	Father William Clarke, for one year. He was replaced by Father James Hunt in 1879 who then stayed for ten years. In 1878, Bishop O'Connell established the parish of Cherokee, taking territory from Downieville and Nevada City. Father Clarke became the founding pastor. He was in his post by November, 1879. He had under his care such places as Birchville, Moore's Flat, Columbia Hill, Graniteville, Sweetland, and Lake City; yet it was not a very prosperous place as Father Clarke had only thirty-five baptisms during the year and a half of his incumbency as pastor of Cherokee.[424]
Yreka:	Father James J. Claire became the new pastor for just one year. He was succeeded by Father Leon Haupts in 1879, who stayed there seven years.
Weaverville:	Father Walrath had been the pastor since 1877, but in 1879 he was to go to Colusa and the young Father Walsh came as pastor.
Eureka:	(California) After thirteen years in Downieville, Father Lynch became the new pastor of Eureka and remained four years.
Crescent City:	Father James J. Claire came here from Yreka, but only for a short stay.
Mendocino City:	The Rev. John D. Sheridan had begun in 1877 a six-year stay as pastor here, the first one of any long duration.
Chico:	This was the new parish Bishop O'Connell established in 1878, with Father James Hynes as the founding pastor. He remained nine years.
Downieville:	Father Andrew O'Donnell, the one whose Latin was so poor, succeeded Father Lynch for a short one-year stay.
Forest Hill:	Father Moloney was still here until March, 1879, when he was replaced by Father Pettit.

ST. BERNARD'S CHURCH, Eureka, California
Photo taken between 1886 and 1892. To be noted is that the rectory had not yet been built, and the old or first church is still standing, used as a parish hall for many years. Church dedicated by Bishop Manogue in 1886.
(Photo courtesy of St. Bernard's Church, Eureka, California)

Truckee: It is difficult to ascertain, since the records of both parishes have been lost, whether Father Pettit was actually pastor of Truckee or simply took care of it from Reno.

Smartsville: Father Coleman succeeded Father O'Sullivan and stayed in Smartsville for nine years.

Rohnerville: Father Kennedy had been here at the college in Rohnerville since 1877 and acting also as pastor. About this time he seems to have established himself as founding pastor of Ferndale with Rohnerville as a mission.[425] The college failed in 1879 and was closed, hopelessly in debt. This caused the move by Father Kennedy from Rohnerville to the nearby Ferndale. It is safe to say that this has the distinction of being the last parish established by Bishop O'Connell. Although Arcata became a parish in 1883 while Bishop O'Connell was still the ordinary, its establishment may have been accomplished by his coadjutor rather than by himself. Father Kennedy remained for twelve years.

Nevada City: Father Meagher's term here was to cover twelve years, from 1873–1885. This parish lost its assistant after Father O'Kane moved from there to Grass Valley in 1877.

In the Nevada portion of the diocese:

Virginia City: Father Manogue had rebuilt his church. He had as his assistants Father O'Sullivan from Smartsville and the newly ordained Thomas Nugent.

Gold Hill: Father Nulty was the pastor with Father Haupts as his assistant until the latter was sent as pastor of Yreka in 1879. It then became Father Nulty's turn to have Father O'Kane as an assistant.

Carson City:	Father Tormey was in the middle of his fifteen-year stay.
Austin:	Father Phelan was well-established and destined to remain many more years.
Eureka:	(Nevada) Father Monteverde was well into his seven-year stay in this parish.

One new priest, Father Bernard McFeeley, was ordained from All Hallows on June 24, 1879. On his arrival in the fall, he was sent as an assistant to Father Lynch in Eureka, California.

Thus, the beginnings of some stability seem to be evident. How this came about is unknown, but it was indeed needed to provide some kind of continuity in the work of the church in these many communities. Priests were in good supply now and transportation had improved. Therefore the need for a change of milieu seems to have lessened.

One final preoccupation of the Bishop during these closing years of his sole responsibility for the diocese was his concern about providing brothers for the education of boys. The first mention of this as a special concern is to be found in a letter written to Cardinal Simeoni in Rome on December 29, 1873.

> What am I to do regarding the education of boys in this Diocese, unless your Eminence orders under the virtue of obedience, the Superior of the Christian Brothers to give some Brothers as has happened to my Metropolitan. There is no lack of colleges or Christian academies for girls, but alas, our boys are in danger in the public schools of this republic because they lack holy teachers.[426]

Five months later, in May, 1874, the Bishop repeated the same request to Cardinal Simeoni. In February, 1878, when making his "ten year report," he wrote to the new Cardinal Prefect:

> That which is the saddest and is a constant grief to me is the lack of Christian Brothers to help in the education of boys. Again and again I have written to your venerable Predecessor begging him to order the Superior of the Christian Brothers to send Brothers to educate our young boys.[427]

This problem came to a head in 1879 when the only institution for the education of boys in the diocese was forced to close its doors. The little college at Rohnerville had struggled on during the late 1870s, beset by problems of extremely small enrollment due to its remote location and the ever-mounting costs of keeping it open. The Precious Blood fathers had striven to maintain it, while its founder Father Henneberry continued to give missions in far-off Australia and New Zealand, sending back to the headquarters in Ohio as much money as he could to help eliminate the debt on St. Joseph's College. In spite of all efforts, the decision was made to close the college on September 17, 1879.

This brought to Bishop O'Connell's attention once again the fact that now there was in the diocese no institution for the education of boys. As a result, he proposed a plan to solve the problem, a plan which he was to oppose vigorously when later it was favored by Bishop Manogue, namely that of changing boundary lines so that the Christian Brothers who had made a foundation in Sacramento would be automatically included. He ended his letter to Rome in these words: "Therefore I beg your Eminence to add a portion of San Francisco Diocese to ours."[428]

Bishop O'Connell was to be unsuccessful in this endeavor. He would not have the pleasure of seeing an institution dedicated to the education of boys in his diocese, a fact which he bitterly lamented and for which he laid the blame on his own inability.

Sources for Chapter XIII

411. Walsh, *Hallowed Were*, pp. 297, 501.

412. AAHC, letter of November 28, 1871.

413. *National Catholic Directory*, 1877.

414. Death Register, St. Joseph's, Marysville; entry of January 19, 1877.

415. Walsh, *Hallowed Were*, p. 527.

416. ASRC, Vol. 27, F672.

417. ASPF, letter of October 13, 1876.

418. *The Monitor*, November 6, 1875.

419. ASPF, letter of December 3, 1878.

420. Weber, "Decision regarding the Pious Fund," in *Documents of California Catholic History*, pp. 153–160.

421. ASPF, letter of December 3, 1878.

422. AALA, letter of October 17, 1878.

423. Gorman, *Seventy-Five Years*, p. 67.

424. Baptismal Records of St. Patrick's, Cherokee, Nevada County.

425. Walsh, *Hallowed Were*, p. 502.

426. ASRC, Vol. 177, F86A.

427. ASRC, Vol. 189, F173A.

428. ASRC, Vol. 31, F764.

Chapter XIV

THE QUEST FOR A COADJUTOR, 1874–1881

Both Archbishop Alemany of San Francisco and Bishop O'Connell of Grass Valley had a long hard struggle to find replacements so that they could retire after their years of pioneering service to the church. Each was required to remain on the job ten years beyond what they themselves wanted. The problem lay in the reluctance of the candidates nominated to take on the burden of the church in California. The other suffragan, Bishop Amat of Monterey, had been successful in obtaining a coadjutor in the person of Bishop Francis Mora in 1873. But for the bishops in the northern portion of the state, obtaining a helping bishop or a successor became a most frustrating quest.

The first time that Bishop O'Connell mentioned a possible successor was in a letter to Father Simeoni at Propaganda Fidei in Rome in 1872:

> I also ask another favor, that the State of Nevada be cut off from this Diocese and erected into a new Vicariate because I haven't the strength to visit the whole of this Diocese. I have informed my Metropolitan of successors in as far as I can judge who are fit for ruling this peculiar Diocese viz. Father Vincent Vinyes O.P. of Benicia or Father Denis Mahoney of All Hallows, Dublin, Ireland.[429]

Again in the month of August he wrote: "Most Rev. Father I

commend myself, already growing old and needing a Coadjutor, to your prayers."[430]

Once again at the end of 1873 he proposed names for the bishopric: again Father Vincent Vinyes and Father Comerford, the former Vicar General of the Mauritius Islands near Africa.[431]

But this was not the accepted procedure as far as Rome was concerned. It was not until April, 1874, that the formalities of such a request were complied with. The occasion was the meeting of the California bishops at the first Provincial Council held in San Francisco between April 28 and May 2, 1874.[432] Both Archbishop Alemany and Bishop O'Connell submitted to the Council formal requests that they be granted coadjutors. The requests were approved by the Council and forwarded to Rome. Since Bishop O'Connell was the writer of Latin letters, he was usually elected secretary on such occasions, as he was in this case. Thus it became his task to forward the request to Rome. He did so in the following words:

> Our Metropolitan, Most Rev. Joseph S. Alemany, Archbishop of San Francisco, wishes no longer to be Bishop and therefore asks me, the least of his suffragans, to extend his request to the Holy See. Gladly I would wish to accede to his petition and to approve it, if I knew anyone more filled with the Spirit of God, wiser and like him. I am of the opinion that the same ruler is needed for the people together with a coadjutor. Likewise I ask you to remove me and to put in my place another who is better for the universal good of the flock committed to me. From my heart I ask this, I beg it, this one thing I ask.[433]

Each of the bishops had such a great admiration for one another's accomplishments that they both undermined one another's chances of retirement. Archbishop Alemany just a few months previously had written:

> Wherefore the two suffragans propose to divide their Dioceses which does not yet seem expedient to me, and the Bishop of Grass Valley has often asked that a Coadjutor be given him, which, considering his age, his health and his

many labors covering vast distances, seems to me to be highly recommended.[434]

When the official papers of the Provincial Council went into Rome, the following official letter regarding Bishop O'Connell's request accompanied the proceedings:

> Since Rt. Rev. Eugene O'Connell, Bishop of Grass Valley in the Province of San Francisco has humbly begged the Holy See that a Coadjutor Bishop be given him and since the Holy See has kindly assented, the praiseworthy Bishop of Grass Valley has proposed, to the Fathers of the same Province, assembled in Synod, the following priests as worthy to assume the office of Bishop from among whom a Coadjutor be given him by the Holy See:
> 1) Rev. Vincent Vinyes of the Convent of St. Dominic in Benicia.
> 2) Very Rev. John Prendergast, Vicar General of San Francisco.
> 3) Rev. James McGill, Rector of St. Vincent's College in the City of Los Angeles and the Diocese of Monterey and Los Angeles.[435]

Unfortunately, Rome did nothing about the requests until Bishop Amat made a plea for both of them while he was in Rome in 1875. When he returned, the bishops met again on July 28, 1875, and renewed the request, once again submitting names. Father John Prendergast, the Vicar General of San Francisco, was on both lists. The members of the Congregation met on July 30, 1875, in Rome and selected him to be the coadjutor to the bishop of Grass Valley.

The letter of appointment was sent on August 20, 1875, and the announcement was made in *The Monitor* on October 16, 1875, in the following words:

> The Catholics of San Francisco will be sorry to learn, and those of Grass Valley glad to hear that the Bulls have been received by which the Holy Father has appointed the Very Rev. John Prendergast, Bishop of Lerba in Pamphylia, and

THE REV. JOHN PRENDERGAST, Vicar General of San Francisco; appointed Coadjutor Bishop of Grass Valley in 1875. (He declined the honor.) (Photo, courtesy of Holy Family Sisters, San Francisco)

THE REV. VINCENT VINYES, O.P., of Benicia, Calif.; appointed Coadjutor Bishop of Grass Valley, 1877. (He declined the honor.) (Photo, courtesy of Dominicans of the West, Oakland)

Coadjutor to Rt. Rev. Eugene O'Connell, Bishop of Grass Valley, who in his declining years will receive most valuable assistance from the able services of such a Coadjutor in the administration of his extensive Diocese.[436]

But matters would not be quite so simple. Between the time of the reception of the appointment from Rome in early September and this announcement in October, Bishop-elect Prendergast had made a very serious decision, namely, to turn down the appointment. In a letter addressed to Cardinal Franchi, written on October 9, 1875, Father Prendergast made the refusal a matter of conscience and enclosed a letter from his Father Confessor. He offered to disclose his reasons if he could do so personally to the Holy Father, a trip which could not very well be made until the following May.[437] Rome accepted the refusal and the first hope that there would be a coadjutor for Grass Valley was dissipated.

Therefore, once again, a new list of proposed candidates had to be drawn up by both bishops since Father Prendergast's name had been on both lists. Once again the name of Dominican Father Vincent Vinyes headed the Grass Valley list with Father Lawrence Scanlan in second place and Father Michael Richardson of Los Angeles in third place. The secretary of Propaganda, in preparing the list of names for submission to the cardinals, wrote to the Master General of the Dominicans for his recommendations which the Vicar General answered in the following words:

> I deem it my duty to report to you that our Dominican confrere Father Vincent Vinyes is deserving of commendation under every respect, and that no complaint has ever been registered in regard to his religious or moral conduct. I also deem him fit for the distinguished office for which Bishop O'Connell of Grass Valley is singling him out. However on the occasion of a similar request for Father Vinyes, I pointed out the fact that his departure from his young Province would cause considerable hardship. Father Villarosa wrote to me on Feb. 4, 1874. "I thank you especially for your help in preventing that Father Vinyes should be named Bishop. In the present circumstances his loss would appear to constitute a great calamity for the Order in California."[438]

In spite of these pleas, the Sacred Congregation met again on January 29, 1877, and this time the bishop-elect of Grass Valley was Father Vincent Vinyes. The Bulls were sent to Archbishop Alemany who, on February 28, 1877, gave them to the Dominican provincial who in turn presented them to Father Vinyes without sharing his thinking on the matter. Two days later, Father Vinyes returned the Bulls saying that he, too, was declining the appointment. In the first days of April, he wrote three letters, one to Bishop O'Connell, one to the Archbishop, and one to the Vicar General of the order.

To Bishop O'Connell he wrote:

> Knowing how unfit I am for this Office, and how incapable to fulfill its duties, I feel compelled to decline the honor. As a student I decided to become a religious principally in order to avoid a Pastor's responsibilities.

To Archbishop Alemany he wrote:

> I received the documents and in my inexperience not knowing what to do with them, after careful thought I believed it would be better to send them back to you rather than return them directly to Rome. I had never given this matter a thought, but now, the more I think of it, the less inclined I feel to accept this burden.[439]

It was his letter to the Vicar General of the order which best portrays the soul of a deeply spiritual man. He wrote:

> I fear that a certain predilection for me on part of the Bishop of Grass Valley (I once helped dissipate one of his perplexing doubts to his satisfaction) and my old friendship with the Most Rev. Bishop Mora, Coadjutor to the Bishop of Monterey, may have prompted them to nominate me and that therefore, this choice may come more from human rather than a divine will.
>
> I have always shied away from every type of responsibility where others are concerned, so that it was mainly to avoid the responsibility involved in the care of souls that I decided to join a religious order. This repugnance became

so deep that I am often sorry not to have become a lay Brother and thus have avoided even the least such responsibility in the Order.

When I stop to consider how many and great are the qualifications necessary for a Bishop, I can't honestly find a single one in me. Unfit as I am to rule even a tiny community, how on earth could I undertake the administration of a Diocese? I am led to say this by truth rather than by humility.[440]

The effort to obtain a coadjutor thus went down to defeat for the second time. This would involve another delay of at least a year under ordinary circumstances.

The California bishops met on March 27, 1878, once again for the purpose of submitting a new slate of nominees. Bishop Amat, being ill, sent Bishop Mora as his delegate. Bishop O'Connell submitted a new list for approval:

1) Father Michael Richardson, the Vincentian from the College of St. Vincent in Los Angeles.
2) Father Patrick Manogue, Vicar General for Nevada and pastor of St. Mary's in Virginia City.
3) Father Lawrence Scanlan, pastor of St. Mary Magdalen's in Salt Lake City.[441]

The assembled bishops approved the list in the order submitted and it was duly sent to Rome by Bishop O'Connell. On the following day, however, Archbishop Alemany followed up with a personal letter in which he wrote:

Bishop O'Connell now prefers as his Coadjutor Father Michael Richardson; besides possessing many good qualities he is an excellent preacher and a very good religious but perhaps not as capable as the Rev. Patrick Manogue with regard to temporal administration even though I know he has much experience in it.[442]

This time the delay between the submission of the names and the actual appointment of the new coadjutor was to be almost two years. During those long months, several events took place which were to determine the choice of the new coadjutor.

For one thing, Bishop O'Connell, now sixty-three years old, instead of becoming more mellow seems to have become more obsessed with little things and more difficult to get along with. As a result, the alienation of his priests became increasingly greater as time went on.

One of the key events which produced the greatest alienation was the manner in which Bishop O'Connell treated Mother Dolores, the superior of the convent in Reno. Perhaps it should be stated at the outset that Mother Dolores had arrived in the diocese somewhat under a cloud, a fact which Bishop O'Connell would not be likely to overlook or forget. Secondly, as we have seen previously, when Bishop O'Connell felt he had the law on his side, he could be very tenacious in his pursuit of the offender.

It all began one day in mid-July, 1877, when Bishop O'Connell received a letter from Father J. M. Mevel, the pastor of Reno. The letter described how he had been informed that there were three nuns in Reno, one of them very ill, that he had visited them and that they were willing to remain and open a much-needed school in Reno. After much correspondence, Bishop O'Connell learned that the sisters were Mother Dolores O'Neale, Sister Aquin Montgomery, and Sister Joseph Cowan, all Dominican sisters who had left Vallejo without permission and were on their way east when one of them fell ill. When the bishop of Grass Valley learned that the sisters had departed from Vallejo without permission, that was enough for him. However, in the course of correspondence with Archbishop Alemany, the archbishop finally wrote: "I give her to you as a present." With the legal aspect settled, Bishop O'Connell consented, but his suspicion of Mother Dolores remained and thus made him quick to reprimand her. He had grown weary over the years with priests who had come to the diocese and then after a few years left. Bishop O'Connell had little understanding for those who did not stay on their original mission. This was his first female version of the type.[443]

On August 20, 1877, Bishop O'Connell established the Reno convent and appointed Sister M. Dolores O'Neale as prioress of the convent. He wrote to Rome for permission for them to keep the Blessed Sacrament in their chapel.[444] A temporary school was opened in the brick home of John Sunderland at the corner of

Fifth and Lake on September 3, 1877, and there were forty-five students in attendance, with a capacity for eighty.

In the meantime, Father Mevel had decided to move on and Bishop O'Connell appointed Father Thomas Pettit as the new pastor. Under his leadership, a fair was held at the end of November for the benefit of the new school. The fair netted $1,067.25.

Property was purchased in January, 1878, for $3,800, on Fourth Street between Center and Lake, and construction began on a new building which was to be convent, school, and boarders' quarters. The building, sixty feet in each direction, a three-story frame structure with a brick basement, was completed on time for the new 1878–79 school year and was named St. Mary's Academy. Within a short space of time, there were thirty boarders and the school was well attended. We already have read about the attention the sisters gave to the Indians of the Reno area and Bishop O'Connell's efforts to obtain grants for them from Propagation of the Faith.

To accomplish her goals, the rather independent Mother Dolores had to borrow heavily. Anyone deeply in debt was always suspect with Bishop O'Connell. But, in addition, Mother Dolores found it necessary to go on begging expeditions even into the remote mining areas of Modoc County and as far north as Alturas. She evidently made these excursions without bothering to ask for permission. Eventually, the Bishop of Grass Valley heard about it and at once informed Mother Dolores that she was violating the rule and that she was to cease and desist and remain home in her convent as the Dominican rule required.

The war was on. Mother Dolores had given ample evidence of her independence. She had left Vallejo for that simple reason. She wanted to head an independent community and not just be a subject of the Benicia convent. The difficulty continued until Bishop O'Connell, rightly or wrongly, invoked his full authority as ordinary of the diocese, by which he ordered the priests of the area who were involved in hearing the confessions of the Dominican sisters to withhold absolution from Mother Dolores until she agreed to stay in her convent.[445] Father James Callan succeeded Father Pettit as pastor of Reno; Father Patrick Kirley succeeded him. Both of these priests were quite disturbed by the bishop's unyielding stand, and wrote letters to Rome in support of Mother

Dolores. Father Kirley testified that when Mother Dolores did leave her convent for one of her trips, "she always did it in the spirit and tenor of the rule, for the sake of charity, and for the good of her neighbor and the community."[446]

Bishop O'Connell was required by Rome to give an accounting of his actions, which he did in a very forthright manner. How the matter was resolved is not known. What is known is that Mother Dolores continued with her school and her indebtedness until finally in 1892 the creditors pressed on Mother Dolores to the point where she had to appeal to Bishop O'Connell's successor for help. The new bishop offered to assist her if she deeded the property to him. Her answer was an indignant, "Never." She was told to go home and pay her debts at once. As soon as the mortgage foreclosure approached, Mother Dolores at once again took off. When she returned on April 23, 1892, she found her buildings securely locked and in the hands of the sheriff. When they were sold at auction on November 9, 1892, they brought $11,479.50. Mother Dolores ended her days in a mental institution.[447] Yet the Reno institution accomplished untold good from its founding in 1877 till its closing in 1892.

This story was used as an example of the poor judgment often used by Bishop O'Connell and especially of the pettiness in the manner he often pursued something which, because of the circumstances of the time, might have been better if ignored. Along with this increase in pettiness on his part went an increasing dissatisfaction on the part of the priests. The most telling of the communications which went to Rome during these years of delay in appointing a strong coadjustor was a letter from one of the Passionists who had been at Divide in Nevada and who had himself incurred the displeasure of Bishop O'Connell. He was Father John Philip Baudinelli, often referred to as Father Philippus, who had returned to the diocese in 1877 at Bishop O'Connell's request to give missions. After making a circuit of the diocese, and therefore having heard what the priests had to say, he felt compelled to forward his findings to Rome to his major superiors. He wrote as follows:

> For the third time I am in the Diocese of Grass Valley, California. This time I am engaged in giving Missions throughout the Diocese in company with two of our fathers.

There is, very Rev. Father, a thing of great importance that I would like to place before your consideration and that of Propaganda. I feel almost duty bound to do so for the good of the Church in this remote part of the world. There is a saintly Bishop at the head of this Diocese Rt. Rev. Eugene O'Connell, and has been for 16 years. Besides being a saintly man he is also a man of learning and knowledge. But this is all that can be said of him—as to prudence and the art of ruling a Diocese he seems to be, and to have ever been a perfect stranger to. I have come in contact with all of the Priests of his jurisdiction twenty-five or twenty-six in number, and there are not *two* in the whole number that are not greatly annoyed at, and dissatisfied with him.

For the last two years he has been working hard to get a coadjutor— Rome granted the petition— Father Prendergast was first appointed by Rome— He renounced the honour and burden— Then Father Vincent, a Dominican Priest, was elected by Rome, and he too refused to accept the mitre— The main reason of their unwillingness to accept the coadjutorship was the difficulties, not to say the impossibility, they saw of ever being able to get along with him. The Bishop has not given up the idea of having a coadjutor still, and he may probably succeed in getting a man from Europe, who will accept the Dignity because he is not aware of the State of affairs of the Diocese. But if a coadjutor is to be given to Bishop O'Connell there is only one priest in this Diocese, that would be welcome and unanimously hailed by the whole Diocese of Grass Valley. This man is the Very Rev. P. Manogue, Vicar General of the Diocese. For the past 17 years he has laboured hard and faithfully in the most important and populous city of the diocese. By his talents, gentleness, charity and rare prudence he has endeared himself to all of the Priests of the diocese in which he lives, and also the Archdiocese of San Francisco— He is, in the opinion of the Priests of the Diocese, the only person fit for the position— He knows the diocese thoroughly, is well acquainted with the clergy, he commands their respect and affection, and he is probably the only one that by his firmness of character and prudence in acting would and could make Bishop O'Connell act differently from his usual ways. I know that Bishop O'Connell would not like the appointment of the said Vicar General, and though he has acknowledged to me [an indecipherable passage here] that he is fully equal to the honour, yet he fears him because of his ability to oppose him in his unreasonable ways of dealing.

Do you think Very Rev. Father that it would be proper to hand this letter of mine to the Cardinal Prefect of Propaganda. I think that there must be Documents already in Propaganda purporting to the same effect, and this letter of mine might be a confirmation to the aforesaid Documents. What ever I have said I do vouch to be true, and my object in this note is no other than the glory of God and the good of religion, as well as the welfare of the Catholic people of this diocese.[448]

Moreover, Propaganda, besides the letter from the Passionist missionary, had received letters from Fathers Lynch, Meagher, and Coleman all favoring the selection of Father Manogue as the new coadjutor.[449] Rome's problem was to get Bishop O'Connell to consent, as Father Manogue had been his second choice. In setting down his opinion of Father Manogue, the bishop of Grass Valley betrayed his concern over legalities. He wrote:

> With regard to my second choice for a coadjutor, viz Father Manogue, I must point out that he is the same priest who some years ago, acting in good faith, after breakfast offered a second Sunday Mass so as not to leave the people without Mass and to protect the good name of his vicar who was laid up due to over drinking. It is for this reason that I did not place his name first on the list.

He then continued:

> Would that his love for Church discipline were as great as that of Father Richardson of Monterey or even of Father Scanlan, both of whom he far surpasses in administrative skill.

Archbishop Alemany had written that Bishop O'Connell did

not particularly favor Father Manogue because he was a bit weak in his preaching, but, he added,

> ... on the other hand Bishop O'Connell thinks he is gifted with charity, meekness, patience and a high degree of prudence, so much so that he has made it clear he would be pleased if Father Manogue were chosen by the Holy See as his coadjutor.[450]

All of these facts, statements, and the whole history of the attempt to find a coadjutor for the bishop of Grass Valley were laid before the assembled members of the Congregation of Propaganda Fidei when they met at the end of June, 1879. With the overwhelming mass of evidence in favor of the pastor of Virginia City, it is no wonder that the Congregation chose him as the new coadjutor and submitted his name to the Holy Father for approval. On October 29, 1880, the official selection of Patrick Manogue as coadjutor bishop of Grass Valley and Titular Bishop of Ceremos was promulgated.

One year later, Bishop Manogue wrote to tell Cardinal Simeoni that he too had almost declined the appointment. He wrote:

> The two priests named for the coadjutorship before me refused— [then follow several unreadable words] especially the disposition of the Bishop, his unpopularity, and particularly with religious Orders. It seemed I was reserved as the long-looked-for victim for the oblation. Knowing all these things I was also after my nomination determined to refuse. The priests of the Diocese aware of this wrote me both publicly and privately, both collectively and individually without single exception, requesting me for the good of religion to accept, and they in turn, gave the most positive assurance of their obedience and cooperation. This document they drew up after their retreat last winter and with all the names of the priests attached, without a single exception they published this memorial in public and before the world. For the good of religion, the diocese and the priests, I sacrificed my own private feelings and convictions. The priests hoped for a change and relief from maladministration.[451]

THE REV. PATRICK KIRLEY, 1841–1901
First Pastor of Alturas, Calif., 1883–1885
Twice Pastor of Crescent City, Calif., 1887–1892 & 1893–1896
Pastor of Weaverville, Calif., 1896–1898
Pastor of Lincoln, Calif., 1898–1901
(Photo, courtesy of Sisters of Mercy, Grass Valley)

The consecration of the new coadjutor took place in (Old) St. Mary's Cathedral in San Francisco on January 16, 1881, with Archbishop Alemany as consecrator, assisted by Bishop O'Connell and Bishop Mora.[452] Both the old Bishop and the new bishop-elect had made a retreat together at St. Ignatius College in San Francisco which they began on January 5, 1881.[453] We can be sure that each must have prayed sincerely for the grace and strength to be able to work together, the one knowing he had to deal with a difficult man who was still the ordinary, the other knowing that he had a very strong and able coadjutor from whom he could expect opposition. Both needed a great deal of grace for the three difficult years which lay ahead.

Sources for Chapter XIV

429. ASRC, Vol. 172, F633.

430. ASRC, Vol. 24, F386.

431. ASRC, Vol. 177, F86A.

432. McGloin, *California's First Archbishop*, p. 246.

433. ASRC, Vol. 22, F664.

434. ASRC, Vol. 1004, F807.

435. ASRC, Vol. 1004, F799.

436. *The Monitor,* October 16, 1875.

437. AALA, letter of Prendergast to Franchi refusing appointment.

438. ASRC, Vol. 100, F804.

439. ASRC, Vol. 27, F1269, Alemany to Franchi.

440. ASRC, Vol. 27, F1271.

441. ASRC, Vol. 1009, F636, Simeoni's Summary to the Cardinals of Propaganda.

442. ASRC, Vol. 1009, F711.

443. Sister M. Gerald La Voy, O.P., "The Foundation and Early Growth of St.

Mary's Hospital, Reno, Nevada," Catholic University, Washington, D.C., 1960, pp. 10ff.

444. ASRC, Vol. 38, F534.

445. ASRC, Vol. 38, F527.

446. ASRC, Vol. 38, F530 and F531.

447. La Voy, op. cit., pp. 15, 16.

448. Ley, op. cit., pp. 155–157.

449. ASRC, Vol. 1009, F695. Summary prepared by the Cardinal Prefect of Propaganda.

450. Ibid.

45.1 Ley, op. cit., p. 162.

452. Code, op. cit.

453. Riordan, op. cit.

Chapter XV

THE UNSETTLED YEARS, 1881–1886

When the month of February, 1881, arrived, it found the bishop of Grass Valley noting the twentieth anniversary of his incumbency as ordinary and the arrival of his new coadjutor, both milestones in the progress of the diocese.

Because it was the twentieth anniversary, Bishop O'Connell was required to make a report to Rome, and for the first time his report was made out according to a form which Rome sent him and which has been preserved in its archives. It is a seven-page manuscript carefully written in Latin in Eugene O'Connell's best handwriting. It was a good time to make a report, just as he was about to end his sole administration of the diocese, a good opportunity to compare with what he began twenty years previously, six parishes and six priests.

The report shows that there were now twenty-five parishes and thirty-one priests. What he does not state in the report is the fact that twice the number of priests presently in the diocese had actually served in the diocese in the twenty years. Of these, eight were deceased, four of them buried in the Marysville priests' plot. Six had served a long number of years and had then departed, such well-known names as Bernard Morris, Bernardine Sheehan, Patrick Henneberry, John M. Mevel, Edward Kelly, and Charles Becker. But there were also another fourteen or more whose stays had been short, some by their own choice, but

STATUS OF THE DIOCESE OF GRASS VALLEY, FEBRUARY 1881, at end of Bishop O'Connell's sole reign of 20 years

	Year of Founding	Parish	Name of Church	Name of Pastor	Catholic Population	Mission Churches and Stations	Institutions
			CALIFORNIA				
1)	1852	MARYSVILLE	St. Joseph	Thomas Grace Asst. M. Dillon	1500	Oroville	NOTRE DAME SISTERS School: 105 pupils
2)	1871	"	Immac. Conc.	L. Buholzer			
3)	1853	WEAVERVILLE	St. Patrick	James J. Claire	no estimate	St. Patricks, French Gulch St. Patricks, Oregon Gulch	
4)	1855	GRASS VALLEY	St. Patrick	Thomas J. Dalton Asst. M. Walsh	850		SISTERS OF MERCY School: 109 pupils Orphanage: Girls 89 Boys 89 Boarders: 40
5)	1855	YREKA	SS Peter & Paul	Leon Haupts	800	SS John & Paul, Callaghan St. Joseph, Sawyers Bar	SISTERS OF MERCY School: 40 pupils Boarders: 23
6)	1856	DOWNIEVILLE	Immac. Conc.	Patrick Kirley	400	St. Michael, Alleghany;Forest City St. Thomas, Sierra City;La Porte	
7)	1861	FOREST HILL	St. Joseph	Thomas Petit	541	Michigan Bluff;Colfax St. Joseph's, Iowa Hill,Dutch Flat	
8)	1863	MENDOCINO CITY	St. Anthony	John F. Sheridan D. Governo	no estimate	Navarro	
9)	1863	BIG VALLEY	St. Turibius	Asst. Luciano Osuna	200		
10)	1863	EUREKA (Humboldt)	St. Bernard	Charles Lynch	750	Arcata	SISTERS OF MERCY School: 90 pupils
11)	1867	NEVADA CITY	St. Canice	Daniel Meagher	700		
12)	1867	RED BLUFF	St. Mary's	James Hunt	350	Assumption, Horsetown Holy Cross, Shasta	
13)	1868	TRUCKEE	Assumption	William Moloney	no estimate		

	Year of Founding	Parish	Name of Church	Name of Pastor	Catholic Population	Mission Churches and Stations	Institutions
14)	1869	CRESCENT CITY	St. Michael	Bernard McFeeley	220	Holy Trinity, Trinidad	
15)	1870	COLUSA	O. L. of Lourdes	Michael Walrath	305	Holy Cross, Grand Island	
16)	1870	FERNDALE	Assumption	Lawrence Kennedy	600	St. Patrick's, Table Bluff	
17)	1872	SMARTSVILLE	Immac. Conc.	Mathew Coleman	500 no estimate	Holy Cross, Cherokee Flat Stony Creek	
18)	1878	CHICO	St. John the Baptist	James J. Hynes	no estimate	St. Thomas, Moores Flat; Columbia Hill	
19)	1879	CHEROKEE	St. Patrick	William Clarke		St. Columbkill, Birchville; French Corrd	
		NEVADA					DAUGHTERS OF CHARITY School: 215 girls; 90 boys
20)	1862	VIRGINIA CITY	St. Mary's	Daniel O'Sullivan Asst: Thomas Nugent	2,000		Orphanage: 135 boys & girls Hospital
21)	1863	GOLDHILL	St. Patrick's	John M. Nulty Asst. Patrick O'Kane	500		
22)	1865	CARSON CITY	St. Theresa	Luke Tormey	200		
23)	1865	AUSTIN	St. Augustine	Joseph Phelan	600	Andrew O'Donnell absent on leave in Ireland	
24)	1871	RENO	St. Thomas	James J. Callan	no estimate		DOMINICAN SISTERS School: 106 pupils Boarders: 12
25)	1872	EUREKA	St. Brendan	Dominic Monteverde	600	Sts. Peter & Paul, Hamilton Cherry Creek; Pioche	
	Parishes in Diocese: 25		Priests: 31	Catholic Population: 15,000		Mission Churches: 32 Total School Enrollment: 800	Convents: 6

also some whom Bishop O'Connell had dismissed for various reasons. In fact, in the report the Bishop states that one of the problems had been that "some Bishops far too easily grant letters of recommendations to wandering priests in order to remove them from their dioceses where they have given scandal." Bishop O'Connell had never been slow to invite such to move on when they gave similar cause for concern in his diocese.

The report further shows that fifteen of the parishes had thirty-two mission chapels; that there was a Catholic population of approximately 15,000 souls. The Bishop then listed for Rome the Catholic population of most of the parishes in the diocese, omitting only six for which he had no statistics. He informed Rome that there were six convents of sisters, teaching about eight hundred children. It is from this document that we learn that Bishop O'Connell had performed only two ordination ceremonies, those of Lawrence Kennedy and Michael Walrath. Especially in the early days he had allowed several of his young priests to be ordained in San Francisco. He ends the report by stating that in the past ten years he had granted 256 dispensations for mixed marriages and 112 from disparity of cult, as well as 7 from the impediment of consanguinity.[454]

It was in the same month that the new coadjutor arrived after a triumphant visitation, following his consecration, to the Jesuit communities at St. Ignatius College in San Francisco and at Santa Clara College. It was decided that Bishop Manogue would continue to reside in Virginia City, but that Father Daniel O'Sullivan would become the official pastor of St. Mary's in the Mountains. One other change among the pastors was to be accomplished by Bishop Manogue which might have been the first sign of a struggle between the two bishops. While still in San Francisco, Bishop Manogue had entered negotiations with Archbishop Alemany for a rearrangement of diocesan boundaries so that the city of Sacramento would eventually be included in the Grass Valley diocese, which lacked any principal city. This arrangement also included agreement that a Grass Valley priest would become pastor of Sacramento's only parish church, St. Rose. Now the one chosen for this post by Bishop Manogue was the pastor of Marysville, Father Thomas Grace. As a solace to Bishop O'Connell, Father James Callan, who seems to have been much appreciated by the old Bishop, was brought back from

Weaverville to be pastor of Marysville for the second time. It was obvious from the start that Bishop Manogue had his heart set on moving the see to Sacramento. This was eventually to cause problems between himself and Bishop O'Connell.

The year 1882 was a busy one for the two bishops. In the spring of the year, Archbishop Alemany called together the Second Provincial Council for the Province of San Francisco, starting on April 30, at which were present the two bishops of Grass Valley and Bishop Francis Mora of Monterey. (Old) St. Mary's Cathedral was the setting for this Council which lasted until May 4, 1882.[455] This time Bishop O'Connell was not the secretary but rather Father Prendergast who had been the first choice as coadjutor of Grass Valley but who had refused the honor. One month before this Council, the bishops had met to propose another list of names for the coadjutor of San Francisco, still an unsettled question, which once again was to meet with frustration. Shortly after the Council meeting, the bishops begans their visitations, O'Connell remaining in California and Manogue covering the Nevada portion of the diocese. Bishop O'Connell went first to Weaverville and Yreka in August. Bishop Manogue began a circuit of Nevada which amounted to a triumphal homecoming. On Sunday, September 3, he was in Austin with Father Phelan. Then, accompanied by Father William Moloney, the two, in a horse and carriage, covered a six-hundred-mile circuit which included all of eastern Nevada, Eureka, Cherry Creek, Bristol, Hamilton, Treasure City, Pioche, and all the small camps and settlements near the Utah border. When the two reached the Central Pacific line, Bishop Manogue boarded the westbound train for Reno and thence back to Virginia City.[456] Bishop O'Connell set out in late September for the most remote California parish, Crescent City. As was his custom, he traveled to San Francisco where he boarded a northbound ocean vessel. The weather was severe and the voyage very rough so that the aging Bishop suffered from seasickness. In Crescent City, Father McFeeley had nine boys and six girls prepared for confirmation.[457] While Bishop O'Connell stayed on in Crescent City to regain his strength for the voyage home, the priests of the diocese had gathered in Marysville for a retreat given by Father Raffo, a Jesuit, at which Bishop Manogue was present. What transpired at the end of that Retreat must certainly have been heartwarming to Bishop Manogue, but since it was written up and publicized, the feelings of the rejected old bishop upon reading it can only be surmised.

On Sunday evening, after the Retreat for the priests of the Diocese of Grass Valley closed at Marysville, a very happy reunion of the clergymen took place for the purpose of making a presentation to Bishop Manogue. A crozier, mitre, and magnificent set of Pontificales were purchased by the priests who anxiously awaited an opportunity for presenting them to the Bishop of their choice.

Accordingly at 8 P.M. the clergy met the Bishop in the parlors of the Episcopal residence at Marysville. The articles to be presented—a handsome serviceable crozier, two mitres and the richly-bound Pontificales—were laid out for inspection. When all had arrived, Father Coleman of Smartsville arose and addressing the Bishop said that they had come together for the purpose of presenting their Bishop with some slight proof of the affection they all entertained for him. No time had been given for the preparation of any formal presentation address, but there was no danger of any lack of words to-night, since every heart was overflowing with joy and satisfaction at seeing Bishop Manogue amongst them. The presentation was made to the Bishop because, in the first place, his priests regarded him as a man, who by his knowledge of the world, his insight into human nature, his deep and varied learning and his profound common sense was eminently fitted for the commanding position to which he was raised; and secondly because he was one of themselves, one who rose from the ranks; and all felt honored and flattered by the choice of Rome falling on one whom his brother priests regarded as the man for the place. No one there that night need be told that in Bishop Manogue the priests would have a Bonus Pastor, a father whose whole care and desire would be to see his spiritual children—the priests—zealous, efficient, and as happy as their lives of toil and privation would permit. Father Coleman concluded by saying that he but voiced the general sentiments of his brother priests by expressing the earnest hope that Bishop Manogue would be spared to rule them for many happy years, with the prudence, the firmness, and the clemency he knew so well how to commingle.

During the address of Father Coleman, who spoke with an earnestness and feeling evident to all, the Bishop was visibly moved. When he arose and began to reply, it was in a voice trembling with emotions. "The duty," said the Bishop, "of responding to the flattering address of Father Coleman is a somewhat difficult one. No one feels more keenly, or appreciates more fully than I do, the motives that actuated you all in making me this presentation. I recognize in it your desire of showing the kindly feelings of friendship that you entertain towards me, and I need scarcely tell you that now as in the past, those feelings are fully reciprocated. I accept the beautiful articles with sincere and grateful thanks, and when using them in my sacred ministrations I shall be reminded of the kind friends whom I am so proud and happy to meet to-night, and for whose welfare I shall ever pray."

When Bishop Manogue had concluded his remarks which were received with the greatest warmth, Father Dalton of Grass Valley arose and said that for himself this was a peculiarly happy occasion, as he had known the Bishop for very many years, and even before his ordination had recognized in him the noble qualities that never changed but were only more fully developed in after years, qualities that Rome had recognized in conferring on him the high dignity for which he was so eminently qualified. After Fathers Callan, Lynch, Grace and O'Sullivan had spoken in a similar strain, Father Buholzer the beloved Pastor of the German Church in Marysville took occasion to say, that he was glad to be allowed the opportunity of offering his congratulations to Bishop Manogue and assured him how pleased he was to be able to co-operate with his brother priests in giving the Bishop some tangible proof of the warmth and earnestness of their friendship for him the Bishop of their choice. Afterwards Father Tanham, a recently ordained priest, spoke in very suitable terms for himself and his class-fellows, two of whom sat by him, assuring Bishop Manogue that he felt honored in being allowed to add his meed of congratulation, and to express the hope that Bishop Manogue would be ruling the diocese in years to come, when himself and his young confreres would be the venerable pastors of flourishing missions.

Altogether the reunion was a most happy one. Bishop Manogue with the ease and tact that he has made his own, entered fully into the spirit of the occasion, and made all the priests feel that he appreciated and heartily returned the kindly feelings that suggested the idea of presenting him with an outfit that is both handsome and serviceable.[458]

The article mentions several priests about whom some comments should be made at this time. It was Fathers Dalton, Coleman, Meagher, and Lynch who were the signers of the letter to Propaganda Fidei on November 23, 1877, asking for Manogue to be the new bishop. Two of the young priests mentioned were the products of All Hallows in 1882, Fathers James Tanham and Michael O'Reilly. Father Cornelius C. McGrath had been ordained from St. Vincent's Seminary, Latrobe, Pennsylvania, on July 6, 1882. All three were men for whom Bishop O'Connell had continued to sacrifice whatever money he had to pay both their tuition and their passage money to the diocese. But it was easy to forget the old Bishop when caught up in the joy of the welcome of the man who was to be their ordinary for some years to come. Father Tanham had been ordained on November 13, 1881, and on his arrival in Marysville had been appointed to serve there as an assistant in May, 1882. Father Michael O'Reilly had been ordained on June 25, 1882; he and Father McGrath were newly arrived at the time of the retreat. Father O'Reilly was to become in December the new pastor of Forest Hill, a post he would hold for ten years. Father McGrath's whereabouts in the early years of his priesthood have not been established.

One other priest mentioned in the article about the clergy retreat was Father Buholzer, the pastor of the German Church of the Immaculate Conception in Marysville. It seems that the decline in the German population in Marysville caused the closing of this parish at about this time. Father Buholzer remained for another couple of years as "pastor at large" of the Germans in the diocese. Bishop O'Connell would send for him the following year to help him during his long visit in Eureka. Eventually Father Grace would receive him as a full-time assistant at St. Rose in Sacramento. He remained until the establishment of the Sac-

THE REV. MICHAEL KIELY, 1858–1936
Pastor of Cherokee, Nevada Co., Calif., 1882–1884
Last Pastor of Eureka, Nevada, 1884–1887
Pastor of Reno, Nevada, 1887–1897
Pastor of Ferndale, Calif., 1898–1912
Pastor of Grass Valley, 1912–1919
Pastor of Colusa, Calif., 1912–1922
Retired in Sacramento until his death in 1936.
(Photo, courtesy of Sisters of Mercy, Grass Valley)

ramento diocese, at which time he left the diocese. The church in Marysville, meanwhile, was dismantled and used in the construction of the new church erected by Father Walrath as a mission chapel in Williams.[459]

One other major change was made at this time. Since Manogue had been Vicar General for the state of Nevada and since he was now the bishop, the question came up of a new Vicar General for Nevada. Whether Father Dalton resigned the post in California or whether the "new broom" simply swept clean is not known, but the newly appointed Vicars General were Father Matthew Coleman for California and Father Daniel O'Sullivan for Nevada.[460] Most probably Bishop O'Connell removed Father Dalton from the position as he was displeased with the pastor of Grass Valley at that time. It seems that Father Dalton refused to send the Cathedraticum for the support of the bishop. "He does not want to give the Cathedraticum to his Ordinary nor even a salary to any assistants I send him. What must I do," he wrote to Propaganda, "to the one occupying the Cathedral Church?"[461] Evidently Bishop O'Connell found his answer.

The year 1882 ended with Bishop Manogue's administering confirmation in Forest Hill on November 5 and in Nevada City on November 12, and on November 19 he was in Red Bluff to dedicate the new church built by Father James Hunt and to bless the newly established convent of Sisters of Mercy which had opened in September with seventy pupils and twelve boarders.[462] The year closed with publication of a joint pastoral letter on mixed marriages issued by the ordinaries of the three California dioceses, Grass Valley, San Francisco, and Monterey–Los Angeles.

The year 1883, Bishop O'Connell's last full year as bishop of Grass Valley, was not a very happy one. To begin with, he became so ill that there was concern he might not live. *The Monitor* sought for prayers in the following words at the beginning of May:

> Our esteemed friend, Bishop O'Connell of Marysville, has been seriously indisposed during the past week and we ask the prayers of our readers that his life may be spared, as the loss of a Prelate possessing such wisdom, prudence and charity would be a serious calamity to the Catholic Community in general.[463]

THE REV. MICHAEL WALSH, 1852–1898
Pastor of Weaverville, Calif., 1879–1880
Pastor of Cherokee, Nevada Co., Calif., 1881–1882
Pastor of Sonora, Calif., 1887–1889
Pastor of Carson City, Nevada, 1889–1890
Assistant in Woodland, Calif., 1890–1892
Pastor of Sacramento Cathedral, 1892–1898
(Photo, courtesy of Sisters of Mercy, Grass Valley)

The aging Bishop recovered, so that by mid-August he embarked on the long trip to Eureka where he spent the month of September in an exhausting visitation and giving of confirmations in Eureka, Arcata, and Ferndale. This was the occasion when he sent for Father Buholzer to come and assist him. On September 8, 1883, he blessed the new altar and tabernacle in the Mercy Convent in Eureka and the newly renovated convent and school.[464]

Bishop O'Connell arrived back in San Francisco at the end of September. Meanwhile, Bishop Manogue was on a three-week tour which took him for the first time to Weaverville and its two missions of Oregon Gulch and French Gulch, in company with Father J. J. Claire, the pastor.[465] The annual clergy retreat was held in Marysville in mid-October in the midst of delightful weather. Possibly at this retreat was the lone ordinand of All Hallows for 1883, Father Hugh McCabe, who began his duties as an assistant in Marysville, the only assignment he ever had. He died on July 6, 1890, after a short priesthood of only seven years, at the age of thirty-nine.[466]

The previous June, word was received that Archbishop Alemany had finally received a coadjutor in the person of Father Patrick Riordan who had been a parish priest in the Archdiocese of Chicago. The way had finally been paved for a completely new administration for the church in California.

Among Bishop O'Connell's last acts for 1883 was the founding of the last parish in the diocese during his administration. Arcata was cut off from Eureka in November, 1883, with Father Thomas Nugent as the first pastor. His final act was the dedication on November 11 of a new mission church in Gridley, a mission of Chico. On this occasion, the famous Jesuit Father Bouchard was the preacher.[467]

Bishop O'Connell ended 1883 by writing a letter on New Year's Eve to Propaganda Fidei asking to be allowed to resign. His letter read as follows:

> From 30 priests ministering in this Diocese scarcely twelve can pay the Cathedraticum. About eight Rectors pay the Ordinary $50 per year, the rest $20 or $25. These meager returns divided into two do not suffice for an Ordinary and a Coadjutor. For me, however, once I have been removed from governing this Diocese, through your Eminence's

help, Mass Stipends and voluntary offerings of the faithful will suffice. Furthermore there is scarcely a Rector either in this Diocese or in the Metropolitan See who will not receive me into their homes.

Therefore I plead that you deign to remove me from my stewardship. Experience has taught your servant that a divided empire not only does not go forward, but actually goes backward.[468]

What Bishop O'Connell was referring to here was the widening rift between himself and the coadjutor. There was no question about the feelings of Bishop Manogue. He was pushing for a change of boundaries and the inclusion of the city of Sacramento into the diocese. Bishop O'Connell stated this in a letter to Cardinal Simeoni on June 27, 1883: "Until it pleases the Holy See to add the city of Sacramento to the Diocese of Grass Valley, my Coadjutor will not be content." Bishop O'Connell at first went along with the proposal.[469] He signed the original petition for the change, which was sent to Rome on February 24, 1881, and which was signed by all the bishops of the Province. But by March, 1882, Bishop O'Connell had reversed his decision. He wrote claiming that he refused to add any more territory to his diocese until "the Holy See would provide a Bishop for the State of Nevada, and until it would please the Lord of the Vineyard to send more workers into our fields." Bishop Manogue later explained this change of heart by stating that Bishop O'Connell had been "censured by some imprudent persons in Sacramento and this provoked his disgust of the people in this city, prompting him to write privately to Rome against the transfer from Grass Valley to Sacramento."[470]

Bishop Manogue, who had his heart set on this transfer, was deeply hurt by the old Bishop's action. When finally the bishops of the Province once again petitioned for the change on July 9, 1882, O'Connell refused to sign. This action split the ordinary and the coadjutor into irreconcilably opposing camps. Aware of the rift, Rome did as it had often done previously. It let the matter rest. Bishop O'Connell was sensitively aware of the problem, and although he had taken his stance from a sincere conviction, he knew the division between himself and the coadjutor was not for the good of the diocese.

A story has been handed down which illustrates Bishop

Manogue's attitude to the old Bishop. Manogue all his life was in the habit of signing his name simply: P. Manogue. When he became a bishop, correct procedure would have called for his affixing a small cross before his name. Always a stickler for detail, Bishop O'Connell, in a letter sent to him in Virginia City, once called this to Manogue's attention. Bishop Manogue answered: " 'It seems to me that one cross is enough in a Diocese.' P. Manogue."

Seeing the impossibility of the situation had prompted Bishop O'Connell's letter of New Year's Eve in 1883. When there was no reply from Rome, he pushed harder again on February 25, 1884, when he wrote:

> Once again I beg your Eminence for my dismissal because a divided rule is not conducive to the good of religion or of peace. On the contrary it does much harm, and various Rectors advise me for the good of souls and the status of their churches. Furthermore my coadjutor a few years ago gave me $2,050 which I loaned to some Sisters. Therefore that I might not be a burden on the Diocese, let me work in the Diocese for my own keep and spend the rest of my days. I can live decently.[471]

This letter provided Rome with the solution to the problem. The request was approved by the Holy Father on March 26, 1884, and Bishop O'Connell was appointed Titular Bishop of Joppa and relieved after twenty-three years of the burden which always weighed so heavily on his shoulders. Bishop Patrick Manogue automatically succeeded as the second bishop of Grass Valley. The way was now clear for him to pursue his goal without opposition.

The following month, Bishop Manogue conducted the Holy Week and Easter services in the Grass Valley cathedral, actually the first time that the ordinary of the diocese had used the cathedral church for those ceremonies.[472] Bishop O'Connell continued to reside in Marysville and conferred the sacrament of confirmation there on a large class on Pentecost Sunday, June 1, 1884.[473] However, he must have left shortly afterwards as he was not present for the funeral of one of his priests, Father Thomas Pettit, who died on July 24, 1884, at Sacramento. Father Pettit

THE REV. PATRICK J. CLYNE, 1859–1912
Pastor of Mendocino, Calif., 1886–1887
Pastor of Placerville, Calif., 1887–1892 (Photo taken here)
Pastor of Carson City, Nevada, 1892–1895
Pastor of Nevada City, Calif., 1895–1911
Pastor of Grass Valley, Calif., 1911–1912
(Photo, courtesy of Sisters of Mercy, Grass Valley)

THE REV. THOMAS TUBMAN, 1859–1931
Assistant at Virginia City, 1884–1894
Pastor of Virginia City, 1894–1904
Pastor of Reno, Nevada, 1904–1929
Affectionately known as "Dean Tubman."
Spent all his priestly life in Nevada State
(Photo, courtesy of Sisters of Mercy, Grass Valley)

had been the new pastor of Willows for about a year but had been ill during all this time. He was only forty-one at the time of his death. Although his funeral took place at St. Rose Church in Sacramento, his body was shipped by train to Marysville where it was buried on July 26, 1884, next to Father Farrelly.[474]

Two events took place in the fall of the year which would have given great joy to the old Bishop had he been present to witness them. Early in September, 1884, three Marianist brothers arrived from Dayton, Ohio, to open the long-sought-for school for boys in Marysville, a school which was to endure for only two years. Likewise, in October there arrived in the diocese the largest contingent of new priests from All Hallows since 1867.

The new arrivals were Father Thomas Tubman, Patrick J. Clyne, and Francis Reynolds who had been ordained at All Hallows on June 24, 1884, and Father Peter McDonnell who had been ordained in July. These four were followed by Father Bernard Kelly who was ordained on October 19, 1884. Their appointments, of course, were the duty of Bishop Manogue, but the credit for these new priests goes to the now-retired bishop who had paid for their support out of the meager funds of the diocese. With the death of Father Pettit and the addition of these five, the number of priests in the diocese now numbered thirty-five. But in spite of such accomplishments, the now-retired bishop poured out his feelings about his stewardship in Grass Valley in a long, undated letter written after his retirement.

> I can claim no credit for the churches erected, or the Missioners that have labored and suffered privations in this poor Diocese since my incumbency. The Convent of the Sisters of Charity in Virginia City, Nevada, the Dominican Convent in Reno, Nevada; the Convents of Mercy in Grass Valley, Nevada Co., and Tehama Co., California; the Convents of Mercy in Humboldt and Mendocino Co., California are not indebted to me except pecuniarily. On my accession to Marysville I found the Notre Dame Academy established since 1855 and flourishing despite the overflow of the rivers Yuba and Feather, first in December 1861 and in subsequent years. Whatever good has been done during my incumbency is to be attributed to the cooperation of my clergy, more especially to my late Coadjutor, the present

Bishop of Grass Valley, whilst I must only blame myself for my innumerable negligences and shortcomings. I failed repeatedly in my attempts to introduce into this Diocese Christian Brothers or Xaverian Brothers. I hadn't the adequate resource and was obliged here and there to hire teachers who couldn't cope with the salaried masters in the public schools. Hence my administration has been a great failure.[475]

During these first few months of his well-deserved vacation, Bishop O'Connell lived in Oakland to be near his brother Patrick and family. On August 28, 1884, he was present at Carmel Mission for the centennial celebration of the death of Father Junîpero Serra.[476] Meanwhile the call had come for the U.S. bishops to gather in Baltimore for the Third Plenary Council. We recall that the vicar apostolic of Marysville had been present for the Second Plenary Council in 1866. Now he was to go as one of the country's senior bishops, himself and Archbishop Alemany being among the oldest. The two friends left for the Council together on November 6, 1884.[477] The Council opened in Baltimore on November 9 and lasted one month. Bishop Manogue of Grass Valley was also present. When the bishops returned home at the end of the Council, Eugene O'Connell did not. He took the long-sought-after vacation he so justly deserved. Evidently Philadelphia was his first destination where, from mid-December for one month, he was the guest of an old friend noted for her poetic talents, Eleanor C. Donnelly.[478] A correspondent wrote that "the erudition and culture of Bishop O'Connell, combined with his singular humility and simplicity elicited the admiration of his Philadelphia friends."[479] He was present in Philadelphia on January 4, 1885, when Archbishop P. J. Ryan was invested with the pallium.[480] The sojourn in Philadelphia was prolonged by some kind of medical treatments which the Bishop needed, there being some evidence that something was wrong with his feet.

Word was received by Bishop O'Connell in February that his good friend Archbishop Alemany had also been permitted to join the ranks of the retired after thirty-five years of service in California. It was the intention of the retired archbishop to return home to his native Spain just as it was the intention of Bishop O'Connell to return to All Hallows.

Bishop O'Connell left Philadelphia on January 24, 1885, and went to Brooklyn to visit a former Maynooth associate, Father Edward Corcoran, pastor of St. Joseph's Church.[481] At the end of the month he left for New Orleans where he spent about three weeks, went to Pensacola, Florida, and then returned to New York.[482] He was back in Philadelphia at Eleanor Donnelly's before the middle of May where it was his great joy to be visited by Archbishop Alemany, who had left San Francisco on May 24, 1885, en route to Spain.[483] The retired Archbishop convinced Bishop O'Connell to accompany him back to New York. Early in June, the two prelates bade one another farewell, knowing they would never meet again in this life. While Alemany set sail for Rome, Bishop O'Connell had plans to go to Ireland in company with his friends Father Corcoran and Father James Taaffe. Something caused him to change his mind and to return to California. He was back in Oakland by the end of September, 1885.[484] In November, he was the guest of Father Patrick Dowling of St. Patrick's Church in San Jose. From there he went to Santa Cruz to visit another old friend.

It was at this time that the bishops of the state, with the exception of Manogue, began to elicit concern for the retired Bishop. Bishop Mora of Monterey–Los Angeles only knew the former bishop of Grass Valley from meeting him at the various Provincial Council meetings and at the Baltimore Council. Yet he was the first to offer him hospitality in his diocese. On November 23, 1885, Bishop Mora wrote extending the faculties of the diocese to Bishop O'Connell and offering him the use of a house in Los Angeles.[485] One month later, Archbishop Riordan, who was still new to the West and scarcely knew the old Bishop at all, wrote extending him the use of rooms in his home.[486] This was quite a contrast to the treatment accorded him by the second bishop of Grass Valley.

Manogue had been a very independent ruler of his Nevada territory from Virginia City. No one interfered with or opposed the pastor of St. Mary's in the Mountains. In other words, Manogue was a bit spoiled. Now, as bishop, he had to live within the restrictions imposed on him by his predecessors and subject to a metropolitan archbishop who was younger and new to the West. The first opposition had come from Bishop O'Connell and Manogue didn't like it. When he met with some resistance from Archbishop Riordan, Manogue retaliated with some bitterness and attacked both of the old bishops, Alemany and O'Connell. As Manogue shrunk in stature by such actions, Riordan grew by showing great respect and consideration for the pioneer bishops who had built up the church which they had inherited to administer. Bishop O'Connell's first struggle with his successor after retirement came from his attempt to have his belongings sent to him. He had written to Bishop Manogue informing him of his wishes in this matter, but Manogue had not only not answered but had made no attempt to oblige the old Bishop. Finally, because Manogue intended to move into the Marysville rectory, Father Callan had written to Bishop O'Connell for instructions. Bishop O'Connell replied that he wanted his books, paintings, and chalice sent to the home of Mrs. Moore in Marysville and that he would arrange matters further with her. Instead, the books were shipped to the Oakland home of the Bishop's brother and a couple of books which the retired Bishop prized were missing, together with the paintings. This treatment very much disturbed Bishop O'Connell.[487]

Meanwhile Father Callan, as pastor of Marysville, had written to Bishop O'Connell on November 25, 1885, lamenting the fact that the Bishop had left Marysville rather abruptly to attend the Baltimore Council and since he had not returned, his many friends in Marysville as well as the clergy had no opportunity to show their appreciation for his many years of service. Father Callan then suggested that since 1886 would be the 25th Jubilee year of Bishop O'Connell's consecration as bishop, he could think of no better time to render such a testimonial than St. Patrick's Day in 1886, and therefore he was inviting Bishop O'Connell to come for that occasion.[488]

But although at first pleased by the invitation when it came in November, by early March Bishop O'Connell did not feel he would be truly welcome. Thus he wrote to his friend Mrs. Moore: "Such high handed proceedings and the detention of what belongs to me give me reason to expect a cool reception at the hands of my clerical friends in Marysville."[489]

Therefore Bishop O'Connell chose not to accept the invitation to celebrate his Jubilee in Marysville. There is evidence that he celebrated the event with the Dominican fathers in Benicia, probably with his friend Father Vincent Vinyes who had been his choice for coadjutor when Father Prendergast had declined the honor.[490] Besides the celebration of the event at Benicia, there is no evidence of further celebration of the completion of twenty-five years as bishop. *The Monitor*, however, whose editors always held Bishop O'Connell in high regard, published two poetical works written for the occasion in their February 17, 1886, issue.[491]

Bishop O'Connell did not let the matter of his meager possessions rest. The paintings of the Blessed Virgin had been gifts of Cardinals Cullen and Moran, and the Baltimore Memorial and the Vatican Council album were prized possessions. He eventually received the Baltimore Memorial but not the Vatican Album. He also had two medals he had left behind which he wanted, the one given him by Pope Pius IX and the other by Mr. Edward McLaughlin.[492]

It was in one of his letters written regarding his possessions that Bishop O'Connell revealed for the first time that he had received no pension from Bishop Manogue since his retirement. "I also reminded his Lordship (who has not paid me *one cent* since my resignation) of my right guaranteed by the Holy See, to a decent support during my declining years. But no reply has come from the Right Rev. gentleman."[493] Eventually both Archbishop Riordan and Bishop Mora found out about the situation and both appealed to Rome for something to be done about it. The word was sent to Spain to Archbishop Alemany who also appealed to Rome on behalf of Bishop O'Connell.

Although it is difficult to sympathize with Bishop Manogue, yet it must be said on his behalf that Bishop O'Connell had, on the occasion of his retirement, knowing the financial status of the diocese, renounced all claim to any support, stating that he would get by on Mass offerings and gifts. However, he found out that this was not possible. Archbishop Riordan wrote to Rome stating that Bishop O'Connell was helplessly destitute, too poor even to buy a winter coat. Cardinal Simeoni responded at once with a letter to Bishop Manogue asking why he had not sent the pension recommended earlier. "This I do not want to believe," wrote Cardinal Simeoni.[494]

This was the last straw as far as Bishop Manogue was concerned. He broke out in a most unfortunate attack on Bishop O'Connell and Archbishop Alemany, the one for being inadequate, the other for his artful cunning who took advantage of O'Connell's ineptitude! Cardinal Simeoni reported these accusations to Archbishop Riordan who rose to the old Bishop's defense.

"He possesses nothing," wrote Riordan. "A priest for nearly fifty years and a Bishop for twenty-seven who had labored selflessly in the poorest Diocese of California, he had made no provisions for his advanced age. The Diocese should allot much more after nearly a quarter of a century of faithful service to its founder," who in Riordan's judgment, was a

> ... learned, saintly, industrious Bishop, a shepherd of his people and a model for his clergy. In the matter of money he always acted with the simplicity of a baby, without regard or estimate of its worth, almost without knowing what to do with it. But it cannot be said that he had ever spent funds in an evil fashion or to his own advantage because he always lived poorly and with great parsimony. He did what he could, not always, it is true with sound judgment, according to hindsight, but always with the best intentions in the world and for the welfare and advance of the Church.

The archbishop then suggested an annual pension of $1,000.[495]

In the same letter, the archbishop attacked the accusation that his own predecessor had been crafty. In defense of Archbishop Alemany, Riordan wrote that the former archbishop was "entirely incapable of any unjust thought or action. He may not have been a brilliant financier but he was a great Bishop and one of the saintliest I have ever known."

Archbishop Riordan explained to Cardinal Simeoni that he had long been aware of the injustice to Bishop O'Connell but that he had kept out of the matter for fear of antagonizing further the new bishop of Grass Valley with whom he still had to get along for the good of the church in the state.

Cardinal Simeoni settled the matter in an astute manner. Rather than write directly to Manogue, he decided to use an intermediary in the person of the rector of North American College in Rome. Monsignor Denis O'Connell let it be known to Bishop Manogue that the retired Bishop must be given a pension at once and that if it were not done willingly it would have to be done by any means necessary. Rome was ready to use reprisals but pre-

THE RT. REV. FRANCIS MORA, 1827–1905
Second Bishop of Monterey–Los Angeles from 1878–1896.
(Photo, courtesy of Archives of Archdiocese of Los Angeles)

ferred to warn Manogue so that the action taken would appear in the eyes of all to be spontaneously his own. Furthermore, Rome was to be apprised of the action he would take. Bishop Manogue sent $500 to Bishop O'Connell, the entire proceeds of the Cathedraticum for 1886, and promised to send regular support thereafter.[496]

Perhaps the fact that Bishop Manogue got his way in the matter of the boundary changes modified somewhat this severe reprimand from Rome. He had first received a cablegram from Rome in December, 1885, that he could go ahead and count on the change. It was made official on May 16, 1886, but the official documents were not received until the end of July. Bishop Manogue continued to sign himself bishop of Grass Valley all through May, June, and July. It was not until the official documents arrived that the public announcement was made of the transfer of the see from Grass Valley to Sacramento. By September, Bishop Manogue was signing himself as "Bishop of Sacramento."

The new boundaries abandoned the 39th parallel as the dividing line; county lines became the diocesan boundaries. The two counties of Mendocino and Lake were transferred to San Francisco and ten counties, mostly in the foothills formerly in the archdiocese, became the responsibility of the bishop of Sacramento. At about the same time, a vicariate apostolic was created in Utah, and the eastern half of the state of Nevada was given to the new vicariate. The new boundaries in California were to endure until 1962 when further divisions occurred. The state of Nevada had become a diocese in 1931.

The old Diocese of Grass Valley had survived two and a half years from the resignation of its founding bishop. As the new Diocese of Sacramento began its life, Bishop O'Connell began a new phase of his life, the "Los Angeles years."

As stated previously, Bishop Mora showed extraordinary concern for Bishop O'Connell. He wrote to the retired bishop in Oakland on May 17, 1886, explaining that he intended to go to Europe and asking O'Connell to come down and help out. There was no hesitancy in Bishop O'Connell's reply, except to ask if he should bring his "Cappa Magna," the large cape worn by bishops when presiding at ceremonies. Bishop Mora replied affirmatively, thereby assuring Bishop O'Connell that he was expected to help out in the diocese.[497] The retired bishop left for Los Angeles in the middle of June to be with Bishop Mora a few weeks before the latter's departure for Europe.⁴⁹⁸ Thus began the final phase of Eugene O'Connell's priestly life.

Sources for Chapter XV

454. ASRC, Vol. 35, F172.

455. McGloin, *California's First Archbishop*, pp. 304–305.

456. *The Monitor*, September 13, 1882.

457. Ibid., October 11, 1882.

458. Ibid., October 18, 1882.

459. Walsh, *Hallowed Were*, p. 358.

460. ASRC, Vol. 35, F991.

461. Ibid.

462. *The Monitor*, November 29, 1882.

463. Ibid., May 2, 1882.

464. Ibid., September 12, 1883.

465. Ibid., October 3, 1883.

466. Death Register, St. Joseph's, Marysville; entry for July 9, 1890.

467. *The Monitor*, November 14, 1883.

468. ASRC, Vol. 39, F1122.

469. ASRC, Vol. 38, F301, O'Connell to Simeoni, June 27, 1883.

470. Riordan, op. cit., p. 148.

471. ASRC, Vol. 40, F392.

472. *The Monitor*, April 23, 1884.

473. Confirmation Records, St. Joseph's, Marysville.

474. *Marysville Daily Appeal*, July 27, 1884.

475. Archives of Archdiocese of Philadelphia.

476. *The Monitor,* September 3, 1884.
477. Ibid., October 29, 1884.
478. AUND, Daniel E. Hudson, C.S.C., Papers, letter of December 13, 1884.
479. *The Monitor,* January 7, 1885.
480. Ibid.
481. AUND, Daniel E. Hudson, C.S.C., Papers, letter of January 24, 1885.
482. Ibid., letter of May 19, 1885.
483. McGloin, *California's First Archbishop,* p. 337.
484. *The Monitor,* September 30, 1885.
485. AALA, Mora to O'Connell, November 23, 1885.
486. AALA, Riordan to O'Connell, December 21, 1885.
487. AALA, O'Connell to Mrs. Moore, March 4, 1886.
488. AALA, Callan to O'Connell, November 25, 1885.
489. AALA, O'Connell to Mrs. Moore, March 4, 1886.
490. *The Monitor,* January 27, 1886.
491. Ibid., February 17, 1886.
492. AALA, O'Connell to Mrs. Moore, no date.
493. AALA, O'Connell to Mrs. Moore, March 20, 1886.
494. James P. Gaffey, *Citizen of No Mean City, Life of Patrick W. Riordan, Archbishop of San Francisco* (Washington, D.C.: Catholic University Press, 1975), p. 159.
495. Ibid.
496. Ibid., p. 161.
497. AALA, Mora to O'Connell, May 28, 1886.
498. *The Monitor,* June 23, 1886.

Chapter XVI

THE "LOS ANGELES YEARS," 1886–1891

The Bishop of Joppa, as he was now officially designated, obviously did not go to Los Angeles to retire. His very active schedule over the next five years demonstrates that the little Bishop had great vitality.

One of his first acts in the absence of Bishop Mora was to lay the cornerstone of the new St. Vincent's Church in Los Angeles on Sunday, July 25, 1886.[499] By the middle of September he had overtaxed himself so that he was listed as seriously ill for about ten days at the end of that month.[500]

Bishop O'Connell lived in the cathedral rectory with the Vicar General, Father Joachim Adam, who was its rector and his very gracious host. Bishop O'Connell was therefore present on June 8, 1887, when Father Adam marked the silver Jubilee of his ordination.[501] At the end of July, Bishop O'Connell was in San Francisco, having been chosen as co-consecrator with Archbishop Riordan of the newly designated vicar apostolic of Utah, Lawrence Scanlan, whose consecration as a bishop took place in (Old) St. Mary's Cathedral on July 29, 1887.[502] This must have been a milestone for Eugene O'Connell, passing on down to a successor the episcopal dignity together with the jurisdiction over Utah and all of eastern Nevada, the territory which was once so underdeveloped and had been the responsibility of Bishop O'Connell.

In the summer of 1888, Eugene O'Connell came north to

visit his brother and his friends. It seems that he paid a visit to Marysville where *The Monitor* states he presided at the closing exercise of St. Joseph's School for Boys, a project he had never been able to realize while he was ordinary and for which he considered himself a failure.[503] By early October, Eugene O'Connell was back in Los Angeles.[504]

Some have wondered why, since he loved Ireland so very much, he did not return to his native country and to All Hallows. Although there exist no statements on the matter, it is not too difficult to understand why he did not return to the place where his heart had been all those years. It had been twenty-seven years since he had left All Hallows. A whole new generation was there now, both teachers and students. His old friends were either dead or on other assignments. His family was gone, with the possible exception of one brother. His sister and his brother Patrick, to whose family Bishop O'Connell was very attached, lived in Oakland. There seems to have been no reason to return to Ireland. A dream of many years, of being able to go back to the All Hallows he knew, just remained a dream as the reality did not exist.

Evidently the esteem of the Los Angeles clergy grew and Bishop O'Connell was welcome and was invited to all functions. On February 5, 1889, he was once again invited to St. Vincent's, Los Angeles, this time to conduct the ceremonies for the blessing of the new parish school.[505] In the same month he was present with Bishop Mora when the latter laid the cornerstone of the new Sacred Heart Church in East Los Angeles.[506]

On February 21, 1889, Bishop O'Connell accompanied Bishop Mora to San Gabriel to attend a Requiem Mass for the father of Father C. Scannell, the rector of San Gabriel. Father Scannell had lived at the cathedral with Bishop O'Connell and had recently been transferred as pastor of San Gabriel. When the news of the death of the father of this priest came from Ireland, the Mass was planned for the repose of his soul.[507] In June, once again Bishop O'Connell accompanied Bishop Mora, this time to Pomona for the dedication of the new church there.[508]

In May, 1889, Bishop O'Connell blessed a new crucifix which was placed over the main altar of the cathedral. On the occasion of the eleventh anniversary of the consecration of Bishop Mora, Bishop O'Connell accompanied him to the entertainment put on for the occasion by the students at the Immaculate Heart Convent.[509] Again in the late summer, possibly to escape the heat of August and September, Bishop O'Connell left for the north to spend some time with his brother's family and his friends in the Bay area.[510] Whether he visited in Marysville is not known.

Bishop O'Connell commenced the year 1890 facing a decision. Two new buildings were under construction: a new rectory for the cathedral and a new convent for the Immaculate Heart Sisters at Pico Heights. Whether Bishop Mora suggested the move to the Immaculate Heart Convent as chaplain or whether Eugene O'Connell asked for it is not known. But by February the decision had been made; he would move to the new Pico Heights Convent that same month.[511] Bishop O'Connell accompanied Bishop Mora for the laying of the cornerstone of the new orphanage of the Sisters of Charity in Boyle Heights and a few days later the two traveled to Pomona to dedicate the Convent of the Sisters of the Holy Names.[512]

Bishop O'Connell's move from the old cathedral rectory to the new convent and school on Pico Boulevard took place in February, 1890, and the first Mass was celebrated in the new convent by Bishop O'Connell on Sunday, February 16, 1890.[513] On Palm Sunday, March 30, 1890, he conducted the ceremony of the blessing of the new institution. In that same week, Bishop Mora and the clergy of the cathedral moved into their new residence.[514]

On Sunday, May 4, 1890, the Vincentian Fathers began a triduum at St. Vincent's Church in honor of their recently beatified Gabriel Perboyre. On the third day, it was Bishop O'Connell who offered the Pontifical Mass. On May 14, 1890, the Bishop attended the housewarming at the new cathedral rectory. There he must have caught a severe cold for he was confined to bed the following week. He was recovered on time to mark his seventy-fifth birthday on June 15, 1890, a remarkably advanced age for those times. Ten day later he presided at the commencement exercises of the Immaculate Heart Academy.[515]

On July 31, 1890, Eugene O'Connell left for the north for his annual visit with his brother and family in Oakland. On September 1, 1890, he returned to Pico Heights, as it was then called.[516]

A big day was marked on September 8, 1890, when Bishop

IMMACULATE HEART CONVENT & SCHOOL
in Pico Heights, Los Angeles
Blessed by Bishop O'Connell on March 30, 1890
(Photo, taken in 1907, courtesy of Immaculate Heart College, Los Angeles)

Mora, assisted by Bishop O'Connell, received five young women into the Immaculate Heart order. They were Sister Lourdes Garvey, Sister Bernard Ward, Sister Counsel Mooney, Sister Montserrat Pollman, and Sister Gertrude Stapleton. The excitement was the result of the fact that these were the first novices to have completed a six months' postulancy.[517]

But this occasion revealed what Bishop O'Connell's presence meant, and what his being there meant to him. After twenty-eight years away from the regulated religious life, away from the classroom and the stimulation of intellectual life for which Eugene O'Connell was so naturally suited, he was now once again in the environment he so loved. One author states that his average day would have exhausted the average man, but Eugene O'Connell thrived on the round of daily Mass, confessions, visiting the sick, teaching the students, instructing the novices, and counseling the religious.[518] He was at home, dealing in the spiritual, without any administrative responsibilities. That he was outstandingly happy is demonstrated by the fact that he repeatedly told all, even Bishop Mora, that this was where he wanted to be buried.

That his wisdom, his holiness, his insight were appreciated is also evident. Father Patrick Harnett, on the occasion of the dedication, congratulated the nuns "in having the good fortune of securing for a Chaplain one whose sanctity is a household word, one whose prudent counsel will be your safeguard, one whose zeal is unbounded, one who will not grow weary in God's service until he has thoroughly imbued others with that love of God and Christian charity which characterizes himself."[519]

The sisters too considered themselves fortunate in having him. "In his instructions, filled with spiritual unction, he strove to impress on them the beauty and joyousness as well as the sacrificial nature of the life to which they were aspiring."

Bishop O'Connell was destined to have almost two full years of this happy life. During 1891 there is little evidence of his taking part in the activities of the diocese, so committed was he to the sisters, the novices, and the students.

There seem to have been two trips north to the San Francisco Bay area in the summer. Bishop O'Connell was one of the bishops present in the sanctuary of the beautiful St. Ignatius Church in San Francisco on June 29, 1891, when the Jesuit Fathers celebrated with great solemnity the 300th anniversary of the death of St. Aloysius.[520]

We know he was back in San Francisco by mid-August to attend the funeral of his very good friend and fellow Dublinite, Stephen James McCormick, the editor of *The Monitor*, who had died on August 12, 1891. The friendship with Bishop O'Connell, who was fourteen years his senior, was very real, as Stephen McCormick kept careful watch on the activities of the retired bishop. It was Bishop O'Connell who performed the final rites at the cemetery.[521]

On one of these two trips to the north, Eugene O'Connell made what was destined to be his last trip to Marysville.

The highlight of this vacation was the return to the family home at 9th and Castro streets in Oakland of his nephew and namesake, the well-known violinist Eugene O'Connell, after a four-year absence in France pursuing his musical studies. In preparation for a concert given by the twenty-four-year-old artist at Hamilton Hall in Oakland on September 10, 1891, there must have been some delightful hours for the old Bishop as he listened to the young man practice, accompanied by his sister Marguerite, who also had a lovely voice.[522] By October 7, 1891, the Bishop was back at Pico Heights and in excellent health.[523] Yet within two months he was dead.

The seventy-six-year-old prelate caught cold in late November and was confined to bed in the infirmary. A few days later he had to be transferred to the Sisters Hospital because he had developed pneumonia. On December 4, 1891, the brave and holy soul of Eugene O'Connell went home to the Maker he had striven to serve so well.

On December 7, 1891, his friend Bishop Mora presided at the funeral Mass at St. Vibiana's Cathedral which was filled with clergy, sisters, and people. In fulfillment of his request, a grave was prepared outside, behind the sisters' chapel. The spot chosen was destined to be directly under the altar when the intended expansion of the chapel was accomplished, an expansion which never took place.[524]

The earthly remains of Eugene O'Connell rested in this grave for nineteen years. When the picturesque old convent was torn down to make place for a high school on November 16, 1910, his remains were removed to old Calvary Cemetery. Here they had only eleven years' rest when again they were disinterred and moved to the newly opened Calvary Cemetery on Whittier

Boulevard.[525] A simple slab marks the grave with the name

Rt. Rev. Eugene O'Connell
1815-1891

There is no evidence to the visitor browsing through the graves of the priests' plot that he is standing over the grave of a bishop, or that he has come into contact with the earthly remains of one of California's great pioneers. His memory is as obscure as his grave. Few, in or out of church circles, are even aware that there was a diocese or a bishop prior to Sacramento and its famous Manogue. Eugene O'Connell in death has been unknown and unappreciated. It is hoped this story of his life will dispel that lack of knowledge and will enkindle appreciation.

Sources for Chapter XVI

499. *The Monitor*, July 28, 1886.

500. Ibid., September 28, 1886.

501. Ibid., June 8, 1887.

502. Code, op. cit.

503. *The Monitor*, July 17, 1888.

504. Ibid., October 10, 1888.

505. Ibid., February 13, 1889.

506. Ibid.

507. Ibid., February 27, 1889.

508. Ibid., June 5, 1889.

509. Ibid., May 22, 1889.

510. Ibid., October 30, 1889.

511. Ibid., February 12, 1890.

512. Ibid.

513. Ibid., February 19, 1890.

514. Ibid., March 26, 1890.

515. Ibid., June 25, 1890.

516. Ibid., September 3, 1890.

517. AALA, Sister Reginald Baggot, "The California Institute of the Sisters of the Most Holy and Immaculate Heart of Mary," 1937, pp. 129, 130, 131.

518. Francis Weber, "California Catholic Heritage," *The Tidings*, (Los Angeles), October 1, 1971.

519. Ibid., January 27, 1967.

520. Riordan, op. cit., p. 294.

521. *The Monitor*, August 19, 1891.

522. Ibid., September 16, 1891.

523. Ibid., October 7, 1891.

524. AALA, Baggot, op. cit.

525. Weber, op. cit.

Chapter XVII

HOLINESS OF LIFE

One characteristic of Eugene O'Connell for which there is uncontestable evidence from every quarter is that he was a very saintly man. Abundant testimony both from his admirers and from those who might be considered his antagonists equally testify that this pioneer bishop was a man of outstanding holiness. In addition, his life itself furnishes many examples of extraordinary virtues which, when added up, give only one conclusion: the bishop of Grass Valley was a man of exceptional holiness of life.

The first indication that Eugene O'Connell might have unusual virtues was given by Archbishop Alemany, himself a saintly man, who had nominated him for the office of bishop. In his letter to Propaganda Fidei, he wrote of Eugene O'Connell as a "man of much prayer, purity of conscience, pious, docile, obedient, humble, of great zeal and charity."[526]

Likewise there is abundant evidence of the opinion of the people, which can be found frequently in *The San Francisco Monitor* from correspondents writing from entirely different parts of the diocese. For example, in 1874 from Gold Hill, Nevada, came a testimonial that "Sunday last our venerable and pious Bishop confirmed nineteen children and four adults."[527] In the same year came a testimonial from the Sisters of Mercy in Grass Valley who "tender to the revered and saintly Bishop O'Connell, thanks for $1,000 given by him to the orphanage."[528]

Last photo taken of the RT. REV. EUGENE O'CONNELL
near the end of his life
(Photo, courtesy of Archives of Archdiocese of Los Angeles)

The following year the Gold Hill correspondent again notified *The Monitor* that the presence of Bishop O'Connell "has been a source of much pleasure to the Catholics of Gold Hill, who are always pleased with the presence among them of their holy and zealous Bishop."[529]

In 1883 the same esteem for his holiness was expressed by a correspondent from the northwest portion of the diocese who wrote from Eureka, California, that "the holy Bishop is still at his labors and up to now has confirmed about eighty with more preparing."[530]

This same veneration of Eugene O'Connell as a holy man was likewise expressed in Los Angeles toward the end of his life. The preacher on the occasion of the dedication of the new Immaculate Heart Convent congratulated the sisters for having as their chaplain "one whose sanctity is a household word."[531]

We recall too that the parishioners of both Virginia City and Gold Hill, when writing to Rome to protest the denunciation of the Bishop by Father Angelo Lugero, stated that "we admire the piety and zeal of the Bishop in rectifying abuses."[532]

Even those who opposed or criticized the bishop always testified to his holiness. The anonymous "Sacerdos regularis" who wrote to complain about the Bishop's administration stated: "Rt. Rev. E. O'Connell is the Bishop of this Diocese, a pious man but most imprudent. . . ."[533]

Likewise, Father John Philip Baudinelli, the Passionist who wrote urging that Father Manogue be made the new coadjutor, stated: "There is a saintly Bishop at the head of this Diocese, Rt. Rev. Eugene O'Connell, and has been for sixteen years. Besides behind a saintly man, he is also a man of learning and knowledge."[534]

Many years after his death, in an interview, Father Kiely, one of the pioneer priests, testified about Bishop O'Connell in these words:

> Notwithstanding the arduous journeys which took him day after day, week after week, and month after month, all over the northern part of the State, and the intense fatigue which they entailed, the good Bishop was never known to return home without spending an hour in prayer before the Blessed Sacrament before he changed his clothing or had a bite to eat.[535]

At the time of his death, the Marysville newspaper wrote of Bishop O'Connell in the following terms: "He led more the life of a saint or hermit than one in the active discharge of his duties. He was a strict disciplinarian and spent many hours in the church."[536]

Even strangers quickly detected this aspect of Eugene O'Connell's character. When Father Hugh Quigley, who visited the West in search of material for his book *The Irish Race in California* wrote about Bishop O'Connell, he stated: "He is a man of very mortified appearance, his austerities evidently showing in his countenance and hence the great veneration in which he is held by his people."[537]

Of course, one would expect that those who admired the Bishop would praise him for whatever good qualities he had. We are indebted to the poet-priest Father Joseph Phelan who, in his encomium of his "beloved Eugene," spelled out some of the characteristics of his holiness. We quote the lines that pertain:

> So learned, so holy, deep and profound.
> His was a life of reflection and prayer.
> Fervor and sanctity he had in store.
> He lived in his faith from morning till night.
> Sound meditations kept holy his heart,
> Our dear Saviour he kept always in view.[538]

The best testimonial to his holiness is to be found in his life itself. If sacrifice of self for the love of God is a sign of holiness, then Eugene O'Connell had this to a heroic degree. For one who was temperamentally so well suited to the quasi-monastic life of a seminary professor to have given up this mode of life for that of a missionary in far-off California was, indeed, a heroic sacrifice. That he found the lonely life at Mission Santa Inez extremely hard is testified to by himself. He looked upon his sojourn at Santa Inez as "just punishment for past sins and negligences" and he prayed that he would be able to "bear it with perfect resignation and accept it as such."[539] But if this three-year period can be considered a heroic sacrifice of himself, what can be said of the twenty-three-year sacrifice he made when he became a bishop? Eugene O'Connell never wanted to be a bishop. He knew it carried a heavy responsibility and he knew well his own limitations.

There is abundant testimony that he did not want this office. He made a special trip to Rome to beg off being made a bishop. And when Pope Pius IX refused to rescind the appointment, Eugene O'Connell's reply sums up his complete sacrifice of himself: "I am condemned to the mines."
We recall his willingness to lay down the burden at the time the letters creating the Diocese of Grass Valley were sent to "Rt. Rev. Daniel O'Connell." He wrote: "Gladly would I cede my right if I have any and my Episcopacy in favor of Daniel O'Connell and I ask that the Holy See excuse me from it."[540] We recall, too, his letters pleading for a coadjutor, and after he received one his pleas to be allowed to resign.

> Likewise I ask you to remove me and to put in my place another who is better for the universal good of the flock committed to me. From my heart I ask this, I beg it, for this one thing I ask.[541]

Likewise, there is abundant evidence of sacrifice of self in the round of visitations to the parishes of his vast diocese, a round he made with scrupulous devotion year after year, enduring the hardships of travel by stagecoach, the long hours by day and by night over the dusty roads in heat and cold, the voyages by ship, including seasickness, as he traveled to Eureka and Crescent City, to Yreka, to Austin, Nevada, and to the White Pine County missions.

Eugene O'Connell suffered within himself an affliction that would be sufficient in itself to merit our admiration. He was a scrupulous man and therefore suffered inside himself about many decisions. He found making decisions about many things to be very difficult and so he sought counsel in Rome. And when that counsel did not come, he suffered all the more. Certainly he suffered from the criticisms of his priests because whatever he did, he did from the purest of motives and found the criticism, the misunderstanding hard to endure. How difficult for him must have been the months when his new coadjutor arrived and even the papers published the acclaim with which he was welcomed and extolled. This on top of a seeming lack of gratitude for more than twenty years of sacrifice of himself must have brought great suffering to Eugene O'Connell.

Bishop O'Connell also practiced the evangelical counsels to a heroic degree. Of his poverty he often spoke, keeping nothing for himself. The best testimonial to his poverty was given by Archbishop Riordan when writing to Rome to plead for a pension for the retired bishop in which he pointed out that Bishop O'Connell was helplessly destitute, too poor even to buy a winter coat and forced to beg for a living. "He possesses nothing," wrote the archbishop. "In the matter of money, he always acted with the simplicity of a baby, without regard or estimate of its worth, almost without knowing what to do with it.... He lived poorly and with great parsimony."[542]

When he died, the Marysville paper commented that "after his many years of service in the vineyard of the Lord he died a poor man."[543]

That he practiced obedience to a remarkable degree is also quite evident. His observance of the laws of the church can only be described as scrupulous. But it is in his obedience to the person of the Holy Father that Eugene O'Connell manifested outstanding virtue. When Pius IX refused to rescind his appointment as bishop, it was obedience that motivated Father O'Connell to accept. This kind of obedience to the Pope continued. In one letter he wrote: "However what the Holy Father decides, I will willingly accept."[544] In Eugene O'Connell's case this was not a rhetorical statement. He meant it.

If zeal for souls is a characteristic of sanctity, then there is abundant evidence that Bishop O'Connell had zeal beyond the normal call of duty. We have witnessed his concern for the people of every nationality and language, his concern for obtaining sisters to open schools and his attempts to secure brothers to teach the boys, his solicitude for the Indians in his diocese, and his efforts on behalf of every soul in his vast territory.

There have not been many writers who have had opportunities to become acquainted with the life of Bishop O'Connell. But the few who have are in agreement that Eugene O'Connell was a man of outstanding holiness. Father Henry Walsh, the first to uncover the O'Connell story, wrote of him in these words:

> It is not wise for us to put ourselves up as judges of character, nor freely to conclude what servants of God may or may not be entitled to the honors of the altar. Like Marc An-

thony speaking over the remains of dead Caesar, I come not to prove nor to disprove anything, but to ask you to recall what you have already gleaned from the letters and deeds of Bishop O'Connell and bid them speak for themselves.

In between the birth and the period of the grave, we have no evidence that he ever performed a miracle, nor like many of the canonized saints of the church, was he ever seen surrounded by the light of glory, nor raised from the ground in heavenly ecstacy; there was no certified testimony that he had been confirmed in grace or had preserved his baptismal innocence, to mark him as a subject of Divine predilection.

But what we do know is that from the time he realized he was called to the service of the Church, all other purposes in life was dispelled like the shadows of night before the bright sun's glorious rising, and he devoted all the powers of his mind and soul to make himself a devout and well-informed priest.

If scrupulous devotion to duty and solid virtue are signs of holiness, then there is all the reason in the world to look upon Bishop O'Connell as a holy man.[545]

The same writer went so far as to say that "no consecrated ring ever adorned a more solicitous hand, no crozier was borne by a more vigilant shepherd, and no episcopal cross ever rested on a more self sacrificing breast." Whether we care to accept such an unrestrained eulogy or not, we certainly have to agree that the pioneer bishop of the northern mines and the Comstock was outstanding for his personal holiness which he acquired through a long life of sacrifice and devotion for the good of the people of northern California and Nevada.

While this presentation of the evidence for his personal holiness seemed warranted because of the abundance of testimony from so many varied sources, it is not to be construed as an attempt to whitewash the obvious human characteristics revealed in the previous chapters. The first bishop of the northern mines and the Comstock, while a very saintly man, was also very human. He was limited in his administrative ability; he never abandoned his professor's attitude toward his priests; he lacked tact in dealing with people and was difficult to get along with at times. Yet this very human man was one who lived a very difficult life from purely supernatural motives, and he was the man destined to be the leader and shepherd of the church in northern California and Nevada for almost a quarter of a century.

What evaluation of his episcopacy should be made in the light of the testimony?

There have been only two other authors who have researched the life of Bishop O'Connell: the Rev. Henry Walsh of Santa Clara University in 1946, who was the first to uncover the story of this pioneer bishop; and Harry P. Ley, who did his Master's thesis on the life of Eugene O'Connell for the University of San Francisco in 1968. Of these, Father Walsh extolled Bishop O'Connell for his very evident holiness of life but did not attempt to evaluate the twenty-three years of his episcopacy.

Harry P. Ley, on the other hand, did evaluate the man and his times in the following words:

> What, then, is the final word in the evaluation of the career of Eugene O'Connell? Was he a heroic and successful frontier bishop? Could a more dynamic prelate coming to Marysville in 1861 have achieved more than O'Connell? The writer believes that because of three factors an extremely vigorous bishop could have accomplished little more than did Bishop O'Connell. First, with few priests, the isolation of a good part of the Catholic population scattered here and there throughout Northern California would have created an unsurmountable problem for any bishop. Secondly, the diversity of the religious backgrounds and religious customs of the Catholics of this area presented a problem that only time could remedy. Lastly, without a firm financial foundation for the vicariate and diocese a hard driving bishop would have been handicapped. As already indicated, without O'Connell's connection with All Hallows College for the recruitment of missionary priests, a different ordinary's problem would have been compounded. A bishop who was better attuned to the times and the country might have achieved more harmony in the diocese, but it would appear that a different bishop would have been but little more successful. Catholics of Northern California owe a debt of gratitude to Eugene O'Connell, and it is unfortunate that

this memory is not better recalled in the area where he labored.

This writer agrees with Harry Ley but is convinced that Eugene O'Connell's role was even more significant. The principal need of the church in the northern mines and the Comstock was for priests to attend the spiritual needs of the people. Eugene O'Connell was in a singular position to achieve this need. As a former professor of All Hallows, as a former missionary in California, he was in a most unique situation to understand the needs of his vast missionary diocese and likewise in an unequalled position to obtain priests for this mission field. How could the authorities or the students of All Hallows resist the pleas of one of their own? And it is obvious that they did not. His pleas included not only his own diocese but also that of "poor Dr. Alemany," so that it can be safely said that the abundance of clergy from All Hallows who staffed the parishes of both the Archdiocese of San Francisco and the Diocese of Grass Valley during the second half of the nineteenth century was chiefly due to one man, and that man was Eugene O'Connell.

It may be true that another bishop might have been more prudent, another might have been a better administrator, or still another might even have managed better financially, but it seems obvious that Divine Providence placed Eugene O'Connell at the head of the diocese for the principal purpose of staffing it with priests, a task for which few could have been better chosen. That he accomplished this goal is undeniable. The record stands for itself.

Likewise, it seems remarkable, at least to the present author, that the same Divine Providence should have provided for the infant church in California two bishops who are outstanding for their personal holiness of life, Joseph Alemany and Eugene O'Connell. Evidently it was very important for the initial start of the church in the very difficult area of the mines, where avarice, loneliness, and intemperance ran rampant, that there be at the head of the two dioceses men whose personal example of poverty, prayer, and self-denial would be an inspiration to the clergy who might be tempted in any or all of these areas. These two bishops certainly furnished remarkable examples of these virtues. Thanks principally to them, the pioneer church in American California and Nevada was furnished with priests of exceptional caliber, led by two bishops whose personal example was an inspiration to these same priests.

Thus it seems to the author that Eugene O'Connell was placed by Providence in this position because he was the man for the season. Perhaps the church in northern California and Nevada owes more to this man than meets the eye. It is about time that his remarkable accomplishment for the church should become known, recognized, and appreciated, and his memory and his virtues be resurrected for our own inspiration and edification.

Sources for Chapter XVII

526. ASRC, Vol. 386, F679.

527. *The Monitor*, August 8, 1874.

528. Ibid., February 7, 1874.

529. Ibid., September 25, 1875.

530. Ibid., September 8, 1883.

531. Francis Weber, "California Catholic Heritage," *The Tidings* (Los Angeles), January 27, 1967.

532. ASRC, Vol. 21, F938, letter of April 19, 1866.

533. ASRC, Vol. 27, F576.

534. Ley, op. cit., p. 156.

535. *The Register* (Sacramento, California), December 16, 1934.

536. *Marysville Appeal*, December 8, 1891.

537. Hugh Quigley, "Rt. Rev. Eugene O'Connell," in *The Irish Race in California* (San Francisco: A. Roman & Co., 1878).

538. Joseph Phelan, "In Memoriam," in *The Poetical Works and Biographical Remarks of.* . . .

539. AAHC, letter of November 21, 1852.

540. ASRC, Vol. 22, F436.

541. ASRC, Vol. 22, F664.

542. Gaffey, op. cit., p. 161.

543. *Marysville Appeal,* December 8, 1891.

544. ASRC, Vol. 24, F440.

545. Walsh, *Hallowed Were,* p. 432.

Appendix A

POETICAL TRIBUTE OF THE REV. JOSEPH PHELAN TO THE MEMORY OF BISHOP O'CONNELL

WRITTEN ON SEPTEMBER 16, 1900

IN MEMORIAM

Right Rev. Bishop O'Connell, who died December 4, A.D. 1891

'Tis often I reflect o'er life's short span,
And the good and bad things performed by man.
Some are not yet able to take a fair view;
Many are false and won't give you your due,
Yet many are biased in every case,
And some oft try each other to debase.
Even the pure and good we criticise,
Pretending, indeed, that we are so wise.
The holy and good can't escape censure;
On all kinds of criticisms we venture.
Man is always an enigma to me—
Him we don't understand or oft agree,
Yet in our presumptions we are so great
To all manner of men we can dictate;
While men of this world we do underrate,
Yet they say that we give much silly prate.

I once had a friend; I thought him perfect;
Nothing mean in him could I e'er detect—
So learned, so holy, deep and profound—
To my mind his equal I never found.
In many things men never coincide;
Some say you are good; others, full of pride;
Our best aspirations are oft denied;
They knew not his worth till after he died;
His was a life of reflection and prayer;
Of letters and study he did his share.
In religious things he was most exact;
For business matters he had no tact;
Theological points he could decide;
The Church lost an aegis when he died.
There were few men who were posted better;
Doctrine and laws he knew to the letter.
From abundance of heart the mouth must speak;
The rose of defense we saw on his cheek;
His lips would quiver, and sparkle his eye;
The hard questions of all he would defy.

Hard questions he had at his finger's ends;
Ne'er so brave as when his creed he defends,
Then his erudition came to his aid.
Of hard objections he was not afraid;
It gave him great delight them to explain—
Those big objections he kept in his brain.
He was soundly versed in all the church lore;
Fervor and sanctity he had in store;
His answers did often myself surprise—
Before him the learned were not so wise.
On all points he was happy and profound;
His instructions never fell to the ground.
What a pity those gifts should pass away.
But like men they were not given to stay;
Yet his life and actions may us inspire,
And by our exertions good things acquire.
His knotty questions, how quick they would speed;
To our answers would say, "That's good, indeed."
He lived in his faith from morning till night;

To propose questions was his great delight.
Profoundest learning filled his humble mind.
To the poor and ignorant he was kind;
Sound meditations kept holy his heart.
From his God or his church he could not depart;
Our dear Saviour he kept always in view,
And his mystifications were not few.
To my poor heart his memory is green;
Peace to your dear old soul, beloved Eugene.

Appendix B

SUCCESSION OF PASTORS OF THE PARISHES IN THE GRASS VALLEY DIOCESE FROM THEIR START UP TO 1900

IN THE ORDER OF THEIR FOUNDATION

CALIFORNIA PARISHES

Marysville

St. Joseph's

Peter Magagnotto	September	1852 – June	1857
Daniel Slattery	July	1857 – October	1860
Robert A. Maurice	November	1860 – May	1861
Eugene O'Connell	May	1861 – March	1868
Edward Kelly		1868 –	1869
James J. Callan	April	1869 –	1870
William Moloney	September	1870 –	1872
Patrick Farrelly	October	1872 – May	1874
Thomas Grace		1874 –	1881
James J. Callan		1881 – December	1887
Matthew Coleman		1888 –	1917

St. Theresa's

Julius Herde	January	1871 –	1872

Immaculate Conception

John Meiler	March	1872 –	1879
L. Buholzer		1879 –	1884

Weaverville

Florian Schwenninger, OSB	1853 – 1856
Thomas Cody	1856 – 1857
John Ingoldsby	February – May 1857
Raphael Rainaldi (at Shasta)	1857 – 1859
Patrick O'Reilly	1859 – 1864
John M. Nulty	1864 – 1867
Patrick O'Kane	1867
Matthew Coleman	1867 – 1873
James Hunt	1873 – 1876
Michael Walrath	1877 – 1879
Michael Walsh	1879 – 1880
James J. Callan	1880 – 1881
James J. Claire	1882 – 1885
Michael Dillon	1885 – 1888
Bernard McFeeley	1888 – 1890
J. T. O'Reilly	1890 – 1892
John B. Ruddy	1892 – 1895
Patrick Kirley	1895 – 1898
Gerald Stack	1898 – 1902

Grass Valley

Thomas J. Dalton	1855 – 1891
Peter J. McDonnell	1891 – 1894
Charles J. Lynch	1894 – 1911
Patrick J. Clyne	1911 – 1912
Michael Kiely	1912 – 1919
James O'Meara	1919 – 1945

Yreka

James Cassin	1855 – 1857
Florian Schwenninger, OSB	1857 – 1858

John K. Handy	1858 –1859
Thomas Crinion	1860 –1863
Guido Matassi	1864 –1865
Patrick Farrelly	1865 –1873
James J. Callan	1873 –1878
James J. Claire	1878 –1879
Leon Haupts	1879 –1886
Patrick Kirley	1866
C. C. McGrath	1887 –1894
John Quinn	1894 –1899
James O'Meara	1899 –1919

Downieville

Cornelius Delahunty		1856 –July	1862
Bernard Morris	August	1862 –December	1864
Charles Lynch	January	1865 –September	1869
William Moloney	October	1869 –September	1870
Charles Lynch	September	1870 –April	1877
Andrew O'Donnell	January	1878 –July	1879
Patrick Kirley	September	1879 –November	1882
Michael Dillon	December	1882 –May	1884
James J. Claire	August	1884 –	1894
Patrick O'Kane	June	1894 –September	1897
James Dermody	November	1897 –September	1903
William Laffan	October	1903 –	1908
Patrick O'Reilly		1908 –	1912
James O'Flanagan		1912 –	1916
John McGarry		1916 –	1926
P. J. O'Donovan		1926 –	1930

became a mission of Nevada City

Forest Hill

St. Joseph's Church dedicated Sunday, June 20, 1858, built by the Rev. Thomas J. Dalton

Church in Iowa Hill dedicated June 10, 1860, built by the Rev. Thomas J. Dalton

Established as a parish by Bishop O'Connell July 14, 1861

Francis Blake	July	1861	– November	1862
George Rigby	November	1862	– June	1863
James J. Callan	March	1864	– September	1868
Daniel Meagher	November	1868	– August	1872
Andrew O'Donnell	November	1872	– December	1875
William Moloney	March	1876	– February	1879
Thomas Pettit	April	1879	– December	1880
Michael Dillon	February	1881	– October	1882
Michael O'Reilly	December	1882	– January	1892
Daniel Meagher	May	1892	– September	1898
Dennis Horgan		1898	–	1900
Gerald Stack		1900	–	1903

(became a mission of Auburn, California)

Mendocino (City)

First church built by Father Sheehan in 1866

Bernardine Sheehan, OFM	1863 – 1866
Vincent Riera	1866 – 1869
James Rooney	1870 – 1871
James J. Callan	1871 – 1873
Thomas Pettit	1873 – 1877
John D. Sheridan	1877 – 1883
Daniel O'Sullivan	1883 – 1886
Patrick J. Clyne	1886 – 1890
William P. Quill	1890 – 1892

Second church built by Father Quill and dedicated by Archbishop Riordan June, 1890

| James Ferguson | 1892 – 1895 |
| Henry K. Whyte | 1895 – 1903 |

(at this time the parish began to be staffed by the Capuchin Fathers)

Eureka (California)

Thomas Crinion	1863 – 1864
Patrick O'Reilly	1866 – 1867
Maurice Hickey	1867 – 1868
Patrick Henneberry, C.PP.S.	1868 – 1871
P. B. Dickman, C.PP.S.	1871 – 1875
Edward Kelly	1875 – 1876
John M. Nulty	1876 – 1877
Charles Lynch	1877 – 1883
John D. Sheridan	1883 – 1893
Lawrence Kennedy	1893 – 1924

Nevada (City)

John Shanahan	1851 – 1853
Peter L. Deyaert	1853 – 1855

(became a mission of Grass Valley)

Established as a parish separate from Grass Valley October, 1867

James J. Claire	October	1867 – March	1873
Daniel Meagher	May	1873 – July	1885
John M. Nulty	January	1886 – December	1886
James Tanham	August	1886 – March	1894
Patrick J. Clyne	February	1894 – January	1911
Patrick O'Reilly		1911 –	1945

Oroville

Thomas Crinion	1864 – 1866
John M. Mevel	1866 – 1868
Patrick O'Kane	1868

Thomas Pettit   1868 – 1872
Lawrence Kennedy   1872 – 1874

(became a mission of Marysville in 1874)
(became a mission of Chico in 1881)

Chico

James J. Hynes   1878 – 1887
James Hunt   1887 – 1888
Daniel Gartland   April-October   1888
Michael Gualco   1889 – 1912
Patrick Guerin   1912 – 1917
James Dermody   1917 – 1937

Red Bluff

Thomas Grace   1867 – 1868
Patrick O'Kane   1868 – 1870
Stephen Kearney   1870 – 1872
Matthew Coleman   1872 – 1874
Patrick Farrelly   1874 – 1877
William Clarke   1877
James Hunt   1877 – 1887
John F. Quinn   1887 – 1894
C. C. McGrath   1894 – 1904
Philip Brady   1904 – 1926

Crescent City

Leon Haupts   1869 – 1871
Daniel O'Sullivan   1871
Joseph Coffey   1872 – 1873
Michael Walrath   1873 – 1876
James J. Claire   1876 – 1880
Bernard McFeeley   1880 – 1883
C. C. McGrath   1883 – 1887

Patrick Kirley	1887 –1892
Leon Haupts	1892 –1893
Michael O'Reilly	1893 –1895
J. B. Ruddy	1895 –1900

Truckee

Instituted as the "Railroad Line Parish to Toana" in 1868

John M. Mevel, founding pastor	
lived for a time at Forest Hill	1868 –1870
moved to Truckee	1870 –1872
Daniel Meagher	
attended the Railroad Line	
from Nevada City	1874 –1875
Charles Becker	
lived in Truckee	1876 –1877
William Moloney	
pastor of Railroad Line Parish,	1877 –1888
spent most of his time in the	
Nevada portion	
Thomas Pettit	
seems to have cared for Truckee	
from Reno	

(The Baptismal Registers for this Parish were destroyed by fire; there is nothing positive until 1885.)

Michael Walsh	1885 –1889
Michael Kiely	1889 –1891
D. Gartland	1891 –1895
James J. Claire	1895 –1900
P. F. Gleeson	1900 –1906
Thomas E. Horgan	1906 –1917

Colusa-Grand Island

Charles Becker	1870 –1871
Andrew O'Donnell	1871 –1872

Edward Kelly	1872 –1873
Joseph Coffey	1873 –1874
James Hegarty	1874 –1876
Andrew O'Donnell	1876 –1877
Michael Walrath	May 27, 1877 –1912

Smartsville

Daniel O'Sullivan	1872 –1878
Matthew Coleman	1878 –1887
Daniel Twomey	1887 –1902
James J. Hynes	1902 –1913
Thomas J. Dermody	1913 –1915
James J. Enright	1915 –1919

(suppressed as a parish and made a mission of Grass Valley)

Rohnerville (Ferndale)

Patrick Henneberry, C.PP.S.	1870 –1876
Joseph Uphaus, C.PP.S.	1876 –1878
Lawrence Kennedy	1878 –1892
Patrick Kirley	1892 –1893
Thomas Nugent	1893 –1898
Michael Kiely	1898 –1912
Jeremiah Gleeson	1912 –1938

Cherokee (Nevada County)

William Clarke	November	1879 – July	1881
William Walsh	November	1881 – August	1882
Michael Kiely	October	1882 – January	1884

(vacant between April and August 1884)

James Tanham	August	1884 – December 1886	

(parish suppressed and made a mission of Nevada City)

Arcata

Thomas Nugent 1883 - 1893
(became a mission of Eureka until 1907)

NEVADA PARISHES

Virginia City

Patrick Manogue	1862 – 1881
Daniel O'Sullivan	1881 – 1883
Charles Lynch	1883 – 1894
Thomas Tubman	1894 – 1904
Francis Reynolds	1904 – 1907
Daniel Murphy	1907 – 1922

(suppressed as a parish in 1922)

Gold Hill

Patrick O'Reilly	May 12,	1864 – January	1866
Daniel Meagher	January	1866 – August	1868
William Clarke	August	1868 – January	1877
Leon Haupts		1877	
John M. Nulty	September	1877 – December	1881
Andrew O'Donnell	January	1882 – June	1911

(suppressed as a parish in 1911)
(became a mission of Virginia City)

Divide

Passionist Fathers December 1863 – September 1865

Carson City

Joseph Gallagher	1858 –	1860
Hugh Gallagher	1860 –	1861
Cornelius Delahunty	1861 –	1865
Vincent Riera	1865 – July	1866
William Clarke	1867 – August	1868
William Gleeson	1868 – May	1869
Thomas Grace	1870 – July	1871
Luke Tormey	1871 – July	1886
Daniel Meagher	1886 – July	1888
Michael Walsh	1888 – August	1890
Terence Sheridan	1890 – October	1892
Patrick J. Clyne	1892 – January	1895
D. Gartland	1895 – January	1917

Austin

Edward Kelly	October 16,	1865 – May	1866
Dominic Monteverde	July 29,	1866 – March	1869
Edward Kelly		1869 –	1870
Dominic Monteverde	September	1871 – October	1872
William Moloney	October	1872 – October	1875
Joseph Phelan	September	1876 – June	1894
James M. Butler		1894 –	1902

(parish center moved to Tonopah)

Reno

Because of disastrous fires, all records destroyed

At times difficult to distinguish Truckee from Reno because both belonged to the "Railroad Line Parish to Toana"

John M. Mevel	1871 – 1877
Thomas Pettit	1877 – 1879
James J. Callan	1879 – 1881
Patrick Kirley	1881 – 1883
John D. Sheridan	1883 – 1885

William Moloney	1885 – 1887
Michael Kiely	1887 – 1897
Francis Reynolds	1897 – 1904
Dominican Fathers	1904 – 1906
Thomas Tubman	1906 – 1929

Hamilton

(White Pine County Missions)

Dominic Monteverde	1869 – 1870
Patrick O'Kane	1870 – 1871
James J. Hynes	1871 – 1872
William Moloney	1872

(parish center moved to Eureka)

Eureka (Nevada)

James J. Hynes	April	1872 – October	1876
Dominic Monteverde	December	1876 – December	1883
William Moloney		1884	
Michael Kiely		1884 –	1887

(In 1887, Eureka was transferred to the Salt Lake diocese)

Cherry Creek

William Moloney	1880 – 1883

Pioche (Lincoln County)

(Technically in the Archdiocese of San Francisco)

Lawrence Scanlan	1870 – 1873
Dominic Monteverde	1874 – 1876

(Attended from that date from the White Pine Missions)

Ten of the priests of the old Grass Valley diocese who could not be identified. Pictures were in the old album of the priests of the diocese owned by the Sisters of Mercy, Grass Valley, California.

Appendix C

BIOGRAPHIC SKETCHES OF PRIESTS FOR WHOM THERE ARE NO PHOTOGRAPHS

THE REV. JAMES J. CLAIRE   1842-1905

Founding Pastor of Nevada City	1867–1873
Assistant at Marysville	1874–1875
Pastor of Crescent City	1876–1878
Pastor of Yreka	1878–1879
Pastor of Weaverville	1882–1884
Pastor of Downieville	1884–1894
Pastor of Truckee	1895–1900
Pastor of Lincoln	1900–1905

THE REV. MICHAEL DILLON   1855-1924

Pastor of Forest Hill	1881–1882
Pastor of Downieville	1882–1884
Pastor of Weaverville	1885–1888
Assistant at Marysville	1890
Assistant at Auburn	1891

(No further trace after that date)

THE REV. PATRICK FARRELLY   1840-1877

Pastor of Yreka	1865–1872
Pastor of Marysville	1872–1874

Pastor of Red Bluff   1874–1877

THE REV. JOHN GRIFFIN   1836–1872

Assistant at Marysville	1862–1863
Acting Pastor of Grass Valley	1863–1864
Assistant at Grass Valley	1864–1868
Assistant at St. Mary's Cathedral in San Francisco	1868
Pastor of St. Leander's in San Leandro	1868–1869
Assistant in Virginia City	1870

THE REV. JAMES HUNT   1848–1912

Assistant at Yreka	1871–1873
Pastor of Weaverville	1873–1876
Assistant at Grass Valley	1876–1877
Pastor of Red Bluff	1877–1887
Pastor of Chico	1887–1888
Pastor of Folsom	1890–1900
Pastor of Angels Camp	1900–1901
Pastor of Woodland	1901–1902
Chaplain, Mercy Hospital in Sacramento	1902–1912

THE REV. EDWARD KELLY

Assistant at Marysville	1865
Founding Pastor of Austin, Nevada	1865–1866
Founding Pastor of Salt Lake City	1866
Pastor of Marysville	1867–1869
Pastor of Austin, Nevada	1869–1870
Pastor of Colusa	1872–1873
Pastor of Eureka, California	1875–1876

(Left Grass Valley diocese in 1876 to enter a monastery)

THE REV. DANIEL MEAGHER   ?–1904

Pastor of Gold Hill, Nevada	1865–1868
Pastor of Forest Hill	1868–1872
Pastor of Nevada City	1873–1885

(This included the Railroad Line Parish)

Pastor of Carson City, Nevada	1886–1888
Pastor of Forest Hill	1893–1898

THE REV. WILLIAM MOLONEY 1843–1903

Assistant at Marysville	1869
Pro tem Pastor of Downieville	1869–1870
Pastor of Marysville	1870–1872
Pastor of White Pine Missions at Hamilton	1872
Pastor of Austin, Nevada	1872–1875
Pastor of Forest Hill	1876–1879
Pastor of Cherry Creek, Nevada	1880–1883
Pastor of Eureka, Nevada	1884
Pastor of Reno, Nevada	1885–1887
Pastor of Sutter Creek	1903

THE REV. DOMINIC MONTEVERDE 1837–1898

Assistant at Marysville	1864
Assistant at Virginia City	1865–1866
Pastor of Austin, Nevada	1866–1869
Pastor of Hamilton, Nevada	1869–1870
Pastor of Austin, Nevada	1871–1876
Pastor of Pioche, Nevada	1873–1876
Pastor of Eureka, Nevada	1876–1883
Pastor of Holy Rosary in Brooklyn, New York	1883–1898

THE REV. BERNARD McFEELEY 1840–1917

Assistant at Eureka, California	1879–1880
Pastor of Crescent City	1880–1883
Assistant at Grass Valley	1883–1884
Pastor of Redding	1884–1888
Pastor of Weaverville	1888–1890
Pastor of San Andreas	1890–1891
Pastor of Placerville	1892–1902
Pastor of Galt	1904–1905
Pastor of Oroville	1905
Pastor of Crescent City	1907–1908
Chaplain at Mercy Hospital in Sacramento	1912–1917

THE REV. CORNELIUS C. McGRATH 1847–1934

Pastor of Crescent City	1883–1887
Pastor of Yreka	1887–1894
Pastor of Red Bluff	1894–1904
Pastor of Willows	1904–1911
Pastor of Colusa	1911–1920
(Retired to Bere Island in County Cork, Ireland)	

THE REV. THOMAS NUGENT 1849–1945

Assistant in Virginia City	1878–1880
Assistant in Grass Valley	1880–1881
Pastor of Reno	1882–1883
Founding Pastor of Arcata	1883–1893
Assistant at Eureka, California	1893–1895
Pastor of Ferndale	1895–1898
Pastor of Willows	1898–1900
Pastor of Folsom	1900–1902
Founding Pastor of Redding	1905–1913
Pastor of Arcata	1913–1945

THE REV. JOHN M. NULTY 1838–1887

Founding Pastor of Weaverville	1864–1867
(moved from Shasta)	
Assistant in Virginia City	1867–1874
Returned to Ireland (for reasons of health)	1874–1876
Pastor of Eureka, California	1876–1877
Pastor of Gold Hill, Nevada	1877–1881
Assistant in Virginia City	1881–1886
Pastor of Nevada City	1886–1887

THE REV. ANDREW O'DONNELL

Pastor of Colusa-Grand Island	1871–1872
Pastor of Forest Hill	1872–1876
Pastor of Colusa	1877–1878
Pastor of Downieville	1878–1879
Last Pastor of Gold Hill, Nevada	1882–1911
In retirement at Virginia City	1911–1913

THE REV. FRANCIS REYNOLDS 1859–1907

Assistant at Colusa	1886–1888
Pastor of Willows	1888–1897
Pastor of Reno	1897–1904
Pastor of Virginia City	1904–1907

THE REV. LUKE TORMEY 1839–1895

Pastor of Austin, Nevada	1869–1871
Pastor of Carson City, Nevada	1871–1886
Pastor of Auburn, California	1886–1895

INDEX

Adam, Joachim, 257
Alemany, Archbishop Joseph, 22, 24, 26, 27, 30, 32, 36, 39, 40, 41, 42, 46, 73, 82, 85, 87, 90, 106, 108, 109, 111, 131, 137, 145, 147, 150, 151, 152, 154, 167, 169, 173, 175, 183, 204, 215, 216, 221, 222, 226, 229, 235, 242, 248, 249, 250, 251, 252, 265, 273
All Hallows College, 6, 13, 24, 26, 28, 31, 32, 35, 36, 39, 41, 42, 44, 45, 46, 47, 55, 58, 65, 67, 70, 73, 74, 75, 91, 96, 98, 100, 106, 108, 109, 111, 124, 125, 131, 133, 136, 140, 156, 163, 173, 175, 181, 186, 196, 207, 212, 215, 238, 247, 248, 258, 272, 273
Amat, Thaddeus, 40, 42, 90, 93, 131, 167, 183, 184, 186, 188, 192, 215, 217, 221
Ancient Order of Hibernians, 166, 167
Auger, Louis, 33

Baltimore, Councils of, 31, 38, 41, 89, 90, 145, 248, 249, 250
Barnabo, Allesandro Cardinal, 40, 42, 43, 88, 90, 115, 145, 166, 188, 220
Baudinelli, John Philip, 111, 115, 224, 267
Becker, Charles, 119, 133, 137, 157, 187, 197, 207, 231
Bedford, Henry, 75
Blake, Francis Joseph, 45, 46, 54, 69, 70, 73, 74
Bouchard, James, S.J., 242, 103, 105

Bowles, Doninic, 35
Brannan, Sam, 19
Buholzer, L., 111, 237, 238, 242
Burchard, J.L., 147, 149, 150, 151, 205

Callan, James Joseph, 54, 55, 67, 70, 73, 74, 75, 98, 127, 133, 137, 157, 196, 207, 223, 234, 237, 250
Carillo, Dona Catalina, 30
Carlow, St. Patrick's Seminary, 24, 26, 33, 35, 75
Carroll, Richard, 35, 46
Certes, Monsieur, 44, 73, 88, 144, 164, 204
Claire, James J., 94, 96, 98, 157, 165, 175, 187, 196, 209, 242
Clarke, William, 74, 91, 98, 127, 128, 129, 131, 157, 165, 175, 197, 209
Clyne, Patrick J., 247
Coffey, Joseph, 175, 194
Coleman, Matthew, 94, 98, 157, 197, 201, 211, 226, 236, 238, 240
Comapla, Juan, 33
Comellas, Juan, 33
Congiato, Nicholas, S.J., 103
Corcoran, Edward, 249
Cotter, James, 46
Crinion, Thomas, 52, 76, 77, 84, 93, 98, 116
Croke, James, 41
Cullen, Cardinal Paul, 44, 136, 251

Dade, Daniel, 161
Dalton, Thomas Joseph, 35, 57, 64, 65, 67, 70, 73, 76, 80, 85, 90, 98, 105,

109, 123, 125, 127, 157, 165, 181, 183, 186, 187, 190, 196, 237, 238, 240
Daughters of Charity, 88, 157, 205, 247
Degnan, James, 160
Delahunty, Cornelius, 52, 54, 69, 70
Dempsey, Denis, 73
Dickman, Bernard, C.PP.S., 140, 157, 160, 161
Diego, Fray Francisco Garcia, 21
Dominican Sisters, 27, 153, 191, 205, 247
Donnelly, Eleanor C., 248, 249
Dowling, Patrick, 249

Ewing, Charles, 152

Faber, Francis, 24
Farrelly, Patrick, 84, 98, 109, 157, 159, 175, 187, 190, 196, 197, 247
Fenstegge, Anthony, 186
Fitzpatrick, Bernard, 45
Foley, Thomas, 41
Fontaine, Flavian, 33
Fox, Bonaventure, 152
Franchi, Alessandro Cardinal, 219

Gallagher, Hugh, 27
Gallagher, Joseph, 87
Gallagher, Neal, 75
Gleeson, William, 128, 187
Gomerly, Antonio, 106
Governo, Dominic, 152
Grace, Thomas, 94, 98, 109, 127, 133, 157, 173, 181, 187, 196, 207, 234, 237, 238
Granzoni, Giancomo Cardinal, 24
Griffin, John, 47, 57, 64, 65, 73, 75, 76, 96, 109, 127, 187
Guadalupe Hidalgo, Treaty of, 18
Guerra, Don Jose de la, 22
Guggenberger, Anthony, 160, 161

Harnett, Patrick, 261
Harrington, John, 33
Haupts, Leon, 137, 157, 173, 197, 209, 211
Hegarty, James, 196

Henneberry, Patrick, C.PP.S., 105, 128, 133, 140, 157, 159, 213, 231
Herde, Julius, 108, 157
Hickey, Maurice, 91, 98, 127, 128, 187
Hughes, John, 21
Hunt, James, 173, 196, 209, 240
Hynes, James J., 136, 173, 196, 209

Immaculate Heart Sisters, 259, 261, 267
Irish College, 43, 44

Kearney, Stephen, 133, 157
Kelly, Bernard, 247
Kelly, Edward, 84, 88, 89, 98, 123, 125, 133, 137, 165, 187, 197, 231
Kelly, Eugene, 186
Kennedy, Lawrence, 55, 96, 98, 127, 157, 161, 173, 196, 211, 234
Kenny, William, 35
Kiely, Michael, 267
Kirley, Patrick, 197, 223, 224

Langlois, Anthony, 24, 32
Largan, James, 44
Lasuen, Fermin, O.F.M., 16
Laufhuber, G., S.J., 108
Ledwith, Mother Gertrude, 161, 163
Lootens, Louis, 129
Losa, Pedro, 75, 80, 106
Lugero, Angelo, C.P., 111, 112, 114, 115, 267
Lynch, Charles M., 80, 82, 98, 133, 137, 157, 187, 196, 209, 212, 236, 237, 238
Lynn, Thomas, 207

McCabe, Hugh, 242
McCormick, Stephen James, 262
McDonnell, Peter, 247
McFeeley, Bernard, 212, 235
McGill, James, 217
McGrath, Cornelius C., 238
McLaughlin, Edward, 186, 251

Magagnotto, Peter, C.P., 47, 85, 111, 131, 185
Mahoney, Denis, 215
Mallon, Thomas, 167

Manogue, Patrick, 59, 60, 65, 67, 70, 74, 77, 84, 96, 98, 105, 109, 125, 129, 131, 144, 157, 163, 165, 169, 178, 181, 183, 186, 187, 197, 201, 207, 211, 213, 221, 224, 226, 227, 234, 235, 240, 242, 243, 244, 247, 248, 249, 250, 251, 254, 263, 267
Marshall, James W., 18
Matassi, Guido, C.P., 76, 77, 111
Maurice, Robert A., 46, 65
Maynooth Seminary, 3, 24
Matassi, Guido, C.P., 76, 77, 111
Meagher, Daniel, 84, 98, 119, 127, 157, 187, 196, 211, 226, 238
Meiler, John, 108, 111, 196, 207
Mercy, Sisters of, 75, 80, 85, 88, 157, 159, 161, 205, 240, 242, 247, 265
Mevel, John Mary, 82, 98, 106, 116, 117, 119, 157, 197, 205, 222, 223, 231
Mission Dolores, 33, 35, 46, 50, 173
Mogan, Mother Baptist, 190, 191
Moloney, William, 119, 133, 137, 157, 175, 197, 209, 235
Monteverde, Dominic, 75, 76, 84, 89, 98, 137, 157, 175, 197, 212
Montgomery, Charles, O.P., 22
Mora, Francis, 59, 167, 215, 220, 221, 229, 235, 249, 251, 254, 257, 258, 259, 260, 262
Moriarty, David, 26, 32, 33, 35, 133
Morris, Bernard, 46, 47, 48, 65, 70, 73, 76, 80, 82, 231
Murphy, P.A., 186
Murray, Archbishop Daniel, 3

Navan, Seminary of, 3, 6
Newman, John Henry, 24
Notre Dame Sisters, 27, 88, 157, 197, 199, 205, 247
Nugent, Denis, 75, 76
Nugent, Thomas, 207, 211, 242
Nulty, John M., 75, 76, 94, 98, 109, 157, 196, 211

O'Connell, Denis, 252
O'Connell, Eugene: birth, 2; baptism, 3; volunteers for California, 26; voyage, 27; at Santa Inez, 28, 30; at San Francisco, 32; at Mission Dolores, 33; sails for home, 35; fluent in Latin, 38; appointed Bishop, 42; goes to Rome, 43; returns to All Hallows, 44; consecrated Bishop, 44; sails for California, 45; leaves for Marysville, 46; dedication of Churches, 58, 167, 173, 242; illnesses, 58, 59, 169; supports All Hallows, 74, 77; owes Archdiocese, 85, 87; rebuilds Pro-Catheral, 87, 88; attends Baltimore Councils, 89, 90, 248; buries his priests, 93, 197; ordains priests, 98, 194; employs Missionaries, 103, 105, 106, 108, 111, 115; becomes ordinary, 123; co-consecrator of Bishops, 129, 167, 229, 257; attends Vatican Council, 131, 133, 134; confirms Indians, 152; sends Holy Father collection, 165; attends Provincial Council, 167, 216, 235; resigns Diocese, 244; takes extended vacation, 248, 249; celebrates Silver Jubilee, 250; receives first pension, 254; moves to Los Angeles, 254; moves to Pico Heights Convent, 259; dies and is buried, 262
O'Connell, Patrick, 3, 31, 32, 186, 248, 250, 258, 259, 262
O'Donnell, Andrew, 136, 157, 188, 196, 209
O'Kane, Patrick, 91, 94, 98, 109, 116, 133, 157, 173, 186, 196, 207, 211
Old St. Mary's Cathedral, 31, 41, 46, 75, 80, 82, 84, 93, 127, 128, 229, 235, 257
O'Neale, Mother Dolores, O.P., 191, 222, 224
O'Neill, Thomas, 161
Ord, Judge, 186
O'Reilly, Michael, 238
O'Reilly, Myles, 35
O'Reilly, Patrick, 52, 71, 76, 77, 82, 84, 91, 93, 111, 187
O'Sullivan, Daniel, 173, 175, 196, 209, 211, 234, 237, 240
O'Sullivan, Jeremiah, 91, 93, 94
Osuna, Luciano, 106, 146, 147, 148,

150, 151, 157, 205

Passionists, 76, 85, 111, 112, 114, 115, 224
Peralta, Don Luis, 16
Pettit, Thomas, 125, 129, 157, 187, 196, 209, 211, 223, 244, 247
Phelan, Joseph, 181, 183, 187, 190, 196, 197, 212, 235, 268
Pious Fund, 203, 204
Poulin, A.Y., 106
Precious Blood, Society of, 105, 128, 137, 159, 160, 161, 194
Prendergast, John, 46, 217, 219, 225, 235, 251
Propagation of the Faith, Society for, at Paris 24, 43, 44, 45, 60, 74, 100, 145, 153, 154, 156, 163, 164, 184, 203, 204, 205
Provincial Councils, 167, 216, 217, 235, 249
Purcell, Archbishop John, 40

Quigley, Hugh, 268
Quinn, John, 33
Quinn, William, 74, 161

Rainaldi, Raphael, 85, 87
Reindl, Joseph, 108
Reynolds, Francis, 247
Richardson, Michael, 219, 221, 226
Riera, Vincent, 82, 91, 98, 131, 140, 146
Rigby, George, 67, 70, 73, 75, 76
Riordan, Patrick W., 183, 242, 249, 250, 251, 252, 257, 270
Rooney, James, 125, 127, 129, 133, 140, 146, 157, 173, 175, 187, 197
Russell, Mother Baptist, 85
Ryan, Archbishop P.J., 248

Santa Inez Mission, 16, 28, 33, 35, 41, 50, 70, 268

St. Francis Church, 24, 28, 30, 31, 32, 111
St. Vincent's Seminary, Latrobe, Pa., 207, 238
Scanlan, John, 32
Scanlan, Lawrence, 137, 157, 175, 219, 221, 226, 257
Schlacter, Godfrey, 160
Schwenninger, Florian, 52, 77, 84, 93
Serra, Junipero, 16, 248
Shea, John Gilmary, 151, 169
Sheehan, Bernadine, 85, 231
Sheridan, John Daniel, 55, 109, 196, 209
Simeone, John Cardinal, 124, 169, 188, 212, 215, 227, 251, 252
Smith, Charles, 186
Sopranis, Felix, 145
Sunderland, John, 222
Sutter, John, 18, 19
Synod, First Diocesan, 30

Taaffe, James, 249
Tanham, James, 237, 238
Tormey, Luke, 133, 157, 173, 183, 187, 197, 212
Tubman, Thomas, 247

Uphaus, Joseph, 161, 196

Vatican Council I, 131, 134, 159
Vinyes, Vincent, O.P., 215, 216, 217, 219, 220, 225, 250

Walrath, Michael, 152, 194, 196, 209, 234, 240
Walrath, William, 161, 194
Walsh, Bishop Edward, 44
Walsh, Bishop James, 44
Walsh, Michael, 207, 209
Woodlock, Bartholomew, 45

Young, Brigham, 89

PHOTOGRAPHS

O'Connell, Rt. Rev. Eugene Official photo	*frontispiece*
1876 photo	170
Final photo	266
Alemany, Archbishop Joseph S.	23
Belmont, Nevada, With Catholic Church	176–177
Bouchard, James, S.J.	104
Callan, James	68
Clyne, Patrick J.	245
Coleman, Mathew	99
Dalton, Thomas J.	72
Gold Hill, Nevada	113
Grace, Thomas	95
Grass Valley Orphanages	189
Immaculate Conception Church, Colusa	138
Immaculate Conception Church, Divide	110
Immaculate Conception Church, Downieville	53
Immaculate Conception Church (German) Marysville	107
Immaculate Conception Church, Smartsville	174
Henneberry, C.PP.S.	104
Hynes, James J.	135
Immaculate Heart Academy, Los Angeles	260
Kennedy, Lawrence	97
Kiely, Michael	239
Kirley, Patrick	228
Lynch, Charles M.	81
Manogue, Patrick	66
Map, Old Grass Valley Diocese	63
Mission Dolores in 1856	34
Mora, Rt. Rev. Francis	253
Notre Dame Academy, Marysville	198
O'Kane, Patrick	92
O'Sullivan, Daniel	172
Pettit, Thomas	126
Phelan, Joseph	182
Prendergast, John	218
Round Valley, California in 1858	148
St. Anthonys Church, Mendocino	83
St. Augustine's Church, Austin, Nevada	168
St. Bernard's Church, Eureka, California	210
St. Brendan's Church, Eureka, Nevada	168
St. Canice Church, Nevada City	118
St. Francis Church (Mission Dolores)	171
St. Joseph's Church (Pro-Cathedral) Marysville	86
St. Joseph's Church, Crescent City	139
St. Joseph's Church, Yreka	158
St. Joseph's College, Rohnerville	162
St. Mary's in the Mountains, Virginia City	202
St. Mary's Hospital, Virginia City	202
St. Patrick's Church, Gold Hill, Nevada	113
St. Patrick's Church, Grass Valley	56
St. Patrick's Church, Weaverville	51

St. Patrick's Rectory, Grass
  Valley 118
St. Theresa's Church, Carson
  City, Nevada 132
St. Thomas Church, Reno,
  Nevada 206
Sheridan, John Daniel 208
Status of Diocese of Grass Valley
  in 1881 232–233

Tubman, Thomas 246
Vatican Council I 58
Vinyes, Vincent 218
Virginia City, early churches 130
Walrath, Michael 195
Walsh, Michael 241